Plato and Aristotle on Poetry

GERALD F. ELSE

Plato and Aristotle on Poetry

Edited with Introduction and Notes

by Peter Burian

The University of North Carolina Press

Chapel Hill and London

© 1986 The University of North Carolina Press

Manufactured in the United States of America

Library of Congress Cataloging-in-Publication Data

Else, Gerald Frank, 1908–1982
   Plato and Aristotle on poetry.

     1. Poetics—History.   2. Aristotle. Poetics.
3. Plato—Contributions in poetics.   I. Burian,
Peter.   II. Title.
PN1035.E47   1986   808.1   86-1475
ISBN 0-8078-1708-2

FOR GLADYS BURIAN ELSE

χάρις χάριν γάρ ἐστιν ἡ τίκτουσ᾽ ἀεί

Contents

Acknowledgments

HELP AND ENCOURAGEMENT have come from many quarters, and I am deeply grateful for so much kindness. Here I can only acknowledge some specific debts. The manuscript was prepared on the Ibycus computer owned by the Department of Classical Studies at Duke University, and I owe thanks to my colleagues John F. Oates, Kent J. Rigsby, and William H. Willis for their cooperation, to Louise Pearson Smith for her assistance, and to David Brafman and Catherine Rine for their painstaking work from a sometimes confusing typescript. I am also grateful to Laura Oaks, whose copyediting for The University of North Carolina Press spared this book a number of blemishes and infelicities. Much of my own editing was done in the library of the American Academy at Rome, and I take this occasion to thank Lucilla Marino and her staff for their flawless hospitality.

A special word of gratitude is due to two people without whom this book would probably never have been completed: Professor George A. Kennedy of the University of North Carolina, whose advice and warm support of this project have been crucial, and Gladys Burian Else, who has shepherded it in a thousand ways, both during Gerry Else's lifetime and after.

Introduction

WHEN GERALD ELSE SPOKE, as in his later years he often did, of the future of humanistic learning in America, he liked to quote a passage from Ortega y Gasset:

> There is but one way to save a classic: to give up revering him and use him for our own salvation—that is, to lay aside his classicism, to bring him close to us, to make him contemporary, to set his pulse going again with an injection of blood from our own veins, whose ingredients are our passions—and our problems.[1]

Else's own work was always animated by this hermeneutic passion to bring close to us the great texts—above all Homer, the tragedians, Plato, and Aristotle—to which he returned again and again all his life. He never forgot the sense of discovery that led him to the classics, never lost the *eros* that he knew was at the heart of humanistic study. His description of a younger generation of classicists could easily be applied to himself:

> They are "outsiders," from all sorts of places and levels in American society; and they are teaching Classics not because it is the most approved or highest-paying thing to do, but out of love: *Eros*, devotion to an ideal which they have perceived as *individuals*.[2]

1. From the essay "In Search of Goethe from Within," reprinted in *The Dehumanization of Art and Other Writings on Art* (New York 1956) 125. Else cited this passage in his presidential address to the Classical Association of the Middle West and South, "The Classics in the Twentieth Century," *CJ* 52 (1956) 8.

2. "The Classical Humanities in the Making of America," a paper presented to the California Classical Association in 1976 and published in *CCA–NS Journal* 2–3 (1977–78) 15.

It may seem paradoxical to speak of a man who was one of the dominant figures of his profession as an outsider, but he certainly thought of himself that way. A son of the western prairies, he found his own way to a most unlikely destination. It is a very American story, and even more paradoxical since this American original became perhaps the Hellenist of his generation who most fully assimilated and embodied the traditions and aims of Continental philology. But he never forgot that the ultimate test of the worth of one's studies is whether they truly promote understanding, whether they help to meet real human needs.

GERALD FRANK ELSE was born to parents of English and German ancestry and of modest means in Redfield, South Dakota, in 1908. German was forbidden in the Else household after the United States entered World War I, but he could recall his mother trying to resuscitate a few phrases on the train so that he could converse with his grandmother, who knew hardly any English. Young Else graduated from high school in Lincoln, Nebraska, at sixteen, then went on to the university there and, when he had absorbed what they could offer him, to Harvard. He graduated *summa cum laude* in classics and philosophy in 1929 and was awarded publication of his senior thesis on Lucretius as well as a European *Wanderjahr*, spent largely at those leading centers of classical learning and Weimar culture, Munich and Berlin. Returning to Harvard, Else took his doctorate with a thesis on the terminology of Plato's theory of Ideas (one of the last to be written in Latin), and went on to become instructor and then assistant professor of classics, and senior tutor of Winthrop House.

The Harvard idyll was interrupted by World War II, which Else spent with OSS in Italy, Greece, Egypt, and Liberia. In Anthony Cave Brown's book on Wild Bill Donovan, the head of OSS, we catch a glimpse of Captain G. F. Else proving his scholarly mettle in a new medium, an intelligence report that revealed how "events that had never happened were narrated in detail by responsible members of the [Greek] government, with all the exact circumstances and a convincing array of sources."[3] After the war, Harvard denied Else tenure and he moved to the University of Iowa as professor of Greek and Latin and head of the Classics Department. Else was understandably hurt by Harvard's rejection, but in the long run the two great midwestern universities he served,

3. *The Last Hero: Wild Bill Donovan* (New York 1982) 426.

Iowa first and then from 1957 to 1976 the University of Michigan, turned out to be nearly ideal for the exercise of his abilities as scholar, teacher, and administrator. At Iowa, Else completed *Aristotle's Poetics: The Argument*, the book that made his scholarly reputation. At Michigan, while helping to make the Classics Department as good as any in the country, he published five more books and monographs, including his Martin Lectures, *The Origin and Early Form of Greek Tragedy*. Many honors came to him. As president of the American Philological Association, he appropriately addressed the Fourth International Congress of Classical Studies, the first to meet in this hemisphere, on "The Classics in the New World." The universities of his home states of South Dakota and Nebraska awarded him honorary degrees. He was perhaps proudest, however, of being elected a corresponding member of the Heidelberger Akademie der Wissenschaften.

Else's life was marked also by great sorrows: the death of his beloved first wife, and then of his son. His last years were marred by the illness that he bore as stoically as he did those terrible losses. But they were also lightened by his second marriage and leavened by hard work on the book that now appears as his memorial. To the end he remained a restless spirit (if he can be said to have had a hobby, it was travel), eager to get on with it, often hard on himself and others, but honest to the very core of his being and full of zest for life.

IT IS NOT for someone linked to Gerry so closely by so many ties to offer a dispassionate view of his achievements. As a scholar, his influence was great and through his commentary on the *Poetics* reached beyond the academic discipline of classics. That was, as he himself called it, his "big book," a work that everyone in the last thirty years seriously interested in Aristotle's views on art has had to come to terms with; few can have read it without being challenged, enlightened, stirred, and perhaps irritated as well. Given its genre (text-translation-commentary) it is remarkable how unconventional it is, how personal a book it turns out to be, how much of Gerald Else the man we can read in it. Its "peculiar pleasure" is perhaps the combination of mastery of philological detail and enormous daring in proposing unorthodox solutions to the central interpretative issues of the *Poetics*. Not surprisingly, the more radical of these have not won universal assent, but none can be simply ignored or dismissed, and it is fair to say that we read the *Poetics* differently after Else than we did before.

I want, however, to emphasize two other traits that permeate this book and everything that Else wrote. First (and this is perhaps his greatest inheritance from his Continental masters) is a buoyant confidence in the power of patient, informed, painstaking research to reveal—to those with sufficient sense and sensibility—definitive answers to the questions that scholarship puts to the great texts of antiquity. In practice, this meant that Else sometimes, perhaps often, overestimated the probative value of scrappy and unsatisfactory evidence, but it meant also that one never finished reading a piece of his with the feeling of having been subjected to an inconclusive rehashing of received ideas. There was always the excitement of discovery, the experience of following where a fine, original, confident intellect leads. The second characteristic is a kind of pendant to the first, though I take it to be a very American trait. Else believed intensely that answers to scholarly questions matter not only for themselves but because they can help us to lead our lives more humanely, to become better citizens and better people. From the point of view of the more hermetic traditions of Continental erudition or the gentlemanly detachment of an Oxbridge common room, this might seem a little naive. It certainly was not a matter of lip service to "tradition." Else believed that the record of human experience at its highest and deepest, if only we listen to it, speaks directly to our own needs and desires; warns, chastises, even offers hope.

This helps explain what one might call Else's second career, as a tireless spokesman for the humanities and promoter of interdisciplinary cooperation. In the late 1960s and early 1970s he served as a member and then vice-chairman of the National Council on the Humanities, lecturing frequently to both university and general audiences. His most ambitious project was the founding and directing until his retirement from Michigan of the Center for the Coordination of Ancient and Modern Studies, with the goal of bringing together the best minds from all the disciplines that might contribute to and profit from genuinely comparative study of the ancient and modern worlds. The Center's conferences and publications, on subjects as diverse as city planning and oral poiesis, remain models of their kind.

I have not spoken of what Else might have regarded as his most important job: that of teacher. I was his student only as an undergraduate, but I have never talked with any of his graduate students who did not share my feeling that he was one of the best—and one of the most demanding. I doubt that he had an inkling of the awe that he inspired. But if he was severe, it was only toward those from whom he had reason to expect more, and only while he was also encouraging and motivating them. Above all, he taught by example. There was no one he demanded more of than himself, and in his teaching he made concrete and believable to many of us what the life of the mind could be. That is a memorial that lives on in the hearts of his students and his friends.

Editor's Note

THIS BOOK has a long and complicated history. Even before finishing *Aristotle's Poetics: The Argument*, Else began laying plans for a sequel that would provide a more systematic treatment of Aristotle's views on literature. Preparation for the task convinced him that the Platonic "background" required independent treatment, and he set out to write a separate book on Plato and the poets. That project in turn burgeoned at both ends. On the one hand, Else found himself delving further and further into Plato's early life, education, encounter with Socrates, and "discovery" of the Ideas, in an attempt to understand the sources of his deeply equivocal attitude toward poetry. On the other, he found that his own ideas about the composition of the "review" of poetry in Book 10 of the *Republic* had outgrown in bulk and technical complexity the limits of a general work on Plato and the poets. He published a separate mono- graph on that subject, *The Structure and Date of Plato's Republic*, the only part of the vast undertaking to have appeared in print during his lifetime.

Perhaps sensing that he would not be able to carry out his entire scheme, Else concentrated after his retirement from the University of Michigan on the book he called *Aristotle's Doctrine of Literature*. Dur- ing 1978–79, when he joined the first group of fellows at the National Humanities Center, he drafted almost all of the projected chapters. Thereafter he made only minor revisions, but shortly before his death he was willing to submit the manuscript to the University of North Carolina Press for a preliminary scrutiny. That manuscript lacked both a promised chapter on the transmission of the text of the *Poetics* and a concluding résumé. Of the former I have been able to discover no trace, which is particularly regrettable in view of Else's strong opinions about successive intrusions into the text. Of the latter I found a draft, clearly less finished than the rest, but nevertheless providing a summary of many leading elements in his interpretation and clearly worthy of inclusion.

The Plato material in the Else *Nachlass* presents different problems. It had grown into an independent work, different in scale and scope from the work on Aristotle. The bulk of the manuscript, constituting a spiritual biography of the young Plato in a vein reminiscent of Wilamowitz's *Platon*, deals only sporadically with the specific problem of Plato's attitude toward poetry and contains relatively little that is original. The second part, on the other hand, provides an account of Plato's views on poetry dialogue by dialogue. Else's treatment of this complex subject is of considerable interest in itself and gains importance from the consistent emphasis he gives in his discussion of Aristotle to the interplay of Plato's and Aristotle's contrasting ideas. Furthermore, although Else himself did not contemplate combining this material with his Aristotle manuscript, its inclusion puts on record all of his views concerning poetry as seen by both philosophers.

The present book, then, consists of a revised version of the Aristotle manuscript submitted to the University of North Carolina Press in the summer of 1982 (Part 2: Chapters 4–13, Appendices 1 and 2), the concluding résumé found in draft (Chapter 14), and the sections of Else's Plato manuscript that deal with Plato's views on poetry (Part 1: Chapters 1–3). As the reader will see, it is a very personal book in both style and substance. I have endeavored as editor to make as few changes as possible, but the differing origins of the various parts, and the fact that none of the book received the *ultimae curae* of its author, have made it necessary for me to intervene on almost every page. Apart from the correction of errors and the clarification of obscurities which I believe Else would have undertaken had he lived, I have occasionally cut material on Plato in Part 2 which is presented more fully in Part 1. (The reader should be aware, however, that a number of substantive discussions of Platonic passages not found in Part 1 are still included in Part 2.) In two places where the manuscript was incomplete, I have made additions. The section on Book 10 of the *Republic* in Chapter 2 is adapted from an unpublished lecture found among Else's papers. In order to complete the survey of Plato's views on poetry, I have provided the paragraphs on the *Laws* that conclude the next chapter. I have kept Else's scattered remarks on that dialogue in mind and believe my remarks to be entirely consistent with his views, but the responsibility for the section is entirely mine.

I have also added the notes, for the very limited purpose of providing references or amplifications explicitly demanded by Else's text (or occasionally by marginal annotations in the manuscript). I have not attempted to bring the bibliography up to date, and thus cite only works I know he consulted. The latest dates from 1981, but it is clear that he never intended to provide systematic coverage of recent bibliography. I have resisted the temptation to use the notes to register my own disagreements, to provide others' dissenting views when he did not explicitly authorize this, or to take up the cudgels for his opinions where recent scholarship has challenged them—as in Richard Janko's stimulating *Aristotle on Comedy: Towards a Reconstruction of Poetics II* (Berkeley 1984), for whose central thesis he would have had scant sympathy.

It is my hope to have represented Else's ideas as clearly and accurately as possible and to have preserved the flavor of his style, more like the man's speech than that of any scholar I know. As is well known, Else had strong views about the text of the *Poetics*; in this book, all *major* differences from Rudolf Kassel's edition (Oxford 1965), which Else recognized as standard, are remarked in the text or the notes, with the exception of Else's extensive excision of interpolations, for which see Appendix 2. The transliteration of Greek names (inconsistent, like everyone else's) is his own. Translations from the *Poetics* are not necessarily identical to those in *Aristotle's Poetics: The Argument* or in Else's 1967 translation. Within the translations, parentheses are used to enclose explanatory material added by the translator, square brackets to indicate interpolations into the original text.

This work may be regarded as the culmination of a lifetime's study, whose main concerns and fundamental assumptions were established early and carried through with great consistency over the decades. I therefore append here a list of Else's earlier publications related directly to its main topics and themes:

"Aristotle on the Beauty of Tragedy." *HSCP* 49 (1938) 179–204.
"Aristotle and Satyr-Play, I." *TAPA* 70 (1940) 139–157.
"The Case of the Third Actor." *TAPA* 76 (1945) 1–10.
"A Survey of Work on Aristotle's *Poetics*, 1940–1954." *CW* 48 (1954–55) 73–82.
Aristotle's Poetics: The Argument. Cambridge, Mass. 1957 [June 1958].
"The Origin of *ΤΡΑΓΩΙΔΙΑ*." *Hermes* 85 (1957) 17–46.
" 'Imitation' in the Fifth Century." *CP* 53 (1958) 73–90.
"*ΥΠΟΚΡΙΤΗΣ*." *Wiener Studien* 72 (1959) 75–107.
Encylopedia of Poetry and Poetics. Ed. Alex Preminger. Princeton 1965. Articles "Classical Poetics" (pp. 128–134), "Imitation" (378–381), "Mimesis" (501), and "Sublime" (819–820).
The Origin and Early Form of Greek Tragedy. Martin Classical Lectures, 20. Cambridge, Mass. 1965. Paperback, New York 1972.

Review of Aristotle, *De arte poetica liber*, ed. Rudolf Kassel. *Gnomon*
    38 (1967) 761–766.
Aristotle. *Poetics*. Translation with introduction and notes. Ann Arbor,
    Mich. 1967.
The Structure and Date of Book 10 of Plato's Republic. Abhandlungen
    der Heidelberger Akademie der Wissenschaften, phil.-hist. Kl., Jg.
    1972, Abh. 3. Heidelberg 1972.
"Persuasion and the Work of Tragedy." In *Tragedy and the Tragic in
    Western Culture*, 63–68. Ed. Pierre Gravel and Timothy J. Reiss.
    Montreal 1983.

Abbreviations

AJP	*American Journal of Philology*
Argument	Gerald F. Else. *Aristotle's Poetics: The Argument.* Cambridge, Mass., 1957
AUMLA	*Journal of the Australasian Language and Literature Association*
CJ	*Classical Journal*
CP	*Classical Philology*
CW	*Classical World*
HSCP	*Harvard Studies in Classical Philology*
JHI	*Journal of the History of Ideas*
JHS	*Journal of Hellenic Studies*
MH	*Museum Helveticum*
NJbb	*Neue Jahrbücher für das klassische Altertum*
RFIC	*Rivista di filologia e di istruzione classica*
Structure	Gerald F. Else. *The Structure and Date of Book 10 of Plato's Republic.* Abhandlungen der Heidelberger Akademie der Wissenschaften, phil.-hist. Kl., Jg. 1972, Abh. 3. Heidelberg 1972
TAPA	*Transactions of the American Philological Association*

PART I

Plato on Poetry

I

The Earlier Dialogues

EVERYBODY KNOWS that Plato treated the poets badly, threw them out of his Republic with no more than a garland or two to cover their nakedness, and told them not to come back until they could prove that their art was not merely pleasurable but useful in public and private life. Actually this final challenge is not addressed directly to the poets but to certain unnamed champions of the art characterized as "not poetical natures, but lovers of poetry" (ὅσοι μὴ ποιητικοί, φιλοποιηταὶ δέ, Republic 10.607d). This strange phrase, with its suggestion of affectionate insult—why should Plato go out of his way to stress the champions' unpoetical nature?—makes one wonder whether the person Plato had in mind may not have been his brightest pupil, Aristotle. In any case, whether the hat was intended to fit him or not, Aristotle put it on and wore it. He wrote a three-book dialogue *On Poets*, which was certainly philopoetic, but has unfortunately been lost. The little treatise or rather lecture script which we call the *Poetics* is in fact, though not in form, a defense of poetry.

Still, the significance of Plato's thoughts about poetry is not exhausted by the role they played in motivating and shaping Aristotle's defense, however important that influence was. For, by an old and fairly well-known paradox, Plato the traducer of poetry had in many ways a deeper understanding of what poetry does than Aristotle its defender. Plato knew things, true and important things, about this matter which were not dreamt of in Aristotle's philosophy. Tradition has it that Plato wrote tragedies and dithyrambs when young, but burned them after he met Sokrates. If we take this tradition seriously—and I think we must—we have to imagine the effect of Sokrates on the young poet as a shattering impact, an overturning of everything he knew and valued. Thus Plato's radical condemnation of poetry cannot be treated merely as an unfortunate aberration, a lapse in "literary criticism." It is rather a particular instance of his radical rejection of Greek culture as a whole. No Greek ever took so much of his own civilization into his heart and soul as Plato did, and none ever rejected it so completely.

From everything we know about the two men, we can say that Plato was a very different kind of person from Sokrates, and equally that he could become Plato only through Sokrates. Without Sokrates, Plato would have remained what he was born to be: an Athenian aristocrat, perhaps a litterateur, perhaps a politician. Plato's experience of poetry was determined initially by two main factors, his own acute sensibility and the central place of poetry in the Athens of his youth. In the absence of either of these, Plato would never have ended by treating poetry as he did. The confluence of the two meant that his experience of poetry was at once intensely personal and intensely political. The shock that Sokrates then administered to his soul brought about a violent reaction against his earlier idolatry, denying and challenging everything that poetry had meant to him up to that time. He found himself faced by a choice between two worlds, two incompatible ways of life, and he chose "philosophy." But the choice necessarily brought with it the banishment of the poets, for they belonged irredeemably to the other world, the one he had rejected.

The vehemence of Plato's rejection of poetry is a measure not only of the ardor with which he had previously embraced it, but of the hold it continued to have over one part of his being. The rejection, like the acceptance, was intensely personal and at the same time intensely political. Plato cannot treat poetry the way Aristotle, for example, does, as one intellectual topic among others. Everything he says about it (at least in his serious moments) takes it as a force, a way of life that one must accept and cleave to or else reject and cast away, but in either case with all the energy of one's being. Plato seldom really discusses poetry; he fights it with whatever weapons come to hand, and on the terrain of his own soul. His utterances on the subject are largely battle plans, commands, exhortations, bulletins from this inward battle, reflecting the shifting tactics of a struggle to the death for his own salvation. It follows that not all the utterances are consistent with each other; only the overall aim of the struggle is consistent.

There are references to poetry in works from all periods of Plato's life up to the last, and in all shapes and sizes from major discussions down to very brief passing allusions. How best to organize and present this large and disparate body of material is a serious problem. If we adopt a strictly chronological order of presentation—so far as that is possible with our less-than-perfect knowledge of Platonic chronology—we are in danger of reducing Plato's remarks on literature to a collection of random comments. On the other hand, a thoroughly systematic exposition would run the opposite danger, that of exaggerating the coherence of what he has to offer, precisely because Plato's statements on the subject do not form a coherent logical whole, much less a complete theory of poetry. To take an example that lies to hand: many of the fuller, more substantial expositions in Plato treat poetry under the headings either of "inspiration" (ἐνθουσιασμός) or of "imitation" (μίμησις), but these two concepts always appear separately (until the very end, in the *Laws*). One might be tempted to take them as positive and negative indicators respectively, but the facts turn out to be less simple. "Inspiration" is not necessarily a term of praise, and "imitation" by itself does not necessarily convey dispraise. Thus a treatment which divided the Platonic corpus into "inspiration" texts and "imitation" texts would be inefficient and misleading. Indeed, most of the references to poetry have a measuarable emotional charge, positive or negative, but the distribution of the charges is eccentric and cannot be plotted on any simple graph. By and large, then, chronology provides as good an organizing principle as can be found, and we shall follow it, while also taking account so far as possible of the occasion, affiliations, purpose, and tone of each dialogue.

Apology, Protagoras, Ion

PLATO'S FIRST CONCERN with poetry, after he became a disciple of Sokrates, was the question of the poet's knowledge. This concern is reflected in the *Apology* and in *Ion* and *Protagoras*, two dialogues which belong early in the roster of Plato's writings, very possibly even earlier than the *Apology*; but it will be convenient to begin with the latter.

The *Apology* betrays no special interest on the part of Sokrates in poetry or poets. He tells us (21bff.) how, after Chairephon had obtained the response from Delphi that no one was wiser than Sokrates, he (Sokrates) set out to "disprove the oracle" by finding someone who was wiser. The result was the one we all know: Sokrates went in turn to the politicians, the poets, and the artisans, and found that "not one of them knew anything worth mentioning." Of the poets he says (22b): "So I soon came to this realization for the poets also, that they were not composing their works out of wisdom, but by virtue of certain natural gifts and being filled with divine inspiration (ἐνθουσιάζοντες, having god in them) like the prophets and givers of oracles; for those too say many beautiful things but have no knowledge of any of them." The word "also," indicates that Sokrates had already reached the same conclusion for the politicians. This fact (which he does not emphasize) will be of interest to us when we come to the *Meno*.

It is obvious that the test which Sokrates administered to the poets was his customary dialectic, based on the principle of contradiction, and that their failure to pass the test was proof in his eyes that they were operating by inspiration, not by knowledge. It is equally clear that the young Plato enthusiastically accepted the "demonstration," since he made it the basis of his *Ion*. That the poet might have another kind of knowledge, which would require another kind of testing, had not occurred to either Sokrates or Plato.

In the *Protagoras*, after the first bout of dialectic has ended in an impasse and the whole conversation appears to be in danger of collapsing (335c), Protagoras is persuaded—with difficulty—to "do the questioning," that is, to play the role of Sokrates. He immediately proceeds to do nothing of the kind; he merely quotes a pair of utterances from a well-known poem by Simonides and asks Sokrates whether they are not mutually contradictory. The sophist having thus played Sokrates' part so poorly, Sokrates turns the tables and delivers (339eff.) a brilliant sophistical *explication de texte* on the poem, showing that Simonides was really promulgating the Sokratic thesis that no one does wrong intentionally. Sokrates' performance is greeted with a "Well done!" from the rather fatuous sophist Hippias, who adds that he too has a nice speech on the subject which he would be glad to "display" to the company. But Sokrates, returning to seriousness, suggests (347b) that they drop all this explicating of poems, since the poets are not on hand to speak for themselves and every man can interpret their work as he likes. Conversation, dialectical conversation between two people (two souls, though he does not say so here), is the only way to get at truth.

It is improbable that Simonides himself, or any poet, would have proved to have knowledge in Sokrates' sense, if Sokrates had been able to interrogate him. In any case we have to make do with a lesser personage, the foolish rhapsode Ion, in the farcical little dialogue that is named after him. Ion (who is identified at beginning and end of the dialogue as an outstandingly successful performer) not only recites poetry but gives lectures on it. He has "the most beautiful things" to say about Homer (530c), but when pressed by Sokrates he has to admit that he does it only for Homer; when other poets are mentioned, e.g., Hesiod or Archilochos, he cannot even stay awake. Sokrates, after a short round of induction (531dff.) to show that anyone who really knows an art is equally equipped and inclined to judge *all* the practitioners of it, proposes (533c) an explanation of Ion's curious difficulty. According to Sokrates, Ion's fixation on Homer proves that what he does is "not an art . . . but a divine power" (τέχνη μὲν οὐκ . . . θεία δὲ δύναμις, 533d; cf. 534c) passed on by the poet the way a magnetic stone passes its attraction to a piece of iron. Furthermore, good poets themselves do not speak "by art but from being inspired and possessed" (οὐκ ἐκ τέχνης ἀλλ' ἔνθεοι ὄντες καὶ κατεχόμενοι, 533e); and analogues that are cited for this state—Bacchants and Corybantic dancers "not in their right minds" (οὐκ ἔμφρονες, 534a)—culminate in the out-and-out assertion that "the poet is not able to compose until he has become inspired and out of his mind and his reason is no longer in him" (534b). All this leaves no doubt that we do indeed have here the notion of poetic madness. Sokrates will not allow the true poet even a shred of rationality; reason must depart before poetizing can begin.

But Sokrates goes even farther. The poet himself contributes nothing whatever to his song; it is all done by a god speaking through him. The poet is a mouthpiece, a conduit, a speaking tube, and god has gone out of his way to advertise this truth by bringing one surpassingly beautiful song out of a certain Tynnichos of Chalkis, otherwise the wretchedest of poetasters (534d–e).

It is not Sokrates' way to launch into a ten-minute discourse when the conversation has barely begun, or to explain to people why they do what they do before he has even asked them how they do it. The speech is a purely gratuitous offering and its irony is, to say the least, premature. Poetic possession or inspiration is merely inferred negatively from Ion's limitation to one poet: it is an absence of art or reason. But then, without warning or further argument, inspiration rapidly takes on positive life, body, color. It is a divine power comparable to the magnet; it takes possession of men, drives them out of their wits, gushes through their mouths, speaks through them to us. A mythology begins to rise before our eyes, couched in the sort of language which one might call Plato's dithyrambic style, complete with images, comparisons, and long, rolling sentences.

This is not Sokrates speaking, it is the young Plato, pricking up his ears and charging into battle before he has even heard the trumpet. The want of logic is supplied by his own enthusiasm—as if he were inspired by the same gods and Muses he ascribes to the poets. Strictly speaking, that is of course impossible, for he is now Sokrates' disciple and a preacher of reason, and he is out to show that the poets and their reciters and explicators are wholly irrational, subrational creatures, not knowing anything of what they do. Very well, to that end he will build up the thesis of "inspiration" to an impossible height of absurdity and lard the whole dialogue with thick irony. But had not Plato been a poet himself, and did he not know that something more than reason is needed for the making of poems? Yes, he knew it well, and that is the very truth he is now determined to discredit and deride, in honor of his new religion. He sets out to hold up to mockery what had been most holy to him before. But somehow in the doing he is carried away and paints so glowing a picture of the poetic afflatus that we almost believe it *is* divine.

Plato's ironic attitude toward the idea of poetic inspiration here often goes undetected, partly because of the eloquence with which he describes it, partly because the idea itself is thought to belong to a sanctified, long-standing tradition. This, however, is not quite the case.[1] Both the Homeric poems begin with invocations of the Muse: obviously a standard gambit, but one with wholly different implications from those suggested by Plato. To the oral bard, Mnemosyne (Memory) and her daughters the Muses do not at all signify irrationality or ignorance; quite the contrary, they are the warrant and guarantee of his art, since he depends on memory for every word he utters. Hesiod's Helikonian Muses were experienced more personally, but their meaning is not very different. They give him his patent of bardship, the warrant of his technical competence and his poetic knowledge. Pindar, Hesiod's fellow-Boiotian, believed utterly in the poet's inspiration, but never at the cost of admitting it to be witless and irrational. He is an artist, *and* he is inspired. Ἐνθουσιασμός as the contrary of art and reason appears for the first time in a fragment of Demokritos (B 18 Diels)—and in the *Ion*. Thus the tradition as a whole is far from sanctioning Plato's dichotomy between inspiration and reason. That he made use of Demokritos is likely but not certain. What counts most is his Sokratic orientation, which leaves no real place for poetry in the life of reason.

There is one implication of Sokrates' teaching of which Plato says nothing in the *Ion*. Since under the convention with which Plato operates only the living (i.e., only those who were living during Sokrates' lifetime) can be reached by dialectic, poor creatures like Ion can be stripped naked

1. On this subject see E. N. Tigerstedt, "Furor Poeticus: Poetic Inspiration in Greek Literature before Democritus and Plato," *JHI* 31 (1970) 163–178; Penelope Murray, "Poetic Inspiration in Early Greece," *JHS* 101 (1981) 87–100.

Kratylos

NOW, in the middle period of Plato's writing, we intitiate a new theme, that of mimesis (μίμησις, "imitation"). The first allusion, so far as we can make out, is in the *Kratylos*.

The *Kratylos* has not been firmly dated but seems to belong in the immediate neighborhood of the *Republic*, either just before or—less likely—just after it.[3] The stated topic of the dialogue is the "correctness" of names, and Sokrates spends much of his time propounding an endless list of etymologies for Greek words, each more absurd and unprofitable than the last. It would appear then that, as Hermogenes maintains, the assignment of names to things is a purely external procedure, a matter of "contract" (συνθήκη) and agreement among men (384d). Yet Plato seems to hanker after some less arbitrary explanation, one that will relate the name somehow to the essence (οὐσία) of the thing, as a kind of tool or instrument (ὄργανον) with which to grasp it (388a). There follows (389aff.) a comparison of the making of names by the "lawgiver" to the making of a weaver's shuttle (κέρκις) by a craftsman.

The essential thing about this craftsman's procedure is that it is not directed at the external appearance of a shuttle but at what we do with it: separate the warp from the woof. In other words, the maker's activity is focused upon what we would call the function of the shuttle. Plato has no specific technical term for this concept;[4] he speaks (389b) of the εἶδος or Form. More exactly, he uses εἶδος to denote the generic form which is common to all shuttles, and φύσις (389c) ("nature") or ἰδέα (389e) for the specific form, the one appropriate to a shuttle meant for working linen or wool or some other particular kind of fabric. The craftsman's procedure consists in "rendering" (ἀποδοῦναι) or "putting" (τιθέναι) the particular form into the material, e.g., wood, which he is using. Plato does not actually say that the craftsman "imitates" the Form or Nature, but he does employ another idiom which, as we shall see later, is highly significant. He speaks of the toolmaker as "looking toward" the Form (βλέπων . . . πρὸς ἐκεῖνο τὸ εἶδος, 389b) with a view to rendering it in the appropriate material; and he uses an exactly parallel locution of the namegiver (νομοθέτης, lit. lawgiver) of the *Kratylos*: in order to make a name a functional tool he must "look toward that which Name really is"

3. Cf. J. V. Luce, "The Date of the *Cratylus*," *AJP* 85 (1964) 136–154.

4. The closest approximation is the use of χρεία (roughly "function") at *Republic* 10.601d.

(389d), in other words, toward the generic Idea of Name—and presumably beyond it to the specific form of the particular thing he wishes to name.

We find here all the terms and concepts which Plato will employ later in *Republic* 10, in the famous passage on the Three Beds—all except "imitation." But "rendering" is very close to "imitating," and the general pattern is perfectly clear: the form is rendered or incorporated in a particular material for a certain purpose.

Later in the *Kratylos*, after endless rounds of etymologizing which come to very little, Sokrates returns to the original question of the correctness of names. This time the problem is viewed in a more restricted context, and the term "imitation," μίμησις (423c), puts in its appearance. We now focus our attention on "first" or basic names, those simplest vocables out of which all other names are formed. The correctness of such a name must consist in revealing (making clear: δηλοῦν, 422d) the essence of the thing it denotes. Now, says Sokrates, if we were deaf and dumb we would have to make things clear to one another by the use of hands, head, and other parts of the body. For example, "if we wanted to make clear that which is above (us) and is light, we would lift our hand(s) toward heaven, imitating (or miming: μιμούμενοι) the very nature of the object; if things that are below (us) and heavy, toward the earth" (432a).[5]

Sokrates next points out (432b) that in fact we *can* imitate things by means of voice, tongue, and mouth, in other words through speech (and

---

5. Hermann Koller, *Die Mimesis in der Antike* (Berne 1954) 12, denies that Plato can be talking about imitation here: " 'Above,' 'light,' 'heavy' can never be 'imitated'; neither can the 'essence' of a thing. Rather, mimesis here is the concretion of a concept into form (*Gestaltwerdung eines Begriffes*), actualization of a spiritual concept (*verwicklichung eines Geistigen*), form and expression of the soul (*Form und Ausdruck der Seele*); only through the latter does it acquire reality." This passage is in fact the cornerstone of Koller's whole theory, according to which *mimesis* in Plato does not denote the copying of an external reality but the bringing to outward view of an internal, spiritual reality. But it is evident that in Plato's view, "above," "light," "heavy" *can* be copied or represented by human bodies. His very next sentence reads: "And if we wanted to make clear a horse running, or some other animal, you know that we would make our own bodies and gestures (or postures: σχήματα) as much like those things as possible." The two sentences are exactly parallel and express parallel ideas; "above," "heavy," "horse running" are all things that we can imitate or mime by the same or similar physical means.

song); and he is just about to accept this as the definition of names ("a name is an imitation by means of voice"), when something makes him pause. It has occurred to him that in that case to imitate the noises made by sheep and roosters and so on would be to name the creatures thus imitated. Naming must be a different kind of imitation, aiming at other objects. Music and painting imitate by means of voice and of shape (or posture: σχῆμα, 423d) and color respectively, while naming aims at the essence (423e). If one could imitate *that* aspect of a thing by means of letters and syllables, he would be revealing (making clear) its true nature.

At 426a–427d Sokrates plays at length with the idea that the "first" or basic names contain likenesses or representations (μιμεῖσθαι or ἀφομοιοῦν are used repeatedly) of basic things, through the sounds of which they are composed: *r* (a trilled sound in which the tongue vibrates rapidly), for example, represents movement in general, *i* lightness, *l* smoothness, and so on. Several times in the passage as a whole (423d, 429a, 430b–d) this hypothetical replicating of "things" by their names is compared and contrasted with imitations through voice and tongue (musical art) and through shape and color (painting) respectively, but especially with the latter. At 432aff. Sokrates pursues an especially close argument involving the images made by painters. These resemble their originals but are not identical with them, possessing their shape and color but not their inward qualities or others such as softness, warmth, etc. In other words painting represents external characteristics of the object. But painting and poetry ("music") were linked at 423d as parallel arts which "imitate" voices and utterances and shapes and colors respectively. Sokrates does not argue this parallel, he takes it for granted. And in fact we find it as far back as the poet Simonides, who spoke of painting as silent poetry and poetry as vocal painting.[6] There is no need to suppose that Plato is directly echoing Simonides; clearly the idea had become a commonplace, though we cannot trace its history between Simonides and Plato.

It is noteworthy that when Sokrates presses his effort to establish names as μιμήματα of things (i.e., of their essences) he repeatedly (429a, 430b–d) invokes the analogy—and contrast—with painting rather than that with poetry, even though the latter uses the same vocal medium as the (hypothetical) art of naming. No doubt Plato feels that the images produced by painting are more tangible and perspicuous than verbal

---

6. Cited as a saying of Simonides by Plutarch, *Moralia* 346f (*De Gloria Atheniensium* 3); cf. *Moralia* 748a (*Quaestiones Conviviales* 9.15e).

images; but there is also something more. The same predilection for visual comparisons will appear in the *Republic* and elsewhere, as an analogue for the activity not only of the poet but of the philosopher. This visual trend seems to be an important one in Plato's thinking, or imaging, and to have important effects on his view of poetry.[7]

7. On this subject see Eva C. Keuls, *Plato and Greek Painting* (Leiden 1978) esp. 33–47.

2

The *Republic*

IT IS A commonplace that the real subject of the *Republic* is not state-craft but psychology and education; and education is the issue that, initially at least, turns mimesis into an indictment against the poets. The parts of Books 2, 3, and 10 which formulate the indictment are among the best known and most assiduously read passages in all of Plato, but few would claim, I think, that they have been fully and satisfactorily explained. Actually a full explanation may not be possible; our analysis will turn up evidence of serious discrepancies and incoherences. But I believe that a satisfactory interpretation can be achieved from point to point, provided one does not (1) require that every Platonic utterance on poetry must jibe with every other; (2) assume that Plato had a complete theory of poetry (and that our job is to find it); or (3) presume that he was infallible.

Book 1 contains nothing of interest to us. The first hint of the coming storm is in the speech of Adeimantos, Plato's older brother, early in Book 2. Glaukon, the other brother, has served notice that they are not content with Sokrates' easy refutation of the sophist Thrasymachos, and lays down the specifications which he and Adeimantos wish to see followed in order to determine the real merits of justice and injustice. Glaukon says that "they" (other persons, identity unspecified, but obviously in-cluding many people, not merely a few sophists) regard justice as a bur-den and a nuisance. They all agree that injustice (i.e., doing as one likes to others) is the best thing, if you are able to get away with it. Glaukon then proposes that we reverse the customary outer trappings of the two kinds of life, giving the unjust man all the usual rewards and honors for justice and the just man all the tortures and penalties for injustice; *then* we shall see which of them is happier (361d).

Adeimantos seconds his brother's attack (362eff.) and brings out still more clearly what is at issue. It is the contrast between justice and injus-tice in themselves on the one hand, and the external rewards and punish-

ments which are conventionally attached to them on the other. Here are
the poets, Homer and Hesiod and the rest (Orpheus, Mousaios, etc.),
singing of the material blessings that the gods bestow on good and pious
men; of endless drinking bouts in Hades, and contrariwise of bodies
buried eternally in mud or drawing water forever in a sieve. But "they,"
both ordinary men and poets, also talk the other way: that justice and
virtue are estimable (καλόν) but burdensome, while loose living and
injustice are more fun and bring more profit. Strangest of all are the
poets' stories about how the gods often allot unhappiness to virtuous
men and the opposite to villains (364b). And then the poets also let on
that the evildoer can always buy off the gods with presents (364d).

Adeimantos's speech continues in the same vein but with mounting
eloquence, ending with the plea that Sokrates show them what justice
and injustice do by themselves, in the souls of their possessors (367b). So
far as the poets are concerned, the crucial point is that they serve up
the same shabby, perverted, externalistic moral code as the rest of so-
ciety, but with greater authority: "For we have no other source of knowl-
edge about the gods," says Adeimantos, "than our laws and the poets"
(365e). It is already clear that whatever remedy Sokrates has to offer
against this disease, it will have to be directed against the poets at least
equally with the others.

These opening remarks have been too little regarded by students of
Plato's "literary criticism," because they are not in a passage which car-
ries that label. Between them, however, they foreshadow directly or indi-
rectly much of what Plato has to say against the poets later.

Sokrates now begins the construction of the ideal state—explicitly
designated as the "large letters" in which we can read the truth about the
soul (368e). Almost as quickly as it can be told, the first simple, healthy
state of five or six producers and artisans is succeeded by the "bloated"
variety, swollen by a motley horde of drones, mainly artists: "huntsmen,
all the various kinds of imitators, those in shapes and colors (painters
and sculptors) and those in music, that is, poets and their assistants,
rhapsodes, actors, members of choruses, contractors; and dealers in
every conceivable sort of wares, especially in the line of female adorn-
ment" (373b); also masses of servants: παιδαγώγοι, wet-nurses, and so
on. This luxurious, cultivated city—obviously modeled on Athens—will
require more territory; that will lead to war; war necessitates a standing
army; and in this breathless, not outstandingly logical fashion we arrive
at the need for selecting and training a corps of Guards or Guardians
(374eff.)

The Guards will need to have two quite different and not always compatible strains of character blended in them: they must be fierce (toward the enemy) and gentle (toward their fellow citizens), or "spirited" (θυμοειδής) and philosophical respectively (376c). How are they to be educated in order to acquire and blend these traits? In the traditional way, through music and gymnastic; and we begin our discussion with music, namely with the tales told to children (377a). By and large these stories are false (ψευδεῖς), "lies," not "fictions," for "fiction" is too polite, and ambiguous to boot. Plato is not above relishing the shock value of saying "lies" in talking about children's stories; and on the other hand he has no qualms of conscience about the telling of lies as such, provided they are told by constituted authority and for a socially beneficent purpose (389b). In any case, considering the softness and impressionability of childish souls, "we will not permit the children to hear any chance tale concocted by any chance teller; . . . we must supervise the makers of stories and license the ones they compose properly, but suppress the other kind" (377b–c).

The literal translation of the word I have translated "properly" (καλόν) is "beautiful"; but Plato is not talking about aesthetic qualities. What he means is made clear a little further down (377d). He has now shifted from the "little" stories to the "big" ones, those told by Hesiod, Homer, and the rest of the poets: "For they, you know, have composed and told false tales to men (grown-ups) in the past, and they still do." "What complaint have you against them?" says the interlocutor. "A very proper complaint, indeed *the* proper one," says Sokrates, "especially if the liar botches his job" (μὴ καλῶς ψεύδηται, "produces an ugly lie"); and he explains that he means "when in his story somebody produces a poor likeness of the character of gods and heroes, like a painter whose portraits bear no likeness to their originals" (377e).

This passage is so exceptionally suggestive that we must pause and look at it with some care. It contains at least five important implications:

1. Story-making (and at the moment poetry is being considered under that rubric) is or includes a process of likeness-making.
2. In this it is analogous to painting.
3. The originals of the likenesses we are talking about at the moment are gods and heroes. The real nature of gods and heroes appears to be known to Plato but not to some (most? any?) of the poets, since he knows that some (most? all?) of their attempted likenesses are not "like."

4. Poetic likenesses are "false" to begin with, not being identical with their originals.

5. But likenesses which do not even resemble their originals are "ugly falsehoods."

It is important to note that the concept of making a likeness or copy of an original dominates the passage and the long argument which follows, even though the word μιμεῖσθαι is not used just here to denote the process. Actually the artists, poets, etc., of the "bloated" city were called μιμηταί in a perfectly matter-of-fact way just above (373b); and we shall see that the idea of mimesis lurks just offstage, as it were, throughout the argument (it turns out that Plato has a reason for keeping the term out of sight).

If gods and heroes are the originals which the poets render (and render so poorly), what kind of originals are they? How can Plato be so sure that the copies are defective, since gods and heroes are not available to him for direct inspection any more than they were to the poets? The answers to these questions will become evident in a moment. Plato gives some examples of poor or botched likenesses (377eff.) but does not argue at this point about their truth; his immediate concern is for their deleterious moral effects on the young. Among them are Hesiod's primitive tale about Kronos's castration (Plato prudishly avoids the word) of his father and his equally unedifying treatment of and by his son Zeus; the binding of Hera by Hephaistos; the occasion when Zeus hurled the latter out of heaven; battles of the gods like that in Book 20 of the *Iliad*, and numerous other tales of wars, factions, and rivalries on Olympos. Even if these stories were true, says Plato later (387a), we would do our best to hush them up. At this point Plato sets his face against the fashionable practice of explaining away some of the immoralities by means of "concealed meaning" (ὑπόνοια, 378d: e.g., that "Zeus" really means *fire* or "Hera" *air*): children cannot judge what is allegory and what is not, and whatever they learn will be indelibly impressed on their young minds.

Plato now proceeds (379aff.) to lay down what he calls his τύποι or guidelines for the portrayal of god(s) in poetry (he adds explicitly: "in epic, in lyric, or in tragedy"). The common premise is that god is to be represented the way he really is, and there are just two points to be observed:

1. God is good and the cause of good only.
2. God never changes form, and never tries to make us think that he does.

The marmoreal simplicity of the first point barely conceals a monstrous problem, which however is no problem for Plato: I mean of course the problem of evil. "For the evils of life some other cause is to be found, not god" (379c). (The principle finds even more magisterial expression in the words of Lachesis in the Myth of Er at the end of the *Republic* (10.617e), referring to the soul's choice of its next life: "The blame is the chooser's; god is blameless.") Plato particularly objects to the famous remark of Achilleus (*Iliad* 24.527) that there are two jars on Zeus's doorstep, one of goods, the other of evils, and that some men—the luckier ones—receive a mixture of the two while the rest receive evils unmixed with good (unmixed good being the lot of no man). Then there is the treacherous dissolution of the battlefield truce by Pandaros (*Iliad* 4.104ff.), instigated by Zeus and Athena; the sufferings of Niobe and Tantalos and Priam; and much more of the kind. If the poet insists on mentioning such things, he must either say that they were not a god's doing, or that the god was righteously punishing the sufferers and they benefited from the punishment. Finally, Plato emphasizes once more (380c) that stories ascribing evils to god, as evils, are neither profitable to the city nor true ("consonant with themselves").

How can Plato dispose so cavalierly of the ancient and deeply serious Greek tradition that all things, good *and* evil, come from the gods? It is his inheritance from Sokrates; in fact it is simply the other side of the Sokratic postulate about evil. The two faiths are already linked in the *Apology* (40c): "You must hold this one truth in your minds, that there is no evil for a good man either while he is alive or after his death; and that that man's welfare is not neglected by the gods." God can only be good and the cause of good; there is an end of it, and in one moment, in the twinkling of an eye, the centuries of contrary belief—and the poetry which enshrined the belief—are annihilated. A perfunctory argument is given. Essentially it runs: god is good; what is good does not do harm but good; therefore god is the cause only of good (379b–c). The principle is not really argued at all; it is a postulate, a self-evident truth.

The second guideline says that god never changes form and never tries to make us believe that he does (380dff.). The first half of the statement refers of course to the transformations of the Homeric gods into various mortal shapes in order to help or hinder the heroes. Here Plato marshals respectable arguments to show that god, being in the best and healthiest state possible, will be least subject to change through external forces and that he least of all creatures will wish to change himself, since it could only be for the worse (381bff.). Now comes the second part: "Well then, are the gods themselves not the kind of creature to change, but do they make us think they appear in all sorts of shapes, with the purpose of fooling and tricking us?" (381e). This leads to the question whether god would wish to deceive either in word or deed, and that in turn to an exposition of how gods and men alike hate the "true falsehood" or lie in the soul: the state of being inwardly deceived as to the way things really are. "The lie in words is a replica (μίμημα) of the perception in the soul, a secondary image, not an unmixed falsehood" (382b). Plato then makes short work of demonstrating that god has no need of the falsehood in words, for any purpose (382c–d). "What use, then, would lying be to god? Would he, not knowing the things that happened in ancient times, tell lies in the endeavor to make likenesses of them?" "That would be absurd." "Well then, there is no lying poet (ποιητὴς ψευδής, 382d) in god."

We should note first of all that the concept of mimesis has now put in its appearance, with the designation of the "lie in words" as a μίμημα of the "lie in the soul"; but it is mimesis in the broad, general sense of representation, not in the special sense of "impersonation" which Plato will promulgate in Book 3. Now, what kind of lying or deception is he talking about here? The gods' quick-change tricks do not really take us in even in the *Iliad*, since the omniscient poet is there to identify them. Does Plato really mean to suggest the possibility of such a deception of "us" in the fourth century B.C.?

The clue to Plato's meaning is in the phrase "lying poet." Throughout the passage, with an implication which approaches explicitness only in that phrase, god is contrasted with the poet. The "lie in words," in this context, is not verbal falsehood in general, it is a poem like those of Homer and Hesiod, or any part of such a poem that contains a misrepresentation of gods or heroes. And the passage gives a reason for the presence of such misrepresentations ("ugly lies," as they were previously called) in such poems: "In the mythical works we were talking about just now, because we don't know how the truth stands with the events of long ago, we make falsehood serve our purpose by making it resemble the truth as much as possible" (382d).

In spite of the "we" (which seems in this case to mean "we men," we human beings), Plato is explaining here why the poet tells his lies: he is ignorant of the truth and tries to make his falsehood "resemble" it. The point is of course that he cannot. Plato has spoken a little obliquely, that is all. Being ignorant of the truth, the poet can only make his "lie" resemble the lie in his soul—his false conception of the truth—and that false conception includes the false notion that gods, and heroes, change, either intentionally or under duress. If pressed hard, this could be taken as an exculpation of the poet: he tells his lies out of ignorance rather than malice. In any case he stands convicted of ignorance, as he was in the *Ion* and as he will be again in *Republic* 10. It is basically the same doctrine. And the answer to the question we asked a moment ago, about the Homeric gods deceiving us into thinking that they change form, is that they may indeed do so, not in their own persons but through Homer's "lie in words."

So much for the two guidelines for portrayals of the gods. There follows a section on the poets' representations of the afterlife (3.386aff.). They must stop making it fearful, since there is nothing fearful about the death of a good man. More stress, however, is laid on the pernicious example to the young Guards than on the falsity of the picture. At one point the verb μιμεῖσθαι appears (386c), its only occurrence in the whole sequence from 377a to 392d. We shall ask the poets, says Plato, not to portray the gods weeping and lamenting over heroes' fates, "and especially not to have the effrontery to represent the greatest of the gods so untruly (ἀνομοίως μιμήσασθαι, imitate him so unresemblingly)" as to make him mourn the approaching death of Hektor (*Iliad* 22.168), or of Sarpedon (16.433). In other words, to make Zeus lament over a mortal is to paint a portrait of him which does not resemble the original: an "ugly lie." We shall come back to the use of μιμήσασθαι in this passage.

The miscellaneous prescriptions which now follow (388eff.) are of no great interest to us either theoretically or practically. There are to be no representations of gods or heroes overcome by laughter; lying will not be tolerated, except from public officials; decency and self-control (σωφροσύνη, 389dff.) will be inculcated, especially with respect to food, drink, and sex; intimations that either gods or men are accessible to bribes will be eschewed; and finally a variety of acts and attitudes will be forbidden to be represented in poetry (391aff.), such as the dragging of Hektor's body or the slaughter of the Trojan captives on Patroklos' funeral pyre. It is noteworthy that at the end of this catalogue, where Plato repeats that such actions are "neither morally defensible nor true," he identifies the heroes as sons of gods and refers back to his "proof" that the gods cannot be sources of evil (391d–e). Thus no separate proof is offered for the heroes qua human beings.

A difficulty presents itself at this point: a difficulty which is acknowledged, in fact emphasized, by Plato. Poets have shocking things to say about ordinary men too: "that many a wicked man is happy and many a righteous man plagued by misfortune, and that wrongdoing is profitable if one can get away with it, while justice means benefit to others and damage to oneself. We shall forbid them to say such things and prescribe the opposite; do you agree?" (392b). But although the interlocutor readily agrees, Sokrates points out that they cannot legitimately do that until they have ascertained the nature of justice and made sure that it is profitable to its possessor; and in fact we remember that that was the aim proposed for the whole *Republic*. "So let our discussion of (the content of) tales end here. The next subject, I suppose, is the manner of their telling, and then we shall have considered both what is to be told and how it is to be told" (392c).

This is a turning point, in more senses than one. The demonstration of the true nature of justice, and that it is profitable—and the opposite unprofitable—to its possessor, will not be finished until the end of Book 9; but then, although Plato returns to the subject of poetry in Book 10, he does not return to it from this point of view. The result is never brought to bear on the poets in any direct way.

The next two or three sentences seem to say that we are now venturing into new and unfamiliar territory. Adeimantos does not understand the distinction between what is said and how. Sokrates asks him whether it is true that "everything that is told by storytellers and poets is a narration (διήγησις) of past, present, or future events" (392d). "Yes." "Well then, isn't it done either by unmixed narration, or by that through imitation (διὰ μιμήσεως), or by both?" Again Adeimantos needs an explanation, and Sokrates gives it at considerable length, using as his illustrative text the first lines of the *Iliad*, about the encounter of the old priest Chryses with Agamemnon. He points out (393a) that as far as line 15 of Book 1 ("and he besought all the Achaians") "the poet not only speaks in his own person (himself), but does not even attempt to turn our thoughts in some other direction (i.e., to make us think) that the speaker is anyone other than himself; but he speaks the following passage (lines 17–21) as if he actually were Chryses, and tries as hard as he can to make us think that it is not Homer who is speaking but the priest, an old man" (393a). Sokrates further establishes that both the speeches and the parts between the speeches are narration, but "when (a poet) speaks a speech as (if) being someone else, we shall say that he then likens his own way of speaking as much as he can to (that of) the person he has announced will speak"; and "to make oneself like (make oneself resemble) another either in utterance or in posture is to imitate (μιμεῖσθαι) the person one likens oneself to" (393c). This, then, is the meaning of doing the narration through mimesis. And Sokrates illustrates by turning lines 12–42 of Book 1 (which contain three passages in direct speech: 17–21, the priest; 26–32, Agamemnon; 37–42, the priest) into uniform indirect narrative: the priest came and prayed that the gods might grant them to take Troy but themselves be saved; and that they release his daughter, etc. That, says Sokrates, is what he means by "simple narrative without any admixture of imitation" (ἄνευ μιμήσεως ἁπλῆ διήγησις, 394b).

At first blush it might appear that the difference in question is simply that between direct and indirectly quoted speech. But Plato is not making such heavy weather over a grammatical distinction. Nor is it a question merely of the dramatic method as such. Implicit in that method, Plato is saying, is that the poet impersonates the characters of his story—impersonates them not merely by putting speeches in their mouths but in the sense that he pretends to be the various characters, tries to make us think that he *is* Chryses and Agamemnon and all the rest in turn. The phrase which I translated above "as if he actually were Chryses" can be rendered more literally "as actually being Chryses," where "as" denotes that his "being" Chryses is the impression engendered in the mind of the hearer. Either way, of course, the impression is false: Homer is not Chryses or Agamemnon, he is Homer. A deception is involved, and the deception is deliberate: "But if the poet should not (try to) conceal himself at any point, his whole poetic narration would stand achieved without mimesis" (393c).

Why does the poet try to deceive us by "concealing himself"? Aristotle, working with what appears to be the same tripartite scheme, uses pure mimesis as a straightfoward designation of the dramatic method. The dramatist "projects" his characters, but not out of himself; they are not he in any sense. But then neither was Aristotle Plato. Plato all his life—consistently, I suppose, since he was a poet himself—felt poetry was a supremely personal communication from one soul to another, just as he always believed dialectic was not a mere canvassing of external truths but a communion between two souls, master's and pupil's. The poet's relationship to his hearers is in fact a kind of devilish inversion of the true relationship between souls. It is a communication of energy all the more potent for being concealed; for the better he conceals himself, the more open and unguarded the listener's soul will be to his nefarious impersonations. It only remains to add that Plato felt this diabolical energy coming from one poet above all others: Homer. His choice of the beginning of the *Iliad* to illustrate his point about impersonation is no accident.

We must now consider Plato's term for that personification, μίμησις. Adeimantos had no difficulty with the idea that poems and stories involve a recounting of events (διήγησις). It was when the term μίμησις was introduced that he asked for clarification, and it was to enlighten him on that score that Plato treated the matter in such detail. Since confusion on the part of the interlocutor presumably signals Plato's awareness of possible confusion on the part of the reader, we have to ask whether μίμησις was likely to be so unfamiliar a term to the readers of the *Republic*. The answer seems to be: in this sense, yes.

Some years ago, in a study of μιμεῖσθαι and related words before Plato,[1] I suggested that three main strands of meaning could be distinguished in the usage of μιμεῖσθαι and μίμησις in the fifth century:

1. *Miming*: enacting a mime-like plot or acting a mime-like character. This meaning, which is presumably the original one (μιμεῖσθαι, denominative verb formed in the regular way from μῖμος), is obviously dramatic in orientation. *Μιμεῖσθαι* appears occasionally in Attic, but only in mimic or comic contexts; it is not used in serious drama.[2]

2. *Imitating*: copying another person's actions or way of doing something, in general. This broader and vaguer (less specifically dramatic) meaning is the predominant one in Attic, especially for the action noun μίμησις.

3. *Copying*: making a replica of something in an inanimate material (wood, etc.). This meaning is especially common with the result noun μίμημα, "replica, copy."

1. G. F. Else, " 'Imitation' in the Fifth Century," *CP* 53 (1958) 73–90 and 245, esp. 79.

2. But we find γυναικόμιμος, "woman-aping" thrice in tragedy, always contemptuously: [Aesch.] *PV* 1005, Soph. frag. 702N² (= *TrGF* 769), Eur. *Bacch.* 980. Senses of μῖμος, μιμεῖσθαι, and μίμημα related to the idea of impersonation are also present at Aesch. *Cho.* 564, frag. 57N²; Eur. *Iph. Aul.* 578, *Iph. Taur.* 294 (?), [Eur.?] *Rh.* 211, 56.

Since these words are latecomers in Attic Greek, since there is no con-vincing Greek or Indo-European etymology for μῖμος, and since the traditional home of the mime was Sicily, it is a not too hazardous infer-ence that the whole word-family was imported into Attic (and Ionic) from the West and was still not wholly domesticated in Athens at the end of the fifth century, except for μιμεῖσθαι and μίμησις in the general meaning "imitate," "imitation."

Our passage is consonant with these facts and inferences. The meaning Plato wants to establish for μίμησις here is the impersonation of dra-matic characters; and he does so by presenting μίμησις in that sense as a particular case of μίμησις = imitation. The subsumption is effected in the sentence already quoted above, 393c: "To make oneself like another either in utterance or in posture is to imitate the person one likens one-self to." The interlocutor readily accepts this subsumption under the broader sense of μίμησις, although he had been puzzled by μίμησις = impersonation. In other words the broader meaning was familiar to him, the narrower one was not. Or at least it was not familiar to him in the sense in which it is used here, as a designation of the dramatic method per se. We noted above that μιμεῖσθαι in its dramatic signification (= "miming") still had a flavor of the mime about it in fifth-century Attic Greek. It was not in use as a general term for the acting of roles in drama—tragedy, satyr play, comedy—much less to describe Homer's kind of "impersonation." In fact Plato is the author of this extension, and in the very passage we are discussing. So far as we can tell, he was the first to proclaim Homer a dramatist and actor, "the teacher and captain of all these glorious tragic poets" (10.595c).

If we now look back over the discussion of poetry since its beginning at 2.376e, we become aware of an interesting fact. We know that Plato was familiar with a view which accepted poetry as a replica-making art (meaning no. 3 in the list above). We found that view in the *Kratylos*, and it will turn up again in *Republic* 10; but it has been excluded from the treatment of poetry here. Excluded, that is, from the discussion as such; but just enough hints, or inadvertent allusions, remain to prove that Plato had not forgotten it.

Thus at 373b, in describing the "bloated" city, Sokrates lumped the poets, painters, and sculptors together under the term μιμηταί, "repre-sentative artists"—clearly a generic term and one he expected to be un-derstood. It cannot be taken either as "impersonators" (meaning no. 1) or as "imitators" in the general sense (no. 2). And at 382b, in the discus-sion of "tales" itself, the "lie in words" was called a replica (μίμημα) of the "lie in the soul." But that is not quite the same thing as calling poetry a mimetic art per se.

Finally, at 388b–c Sokrates says, "We shall ask the poets not to portray (ποιεῖν, compose) gods uttering lamentations," or "at least not to have the effrontery to represent (μιμήσασθαι) the greatest of the gods in so implausible a fashion (ἀνομοίως, unresemblingly) as to make him say . . ."—what follows is from Zeus's lament over Hektor, *Iliad* 22.168–169. Since Zeus's words are quoted in direct speech, one might be tempted to take μιμήσασθαι as "impersonate." But that is negated by the exact parallel with ποιεῖν, which never means "impersonate," and by the important parallel passage on "ugly lies" at 377d (see p. 19 above), where no reference was made to μίμησις.

Everything considered, it seems clear that except for the (inadvertent?) μιμήσασθαι at 388e Plato has deliberately kept μίμησις out of the discussion up to 392d. And his reason for doing so is not hard to see: he wanted to keep the ground clear for his innovative use of μίμησις = dramatic impersonation. To have used it from the beginning in the broad sense of mimetic art, including all or most poetry and the graphic arts as well, would only have muddied the waters. But it is important to notice, as we shall later, that Plato's scheme does not really work after all. *Μίμησις* = impersonation remains an episode, and when the discussion of poetry is resumed in Book 10, it is tacitly dropped.

In hailing—or stigmatizing—Homer as the inventor of the dramatic method, Plato is referring to something which could be analyzed in other ways. One part of a sentence which has already been quoted (393b; see p. 24 above) hints at the basic phenomenon: Homer "tries as hard as he can to make us think that it is not Homer speaking but the priest, an old man." In other words Homer somehow makes it sound like an old man speaking instead of the (presumably younger) poet; and we must assume that he does the same thing for Agamemnon (tactless king), Achilleus (irascible warrior), and so forth. How does he do it? Unfortunately Plato does not identify or describe the old-man-like quality in Chryses' speeches, but it seems that he must be referring to the phenomenon which Aristotle, approaching the matter from a very different point of view, subsumes under the poetic "universal" (*Poetics* 9.1451b8): the kinds of things a certain kind of person is likely to do or say according to probability or necessity. An older term for this fidelity to type, one destined for a long career in rhetorical and poetic theory, was τὸ πρέπον, "the appropriate" (Latin *decorum*). The unfortunate Ion had made a sally in that direction, suggesting (*Ion* 540b) that a rhapsode knows what is πρέπον for man and woman, slave and free man, ruler and ruled, to say. It was in trying to particularize the principle, specifying what kind of "ruler" (ἄρχων) he meant, that Ion arrived at the apparently absurd claim that he (and, by implication, Homer) knew what is fitting for a general to say. This lends itself easily to ridicule but had its point nevertheless in a polity like that of Athens, where the topmost elected magistrates (ἄρχοντες) were in fact generals (Perikles held much of his thirty-year hegemony through annual reelection as general).

Ion's claim was quickly set aside and the dialogue ended with his—apparently total—discomfiture. A better statement of the case (for which an abler spokesman would be needed than that dim-witted rhapsode) would claim that poetry is a part of or akin to the "political" art, the master art which regulates and maintains the relationships between men in society, and that it is from that source that the poet knows how it is fitting for a king or a general or a hero to speak. We shall see that something like such a claim is made for Homer in Book 10 of the *Republic*, though it too is disallowed and set down before it is properly made. Plato cannot admit that there is any political art except his own.

To return to our text: At 392d, introducing the section on the manner of telling (λέξις) of tales, Sokrates has established narration (διήγησις) as the genus and then identified its species as (1) "simple," i.e., unmixed, διήγησις, (2) διήγησις by means of μίμησις, and (3) διήγησις by means of both. It cannot be said that the scheme is outstandingly logical. Narration appears as one basic species of itself while mimesis constitutes the other. A more consistent division would have given the species as (1) διήγησις, (2) μίμησις, and (3) their mixture. But then what would the genus have been called? Simply ποίησις?

The summary which follows (394b–c) is as hasty and casual as the introduction. One form of poetry, the drama, operates entirely through mimesis, "another through narrative by the poet himself—you'll find it particularly in dithyrambs, I think—and another works through both, in epic poetry and several other places, if you know what I mean." The vague indications ("I think"; "if you know what I mean") make it evident that Plato is not out to achieve a complete, tested classification of all poetry here. He is out to show that mimesis in the sense of impersonation is the most dangerous mode; for the rest, he does not care where the chips may fall. The passage does not offer an objective classification of poetry; it is a fighting maneuver against Homer and the drama. (Only the purely narrative method, here identified with the dithyramb, can be considered completely harmless.)

One wonders whether Plato's experience of the mime on its native ground, Sicily, may not have contributed to his innovative definition of μίμησις = impersonation. His connection with the island began around 390 and continued throughout his life. One of the fruits of his first sojourn there was a lifelong fondness for Sicilian mimes, especially those of Sophron. Legend says that a copy of that author was found under his pillow after his death; and there appears to be a covert allusion to Sophron's "men's" and "women's" mimes in the *Republic* itself, 5.451c.[3] These modest productions showed much greater similarity to Plato's own earlier dialogues than did the other forms of drama known to him (tragedy, satyr play, Old Attic Comedy, and perhaps the so-called Middle Comedy). They presented scenes of everyday life, eschewing heroic fates and passions; offered humorous sketches of general types rather than satirically etched portraits of individuals; and were in rhythmical prose rather than verse. Plato must have been especially taken, I should imagine, by their focus on reality and their avoidance of poetic bluster and bombast. He himself had, if not invented, at least perfected a new form of drama centering in the antihero Sokrates, and Sokrates was a new incarnation of a type long known in Dorian farce: the εἴρων, the self-deprecating fellow who plays down his wit and knowledge while other people play theirs up. The mime cannot have inspired this development; Plato's acquaintance with it came too late for that. But he could have gotten from it a pleasurable confirmation of the new literary, or anti-literary, taste he had acquired since he turned toward Sokrates and away from tragedy and poetry.

It is possible, then, that Plato's familiarity with and predilection for the mime may have encouraged his extension of μίμησις to signify the dramatic type of impersonation specifically. If so, the mime must also have stood in his mind for a fresh and undangerous—an un-Homeric—kind of impersonation. The impulse for the extension did not come from the mime, however, or from the drama at all, but from Homer. It was in the *Iliad*, not in Euripides or Aristophanes or Sophron, that Plato had made or thought he made the discovery that the characters of the poem are really the poet in disguise. The hypnotic power that Chryses and Agamemnon and Kalchas and Achilleus and Thetis—and Zeus and Hera and Athene—exert over our souls really comes from Homer. The author of the *Iliad* lurks behind these many disguises, a mighty enchanter.

To be sure, Plato never explicitly calls Homer a sorcerer or wizard

3. See, e.g., James Adam's edition of the *Republic* (Cambridge 1902) ad loc.

(γόης), but the extent of the poet's power can be gauged by the severity of the measures which Plato takes against it; and we can cite evidence from an unexpected quarter to show that Plato did in fact consider Homer to be a kind of γόης. Introducing his second guideline for representations of god—that he neither changes form nor tries to make us think he does—Plato asks (380d) whether god is a γόης who changes his appearance from one form to another ("himself becoming (it)," αὐτὸν γιγνόμενον) and deceives us by making us think such things about himself (ποιοῦντα περὶ αὐτοῦ τοιαῦτα δοκεῖν). These phrases have unmistakably precise echoes in Plato's description of Homer's dramatic procedures. Homer does not actually become Chryses, but he speaks as if he were Chryses (ὥσπερ αὐτὸς ὤν) and tries as hard as he can to make us think (ποιῆσαι . . . δοκεῖν) that it is not Homer who is speaking but the priest (393a–b; cf. 393d, ὡς Χρύσης γενόμενος). At the end of this whole sequence, 398a, the person upon whom the sentence of banishment is pronounced is one so clever that he can take on every kind of shape ("become of every sort," παντοδαπὸν γίγνεσθαι; cf. παντοδαποὺς φαίνεσθαι, 381e). Such is the climax of the poet's becomings. He, not god, is the one who would use his powers of enchantment to make us think that he has become all sorts of persons, human and divine.

The indictment against the poets, especially Homer, has now been framed; Plato proceeds to make the application. Sokrates asks, 394e, "whether our Guards should be mimetic (μιμητικούς) or not." Is "mimetic" general or specific here: "tending to imitate other people," or "given to playing dramatic roles"? It is impossible to say, and it does not matter, since the one tendency is merely a subcase of the other: "Imitations, if carried on continuously from childhood, turn into habits and become second nature, in our bodies, our utterances, and our minds" (395d). But this is a standing threat to the Platonic community, which rests on the principle of "justice": one man, one job. If a man can only do one thing well, he certainly cannot imitate many things well; and to back this up Plato points out that the same person cannot even produce two μιμήματα as close to each other as comedy and tragedy (395a). (The contradiction with the end of the *Symposion*—see above, p. 12—disappears when one remembers that there Plato was not talking about actual dramatists but about the ideal kind, i.e., himself.)

If the Guards imitate anything, they should imitate brave, self-controlled, pious, free men and the likes (395c)—i.e., men like Sokrates. There follows a long list of persons, animals, etc., whom the Guards are *not* to imitate: women abusing their husbands or insulting the gods, or in illness or love or childbirth; slaves doing what slaves do; common men cursing each other, using foul language, getting drunk, going mad; people forging metals or rowing triremes; horses neighing, bulls bellowing, brooks gurgling; and so on. Sokrates ends with the formulation that they may imitate a good man when he says or does something good, but not other kinds of men in other situations, so that "their imitation will partake of both, namely mimesis and the other kind of narration, but with a small portion of mimesis in a large amount of discourse" (396d).

Two views of mimesis are commingled here: (1) that the Guards should imitate only good men, and (2) that in any case they should imitate as little as possible. The two views are mutually compatible though distinct, and it is evident that Plato is urging both. He is not merely trying to limit mimesis to worthy objects, he is trying to limit it altogether, because it means variousness and multiplicity, and variousness and multiplicity are bad. He is out to breed and train a uniform, simple kind of men and is excluding anything that might defeat that purpose. (The fact that Plato himself would perish of boredom if he were condemned to live among such monolithic minds is not, I suppose, strictly relevant to the question.) And the same preference for simplicity and uniformity appears again very clearly in the following section on "harmonies"—musical scales, and rhythms (398c–400c).

Historians of literary criticism tend to pay too little attention to this simplistic tendency in Plato's objections to poetry. It is grounded very deeply in his view not only of justice and the good life but of the structure of reality. In his characterizations of the Forms, in all dialogues down to *Parmenides* and *Sophist*, Plato harps untiringly on their unity and eternal self-identity. Back of the buzzing multiplicity of the world of Becoming stands the divine simplicity of the Idea; and back of the multiplicity of Ideas in turn stands the Good, which is also the One. The philosopher Alfred North Whitehead used to say that we all like to believe the truth is simple; it was surely so with Plato, at least down to the philosophical crisis which seems to be heralded by the *Theaitetos*, the *Sophist*, and the other late dialogues. Then multiplicity—the Many along with the One—began to have its day in court.

There was also the personal example of Sokrates, the Unvarying Man, who was "always saying the same things about the same things" and who preserved the same tone and attitude unchanged through all the vicissitudes of life—and death. Sokrates' presence in the dialogue prevents him from pointing to himself and observing that a man like himself offers very little purchase to an imitative poet because his way of speaking shows hardly any variations: nothing to imitate. But the gist of the idea is conveyed at 397c, as we shall see.

The long catalogue of human beings, craft activities, animals, and natural elements which the Guards are forbidden to imitate (395b–396b), and the shorter but equally heterogeneous list of things which the thoroughly imitative man will want to imitate (397a), have one marked trait in common in addition to their kaleidoscopic variety: few of the items mentioned, and fewer as the list goes on, have any discernible connection with tragedy, not to speak of the epic. A woman reviling her husband may pass as a tragic figure (Medeia); or one boasting and vying with the gods, thinking she is "happy" (Niobe), or "overwhelmed by sufferings, griefs, and lamentations" (Hekabe in both *Trojan Women* and *Hekabe*), or ill (Alkestis), in love (Phaidra), in labor (Auge). But slaves, male and female, doing what befits slaves, or low characters exchanging insults and foul language, drunk or sober, "and all the things they do"? We may assign these gentry to comedy if we like, although Attic comedy seems on the whole to have been less free and foul-spoken in the fourth century than in the fifth. But what are we to make of smiths at the forge, coxswains calling the stroke for rowers, "horses neighing, bulls bellowing, rivers rushing, sea beating on the shore, thunderbolts, and all that kind of thing"? What has this phantasmagoria to do with the drama, or with Homer? We shall come back to this puzzling question in a moment.

The interlocutor readily agrees that the Guards have no business engaging in imitations of this kind, since "they are not permitted either to be madmen or to act like them." "If I understand what you mean, then," says Sokrates, "there is a kind of narration which the true gentleman will use when it is necessary for him to tell something, and another, very different kind which will be used by his opposite in character and training" (396b–c, translation condensed). Ah yes, we think, here are our old friends again: straight narrative, which "you'll find particularly in dithyrambs, I think," and "narrative through imitation," i.e., in tragedy and comedy (394c). But in fact that is not what Plato offers here, and it behooves us to watch him very closely, for he is about to pull off a spectacular trick before our eyes. A change of angle has been introduced which alters all the relationships:

The man of well-regulated character, I think, when he comes in his narration to an utterance or action of a good man, will be willing to report it as if he were that man himself (ὡς αὐτὸς ὢν ἐκεῖνος) and will not be ashamed of that sort of mimesis, playing the part (μιμούμενος) of the good man especially when he is acting sensibly and in full possession of himself (ἀσφαλῶς), but less when in the grip of illness or love or drunkenness or some other misfortune. But when he comes to somebody unworthy of himself, he will not be willing seriously (σπουδῇ) to make himself resemble that inferior person, unless perchance for a short stretch while he is performing some virtuous act, but will be ashamed; for one thing because he has no practice in imitating (μιμεῖσθαι) that kind of person, and for another because he finds it repulsive to force and press himself into the mold of the worse kind (since his mind has no respect for them), except in fun. (396c–e)

So, says Sokrates, the moral man will use the kind of narration we illustrated from Homer—the mixed—but with "only a small proportion of imitation (impersonation) in a lot of discourse" (396e). And now his opposite appears: a man who "will think nothing unworthy of him; so he will undertake to imitate anything and everything, seriously and in the presence of crowds of people; not only the things we mentioned just now, thunderbolts and the sounds of winds, hail, wagon wheels, creaking pulleys, but the voice of trumpets, oboes, pipes, all musical instruments, and the cries of dogs, sheep, birds" (397a). In this carnival of mimetic lust we are hard put to identify the new kind of man. Is Plato saying in effect that this is what it all comes to? Let the mimetic man into your city, give him his head, and you'll see: he'll end up barking like a dog or cooing like a pigeon. He has no higher aim in life. "His utterance, then, will be entirely by imitation through voice and gesture, or with only a small portion of narrative" (397b). Furthermore, indiscriminate mimicry necessarily involves frequent variations not only in content but in whatever rhythms and harmonies accompany it, whereas the virtuous man's discourse will be uniform and almost unchanging in that respect also.

Now comes the moment when Plato engineers a quick change that would make Homer envious. All poets use one or the other of these kinds of utterance, or a mixture of the two. "What shall we do, then? Shall we admit all of them into the city, or the first of the unmixed ones, or the mixed?" "My vote is for the unmixed imitator of the good man." "Well, but the mixed one is enjoyable (ἡδύς) too, Adeimantos; and much the most enjoyable (ἥδιστος) to boys and their slave attendants, and to most of the rabble, is the opposite of the one you chose." "He is indeed" (397d).

What poets are we talking about here? The "mixed" one should be the epic poet, i.e., Homer; that identification was explicitly repeated at 396e. But who are the "unmixed" ones? By our former guidelines (394c) they ought to be the dithyrambist (all narrative) and the tragic or comic poet (all mimesis) respectively. But that cannot be, for several reasons. In the first place the two kinds of utterance which Plato has just described in detail (396c–397b), and has now explicitly made the basis of his classification (397c), are not unmixed. The good man will use mimesis on occasion, when the person and the action represented are worthy (396d), and his opposite may make some use of narrative (397b). Granted that the amount may be slight in each case, all we have left are procedures that are more or less mixed.

But that is not the worst. The way in which the good man's procedure is described (396c–e) has nothing to do with the dithyramb, old, new, or reformed; and his opposite number, the imitator of winds, trumpets, dogs, and pigeons, has nothing to do with either tragedy or comedy. He is a different breed of man entirely. I think we can gain a clue to his identity from a passage in the *Laws*, 2.658aff., where the Athenian asks what would happen if the city should announce an open competition "for pleasure only," one in which the winner would be the person adjudged to be most enjoyable, ἥδιστος, to the spectators. Competitors would come representing epic, lyric poetry, tragedy, and comedy; "and it would not be surprising if somebody should think he would be most likely to win by displaying tricks and marvels" (θαύματα, wonders), 658b–c. We know a little about these gentry, the θαυματοποιοί or θαυματουργοί. Their history goes back to the beginnings of civilization and comes down unbroken to the present day; they earned a living on the fringes of Greek life, as they had before in the Orient, as jugglers, acrobats, conjurers, magicians, but on a modest scale: they made no claim to the glamor or the occult powers of the higher type of magician.

Now, says the Athenian, *Laws* 658c, if the judgment rested with the small boys, the juggler would win the competition hands down. The parallels with our passage seem to me sufficient to establish the identity of the man who is ready to imitate anything and everything; he is the θαυματοποιός. But then what is he doing here? We have already hinted at the answer: if you open the doors of your city to the epic poet and the tragedian, you will end by opening them to the θαυματοποιός, the juggler, and so far as ordinary men and boys are concerned he will win the competition, because he is the mimetic specialist *par excellence*.

After reminding us that there is no room in our state for "duplex or multiplex" man, Sokrates proceeds to sum up this whole sequence:

"Well then, I think, if a man so talented that he can assume all kinds of shapes, that is, imitate anything and everything, should come to our city, to make a display of himself and his poems, we would prostrate ourselves before him as holy, magical, and enjoyable (ὡς ἱερὸν καὶ θαυμαστὸν καὶ ἡδύν), would tell him that there is no one like him in our city—our law does not allow it—and would send him off to another one, heaping myrrh on his head and loading him with sacred fillets; and we would employ the drier and less enjoyable poet, for the public welfare . . ." (398a).

This then is the famous "expulsion of the poets" from the new state. I hesitate to call it dishonest, but at the very least it is unforgivably oblique and imprecise. The real question at issue is the status of Homer and the other serious poets; and the seedy music-hall character who has been put up for the role of scapegoat here has little or nothing in common with any serious Greek poet. He is the same man who appeared at 397b, ready and willing to imitate anything: thunder, winds, horns, pipes, and animal cries; a list which was an obvious echo of the even more elaborate one at 395d–396b. Earlier, at 394d, when Sokrates asked whether the poets should be allowed to perform their narratives through mimesis, wholly or in part or not at all, Adeimantos thought that the question was "whether we shall receive tragedy and comedy into the city or not"; to which Sokrates made the mysterious reply, "Perhaps; and perhaps more than that, too." How are we to take this Delphic utterance, and has it now been fulfilled? Have tragedy and comedy been banished? All tragedy and all comedy? Or only those specimens which involve too much imitation of a low and unworthy kind? And Homer? He represented the mixed species, which was not explicitly included in the damnation. Is he banished entirely, or only that part of his work that consists of impersonation, or everything that represents anyone except the virtuous man in outstandingly virtuous moments?

Plato himself is no mean magician. He has set up a miserable mountebank, a cheap juggler and conjurer, to be his target, and then with a few passes and abracadabras has conjured us—and presumably himself—into believing that he has banished all the great poets, Homer and Hesiod, Aischylos and Sophokles, Euripides and Aristophanes, from his new city. There is nothing to prevent Homer in particular from bringing a suit for mistrial, since his "mixed" method was specifically distinguished (397d) from the one that was "sweetest" to boys and groundlings; and the latter is the one that is pilloried at 398a. As for Aischylos or Sophokles, or Homer too for that matter, any of them could say to

Plato, "I do not recognize myself in this caricature that you are pleased to expel from your city. I have never stooped to the abject and indiscriminate mimicry you ascribe to him, and therefore I deny that your verdict applies to me." And what could Plato say in reply? That they were "imitators" of that sort? Or would he say, "You are right. I didn't mean you, I meant the cheap entertainers who are corrupting the taste of the public nowadays"? No, it is clear that he *does* mean Homer and Sophokles and the rest. Precisely the greatest are his targets, because they present the richest and most varied portrait gallery of divine and human types: gods who do not accord with Plato's norms, men who do not exemplify the bland simplicity of Sokrates.

If our long and laborious pursuit of Plato's meaning in this passage has accomplished anything, it has demonstrated that Book 3 of the *Republic* is not the place to look for an objective, impartial classification of poetry. To order the poets in a neat taxonomic scheme was the least of his motives here.

The next section (398c–400c), on song (μέλος) and its musical components, melody and rhythm, adds nothing significantly new to Plato's account of poetry. The words of a musical piece should establish the guideline for its melody and rhythm. (Plato clearly abhorred the musical innovations of his day, which were attempting to free music from subservience to the verbal text.) At all points simplicity is to be the keynote. At 400a the question is raised what "harmonies" (modes or scales) are "imitations" (or replicas, μιμήματα) of what kinds of life, and Sokrates says that the answer will have to be worked out in consultation with Damon, the writer on music. It has been claimed that a complete Damonian-Pythagorean theory of musical *mimesis* lies behind this allusion.[4] In any case the discussion of music here presents itself as a supplement to what has already been said about poetry; no really new principles are invoked.

There follows (400c–403c) a summing up of the aims of the Guards' education in music, in the broad sense of education of the soul as opposed to the body. This is the real conclusion to the whole sequence that began at 2.376e. It hymns the praises, not of intelligence and understanding—such intellectual attainments are still far in the future for the young Guards—but of grace and harmony in posture and movement and (musical) utterance (400dff.). Here the idea of imitation still floats before

---

4. This is the view of Koller, *Mimesis* (above, chap. 1, n. 5); Else discusses it at length and rejects it in the article cited above, n. 1.

us. Grace of movement (τὸ εὔρυθμον) "follows noble utterance, in like-
ness (as a likeness) to it" (400b). "Painting and all the arts of that kind
are full of these qualities; weaving is full also, and embroidery, and house
construction and the making of every kind of manufactured product,
and all human and animal bodies and those of plants. . . . And lack of
grace and rhythm and harmony are sisters to vileness of speech and
character, while their opposites are sisters and replicas (μιμήματα) of
their opposite, the character that is temperate and good" (401a).

> Therefore not only must we charge and compel our poets to embody
> the image of this good character (τὴν τοῦ ἀγαθοῦ εἰκόνα ἤθους
> ἐμποιεῖν) in their poems or not to compose in our state at all, but
> we must issue orders to our other craftsmen also and forbid them to
> embody (ἐμποιεῖν) that vile and dissolute and slavish and ugly char-
> acter either in images (ἐν εἰκόσι) of living creatures or in buildings
> or in any other product made by hands, on penalty of not exercising
> their crafts among us; so that our Guards may not grow up among
> images of corruption (ἐν κακίας εἰκόσι), as in a foul pasturage, . . .
> but we must seek those craftsmen who are nobly equipped by nature
> to track down the nature of the noble and shapely, so that the
> young, dwelling as it were in a healthful place, may draw benefit
> from whatever effluence strikes upon their sight or hearing from
> works of beauty, like a breeze wafting health from salubrious re-
> gions, and straight from childhood, without their being aware of it,
> brings them into likeness (εἰς ὁμοιότητα) and love and harmony
> with the beauty of reason. (401b–d)

I have translated this famous passage at some length (though still not
at full length) with a specific purpose in mind. It is a splendid example of
Plato's full-blown dithyrambic style, but I fear that precisely for that
reason most readers allow it to blow over them "like a breeze wafting
health from salubrious regions," but bringing only vague notions of
beauty and moral uplift: in other words, like an inspiring but not very
well focused sermon. Its interest for our purpose is quite different.

Throughout the passage the terms "image" (εἰκών, 401b2, 5, 8), "rep-
lica" (μιμήματα, 401a8), and "likeness" (ὁμοιότης, 401d2; cf. ὁμοιού-
μενον, 400d2) are fundamental. What Plato is saying here, not with
philosophic calm but with all the eloquence at his command, is that
poets, and indeed craftsmen of all sorts down to makers of furniture and
other items of everyday use, are to be not merely permitted but bullied

and coerced into incorporating (literally, building in) "the image of good character" in their varied products. The whole environment thus created goes to make up the "healthful place" in which the young Guards will grow to maturity.

The theme of images brings us back to the third aspect or dimension out of which Plato's total concept of mimesis was formed: the idea of poetry as an image- or replica-making art. We found this idea present, though not elaborated, in the *Kratylos*, and there too poetry was set in close parallel with the other image-making art, painting. In the passage we have just been considering, the association has been broadened to include sculpture (perhaps already implied in the *Kratylos*) and the other arts that make visible artifacts. All these arts produce εἰκόνες, images; and that term and its congeners give Plato's words a predominantly visual cast, although both kinds of art are included ("whatever effluences may strike upon their sight or hearing").

The most important aspect of the passage, however, is the way it proceeds from negative to positive: from prohibitions and inhibitions to the vision of the young Guards surrounded by infuences of health and beauty. Objectively, what Plato says is still compatible with, and even echoes, his threat to expel the poets, but the tone is quite different. It is not implied that all poets and craftsmen will fail in their endeavor; quite the contrary. Their work is part of an overarching plan, and they will be fired and sustained by the enthusiasm of the master artist who has designed the plan: that is, by Plato.

One has to look closely at the passage before one notices that in spite of all the allusions to images and copies the actual word μίμησις does not appear, either in the sense of dramatic impersonation or in the sense of (moral) imitation in general. In the following passage, 401d–402a, where Plato sums up the educational effect of music on the young soul, one might expect some reference to the latter "imitating" the good. One finds instead, 401e, "He would praise the beautiful and, receiving it into his soul with rejoicing, would be nourished by it and grow true and noble," but no allusion to mimesis. "Imitation" as impersonation was a special concept introduced for a special purpose, to discredit Homer and the drama. It has now served that purpose and is quietly dropped, not to be mentioned again in the *Republic*. (Μίμησις in the broader sense of imitation will meet us once more, in a moment.)

Concurrently, however, with this deemphasizing of mimesis we can observe, both in the passage we quoted at length (401b–d) and elsewhere, the emergence of another, similar idea: the idea of the philosopher-designer and his Guards as artisans and copiers of the ideal, which they view and reproduce in the institutions and activities of the new state. In this regard, after pointing out that the ability to recognize letters is prior to the ability to recognize their images in water, mirrors, or the like, Sokrates asserts that "neither we nor our Guards will be μουσικοί (i.e., educated in the arts) until we recognize the Forms of self-control, courage, liberality, greatness of spirit, and their congenors and opposites as they circulate about us, perceive them in the places where they are present, both them themselves and their images, and pay respectful heed to them, whether in great or humble surroundings" (402c).

The passage is a notorious crux and stone of offense to those who maintain (following Aristotle) that the Platonic Forms, at least in the mature Plato, are always "separate," cut off from direct human experience and observation. Clearly the Forms are thought of here as in the world, in fact they are "moving about" (περιφερόμενα) in it. And what would their images be? Literary or visual portrayals, or righteously lived lives? Possibly—just possibly—both. In any case it is clear that some of the images must be true ones, if we are to attend to them respectfully. It will be well to remember this when we come to Book 10.

At the beginning of Book 4, after the first sketch of the Guards' style of life has been given, Adeimantos objects that they are going to get no advantages from the city: no houses or private property, no money, nothing. They will not be "happy." Sokrates replies that our purpose is the happiness of the whole, not of a part, and he offers an analogy from the arts. If somebody criticized our painting the eyes of a statue black, on the ground that those most beautiful parts of the body should be painted the most beautiful color, namely purple, we would say, "My dear friend, don't ask us to paint eyes so beautiful that they don't look like eyes at all, and so on, but see whether we are making the whole beautiful by assigning the appropriate traits to each part" (420c). This passage shows again how easily and naturally the analogy with painting comes to Sokrates-Plato.

Similarly, the famous passage on the Divided Line at the end of Book 6, although it does not deal directly with poetry or painting or any of the arts, is of interest to us because it makes significant use of the concept of images. The lowest segment of the line (510a) includes shadows and reflections of things in water, mirrors, and bright surfaces generally. The next segment represents the things which were shadowed or reflected in the previous one; they are defined here as animals, plants, and artifacts. Thus in this case the class of images or likenesses does not include any artifacts, and the originals which are reproduced are limited to natural bodies (animals and plants) and some but not all artifacts. Beds, boats, and harpoons are potentially included, but not hymns or heroes: only objects which cast a shadow, since these first two portions of the line are explicitly said (509d) to embrace the visible (ὁρατόν) realm as contrasted with the intelligible (νοητόν). Here again we find the bias toward visual imagery in the embodiment of truth.

In the Parable of the Cave in Book 7 the visual orientation is still more conspicuous. The parable itself is an εἰκών (517a; cf. 514a, 533a), devised to make the situation represented by the Line graphically visible to the eye of the mind, and the main elements—the central fire, the objects (= "real" objects) carried past out of sight of the prisoners, the shadows they cast on the wall of the cave—are visual symbols. In this imagery the sun's light represents the Good (516a), as it had previously in Book 6 (507eff., where, incidentally, sight was glorified as the highest and most philosophical of the senses). So in the continuation and explication of the Cave (532aff.) the development of the freed prisoner's power of sight, culminating in his ability to look directly at the sun, is explicitly identified with the soul's progress in dialectic, ending in its vision (θέα, 532c) of the Good. And at this point we recall the comparison Plato used in the Seventh Letter, speaking of the final revelation: "a light kindled as if from a fire that has leapt up, which from then on nourishes itself."

Plato's imagery of sight, light, and fire as a parable of the soul's progress in knowledge (out of which came the Platonic-Aristotelian conception of philosophy, and indeed of all intellectual activity, as θεωρία, a "viewing" of truth) is much too large a theme to be treated here. I shall merely point out that Plato's increasing preoccupation with sight as *the* intellectual sense inevitably led to a proportionate downgrading of auditory perception as an avenue to truth. The scandal over the explicit banishment of the poets has tended to make us overlook the implicit fact that the ear arts, music and poetry, important though he considers them to be, have no place in his educational scheme except at the elementary level. There were no courses in literature—no matter how purified—in the Akademy, and none are included in the secondary and higher curriculum for the training of the Guards and future philosopher-kings. Those who are called to rule will have no further contact with poetry (save for the modest exceptions admitted in *Republic* 10) after they leave childhood.

It seems evident that the most potent force behind the master change in Plato's attitude toward the verbal and visual worlds was his discovery of mathematics as the necessary propaideutic to philosophy. We must not forget that the mathematics he learned from Archytas, Theodoros, Theaitetos, and the others was primarily geometry. Although Plato is never weary of extolling its capacity for lifting the soul to the realm of abstraction, it dealt initially and in its own right with visible forms: circles, squares, triangles, cubes, and so on. One does not gain understanding of the circle by meditating on the word κύκλος. The modern mathematician, with his infinitely more sophisticated, mobile, and abstracted subject matter, may speak of mathematics as a kind of language; Plato saw it as a repertory of eternally subsisting shapes. Triangles and octahedrons do not *say* anything, they are there to be seen; they are objects of θεωρία.

Compared with the abstractive power of this luminous, wholly logical world of shapes, the old realm of words and names loses its magic; and indeed Plato never engages in the Sokratic kind of dialectic again after the *Republic*. The new higher dialectic is a very different kind of procedure, having little more than the name in common with the old. It is not accident that modern systematic philosophers tend to take Plato seriously as a philosopher only from the *Theaitetos* on. It is also no accident that the role of the verbal arts, in the *Republic*, is strictly confined to primary education. The secondary and higher education of the Guards (mathematics and dialectic respectively), which only they will receive because only they are going to rule, has no tincture of poetry.

Before we go on to consider Plato's final broadside attack on the poets, in Book 10, another passage claims our attention, both as a confirmation of what we have been saying and as a convenient point of departure for the transition. In Book 6, after repeating the famous pronouncement that there is no hope for human societies until either philosophers become rulers or rulers philosophers, and after speaking of the widespread popular prejudice against philosophy, Sokrates remarks (500b–d) that the true philosopher has no time to "look downward into the preoccupations of men." Instead he will "see and view things which are ordered and always the same"—the Forms—and will "imitate (μιμεῖσθαι) and liken himself (ἀφομοιοῦσθαι) to them as much as possible." Then, if he is required "to put (τιθέναι) what he sees there into men's characters, as a public duty, and not merely to mold his own character," he will become a fine "artificer (δημιουργόν) of self-control and justice and civic virtue as a whole."

These expressions, especially the striking one about the philosopher and future Guardian being an "artificer" of civic virtue, seem deliberately intended to remind us of the passage in Book 3, 395b–d, where the question was what kind of models the young Guards should imitate. In that passage the moral or general meaning of mimesis was uppermost, and the parallel is especially close when Sokrates says here, "Is it possible for a man not to imitate something with which he is in close contact and which he admires?" (500c). We may also be reminded of the slightly cryptic phrase "artificers (δημιουργούς) of freedom for the city" (395c). No emphasis was intended there on freedom as a particular political goal; it simply stood for civic virtue in general. And the words "put what he sees there into men's characters," especially as this operation is contrasted with "merely molding his own character," remind us of that other artisan the shuttle-maker, at *Kratylos* 389c, whose job was to render or "put" (the same verb: τιθέναι) the particular form of shuttle he needed into the material he was using. The Guards are to be artificers of character in the state just as the shuttle-maker was an artificer of shuttles. And, most important of all, they are to do it as he did, by "looking at and viewing" the appropriate Forms—in this case, those of Justice, etc.

In the present passage, as in the *Kratylos*, the reference to looking off at a model or original which is to be reproduced in the given material makes it obvious that we are dealing with a process of making copies or replicas. But there is a gain in clarity over both the *Kratylos* and the earlier *Republic* passage, in that personal imitation ("molding his own character") and character formation in others ("putting what he sees there into men's characters") are now distinguished and stand side by side under the heading of "imitation."

Plato now expands the reference to "artificers of civic virtue" into a full-fledged metaphor, and one which places the idea of image- or copy-making in particularly sharp relief. The Guard-philosophers are now (500e–501c) "the painters who employ the divine model," and their procedure is set forth in outline, but with no essential element missing. They take as their tablet (ὥσπερ πίνακα, like the piece of board on which the picture is to be painted) the city and the characters of its citizens; they scour and clean it; they sketch in the outline (σχῆμα) of the constitution; they look back and forth frequently from the model—the Forms of Justice, Beauty, Temperance, and so on—to "that which they are building into (ἐμποιεῖν) their men"; they "mix and blend the human likeness out of the corresponding moral practices (i.e., justice, beauty, etc.), basing their judgment on (τεκμαιρόμενοι, taking their mark from) that which Homer too called a divine image and likeness appearing in men"; "and they rub out a feature here and paint one in there, until they

have made human characters which are, so far as that is possible, accept-
able to god."

This elaborately designed and executed passage proves beyond any
doubt that to Plato's mind a successful imitation, i.e., copying, of the
eternal Forms is quite possible—for the philosopher or someone under
his guidance. But the most surprising feature is the reference to Homer.
Although the verb ἐκάλεσεν ("called") is faintly ambiguous, the context
really leaves no doubt that Homer saw and represented the divine image
embodied in human flesh, i.e., in the heroes, long before Plato's philoso-
pher-artists were heard of. The inconsistency with everything else that is
said about the poets, and especially about Homer, in the *Republic* (ex-
cept in 401b–d) is breathtaking. Can these divinely modeled heroes be
the masks under which the poet concealed his black magic? And is this
the poet who will be demonstrated, in Book 10, to have no access to
truth? There is no rational answer to these questions. Plato has simply
allowed himself an inconsistency of heroic proportions. Nevertheless,
the message is clear: the philosopher *can* see and "imitate" the Forms
directly.

When Plato resumes the discussion of poetry in Book 10, imitation is
once again seen as the source of danger.[5] Now, however, mimesis is no
longer understood in the peculiar, restricted manner of Book 3 as imper-
sonation, being or pretending to be some other person, but has rather the
broader (and less emotionally charged) sense of producing a copy of
something else. Returning to poetry as imitation, Plato points not to its
sympathetic or magical character as influence passing from one person
to another, but to its objective status as reproduction. Here, for the first

5. The following paragraphs, drawn largely from a lecture script of 1969,
merely summarize the argument of Book 10 as regards mimesis and the expul-
sion of poetry from the ideal state. For a more detailed analysis, the reader is
referred to *Structure*, where Else propounds a number of novel ideas about the
composition of Book 10 not directly reflected here, but taken up in part in
Chapter 4 and alluded to elsewhere in the discussion of the *Poetics*. Else's views
in *Structure* may be summarized as follows: the unexpected appearance in Book
10 of a defense of the banishment of poetry (595a1–608b3), certain inconsisten-
cies between it and the related passages of Book 3, and certain peculiarities in the
language and form of the arguments it employs point to (1) late composition (at
least after the *Sophist*, to which it refers overtly or covertly; i.e., not earlier than
the late 360s); and (2) composition in answer to an early version of Aristotle's
Poetics for the benefit of Plato's inner circle in the Akademy.

time, Plato brings the concept of imitation into relationship with the theory of Ideas.

At the beginning of Book 10, Sokrates refers with approval to the previous rejection of poetry: 595a, αὐτῆς ὅση μιμητική, "so much of it as is mimetic." Actually, Plato seems here to misquote himself, since at 3.39b–c–398a not all mimesis was banished, only imitations of bad or unworthy persons. In fact, of course, banishing mimesis of unworthy objects means, practically speaking, banishing mimetic poetry as a whole. And if ὅση μιμητική is meant as a limitation, it does not seem to make much difference. Epic and tragedy are condemned over again for their mimesis, and there is no mention of possible nonmimetic genres until at 607a "hymns to the gods and praises of good men" are stipulated as the only forms of poetry to be allowed into the city. We get a strong impression that all poetry that amounts to anything as poetry is mimesis.

Plato attempts to demonstrate the necessary distance from the truth of imitation by reference to the theory of Ideas. For this purpose he adduces a pair of Forms: Table and Couch. There are many tables and couches, but only one Form (εἶδος, 596a) or Idea (ἰδέα, 596b) of each. The craftsman does not make the Form, but produces the tables and couches we use by "looking at" (βλέπων, 596b) the Form. There is another kind of craftsman, however, of whom the painter is an example. He too makes a couch "in a certain sense" (596e). There are in fact three couches: the Form of Couch, which no craftsman produces (it was made, if by anyone, by god, 597c, and there is only one); the particular couch produced by the carpenter by reference to the Form; and the painted couch which is made by reference only to the appearance of the particular manufactured couch—and is therefore but the "imitation of a phantasm" (φαντάσματος μίμησις, 598b). And this remoteness from reality applies with equal force to the poet: "The tragic poet, if he is an imitator, will also naturally be three removes from the king and truth; and so will all other imitators" (597e). Plato goes on to point up the moral from his comparison: the poet knows nothing about the various arts and crafts or the various persons he imitates (598dff.). As imitator he is irrevocably cut off from truth.

This argument contains much that is questionable. As regards the painter, we may well ask (to go no further) why he is of necessity limited to imitating visible particulars. Elsewhere in the *Republic* (3.401c, 5.472d; cf. 6.500b–501c) Plato indicates he is not. Plato's primary reason for asserting the limitation here would appear to be the analogy with which he depreciates the poet. But that poets have no direct access to Ideas cannot be proved this way, and indeed Plato offers no proof. Furthermore, the analogy itself breaks down at a number of points. The chief of these is a consequence of the fact that the craftsman "looks to" the Form and must be assumed to produce, in principle, sound, workmanlike copies of it. Thus, although the painter necessarily distorts the particular couch in the process of painting it, a real, honest imitation of the original stands behind his painted imitation. But the realm of the poet, to which the analogy is supposed to apply, is not like that at all. There is no solid middle term at all, nothing really corresponding to the particular couch as an honest copy of the Form of Couch.

What corresponds to the Form of Couch in the realm of poetry? Plato never tells us, but we can deduce an answer from the passage in Book 10 where he describes "the noblest and most important things" that Homer talks about as "wars and generalships, the management of cities, and the education of men" (599c–d). In other words, the poet ought to look to the Forms of Justice, Courage, and so on: the standard Forms with which the theory of Ideas began. Plato has indeed presented the Guards in Book 6 as viewing and copying just these Forms (500b–501c), but that very fact reveals the weakness of the analogy as it applies to poets. The Guards copy the Forms direct and are therefore like the makers, not the painters, of couches. If the poet does not have direct access to the Forms, there simply *is* no sound, well-made imitation of them that he can imitate in turn. Plato has memorably proclaimed, in the *Republic* itself (5.473d), that until the cities of this world are ruled by philosophers, there is no health in them. Evidently the poet, unlike the painter, has no adequate model in the world of particulars at all, only states and human characters that are already hopelessly degraded and distorted.

Might not, however, the poet leap the gap and imitate the true heavenly model directly? Yes, but only if he is willing to go to school with Plato and learn philosophy. Then the poet might proceed to frame an honest imitation. But he could not and would not imitate a tragic fate like that of Achilleus or Oidipous, for philosophy would have shown him that these are products of misconception. A direct poetic imitation of the Forms that stand behind the good life and the good city could bear no resemblance to the *Iliad* or the *Oidipous Tyrannos*. The requirement is, in effect, impossible. It will end by destroying tragedy and its congenor and ancestor, the epic; and that is precisely Plato's intention.

3

The Later Dialogues

Phaidros

INCOMPLETE AND UNSATISFACTORY as was Plato's treatment of poetry in the *Republic*, he never again devoted anything like as much space or consecutive discussion to it—in the dialogues, at least. We shall find certain ideas from the *Republic* reasserted with very little change in the *Laws*, but no more there than before do we find a complete theory of poetry. Meanwhile, however, the *Phaidros* reestablishes a certain balance by bringing back to our attention an idea which was totally passed over in the *Republic*: the idea of poetic inspiration.

The place of the *Phaidros* in the chain of dialogues, after the *Republic* and either just before or just after *Theaitetos* and *Parmenides*, is pretty well agreed on nowadays. But it is not closely linked with any of those dialogues in subject, mood, or method. Rather, Plato's soul being the capacious vessel it was, the *Phaidros* brings a host of quite different ideas and feelings, both new and old, to expression; such a host of them, in fact, that the commentators have never quite agreed on what the dialogue is about. The answer is of course, in one sense, the same as for all the other great dialogues of the middle period: it is about everything that matters. But in this case, as in the others, the "everything" has its own particular focus and tonality. We can sum up the essentials for our purpose by saying that the *Phaidros* is about (1) love, (2) human discourse, and (3) the soul. Of these three master themes, the soul occupies central place, and Sokrates' great speech on its life and powers is the fulcrum of the whole. But the course we follow through the dialogue is no simple logical development or unfolding of clear, neatly delimited ideas. In its advances and returns, its recapitulations and foreshadowings, its interweaving of themes and developmental material, the *Phaidros* is more like a Beethoven symphony or a long complex poem: the *Aeneid*, say, or Eliot's *Four Quartets*. And over the whole there rests a golden equanimity, a sovereign mingling of lights and shadows, earnestness and gaiety, which has no equal elsewhere in Plato, not even in the *Symposion*. As a work of art and as a personal confession, the *Phaidros* is his ripest masterpiece.

The place of poetry in this intricate web is to all appearances high and honorable, but not much is said about it. The one explicit utterance on the subject comes near the middle of the dialogue and in intimate connection with what is said about the soul. But poetry has to share this conspicuous position with three other varieties of beneficent, divinely inspired "madness"; for it is only as a species of madness (μανία) that it is mentioned here at all.

The talk between the two companions had begun—after they were comfortably settled under their plane tree, with the cicadas chirping overhead and their toes dabbling in the cool water of the Ilissos—with Phaidros reading to Sokrates a specimen of sophistic oratory by Lysias, advising the young recipient of erotic attentions to favor the "lover" who is not in love with him, because such a person is more rational. This wretched piece of sophistry stimulates Sokrates to do better, in a speech which sets forth in rational order why reason is better than the irrationality of love. But suddenly, Sokrates confesses that even during his speech he has been troubled by doubts (242c), and beset by an unaccountable change of heart he launches into his "palinode" (244a–257b), a much longer and more elaborate production in which he recants his heresy against love and sings the praises of god-sent madness, of which love is one variety (and the most important). This is the context in which the theme of poetic inspiration returns to our notice, after having been suppressed since the *Ion* and the *Meno* (not even the *Symposion* with its open attitude toward poetic creativity said anything explicitly about inspiration).

The new speech begins with a proemium in solemn, hieratic style and proceeds on various levels between that and plain, unassuming prose, but more often on the high than the low side. Sokrates' first speech was wrong, we are now told, in advising the young person to favor the non-lover, because it assumed that madness (= love) is an unmixed evil, whereas it is the source of our greatest blessings provided it comes through divine dispensation (θείᾳ δόσει, 244a). And Sokrates now expounds (244b–245a) three varieties of god-sent, beneficent madness: (1) the oracular or mantic; (2) the kathartic and telestic, i.e., the frenzy in which "purifications and rites that will release a sufferer from affliction are revealed"; and (3) the "possession and madness from the Muses."

This last section is then followed by a marked caesura before the elaborate treatment of the fourth madness, love, begins.

The actual statement of the third variety runs as follows:

> Third, a possession and madness from the Muses (ἀπὸ Μουσῶν κατοκωχή τε καὶ μανία), capturing a tender, unspoiled soul and rousing it and firing it to frenzy (ἐκβακχεύουσα), both through songs and through other forms of poetic composition, educates the oncoming generation by giving luster to (κοσμοῦσα, adorning) countless deeds of the men of old; but he who approaches the poetic gates without Muses' madness, confident that he will become a real poet by dint of craft alone, remains outside (ἀτελής, uninitiated; i.e., into final grace): the creative effort of the safe-and-sane man is left totally in the shade by that of the madmen. (245a)

This sounds powerfully like the great speech on poetic inspiration in the *Ion*, and has of course been so interpreted. It also sounds like a rehabilitation of poetry, after the severities of the *Republic*, and has been so interpreted. But neither interpretation will hold up to intensive scrutiny of the *Phaidros*. Unlike the treatment of inspiration in the *Ion*, this passage is wholly serious; but it is not directed to all poetry, as such, but to certain spiritual efforts and tendencies which are very broad indeed, yet in some ways strictly delimited.

The first step toward placing Plato's remarks in the right context is to recognize that what is said about the "Muses' madness" does not have to do with poetry alone but with any and every artistic composition in words, including prose as well as verse, rhetoric as well as poetry. Once we recognize this basic fact, we begin to perceive that a web of allusions to inspiration and alleged inspiration pervades most of the dialogue. It begins early, at 228b, where Sokrates says he suspects that Phaidros has retired to the country to practice reciting Lysias' speech and is now delighted to find somebody who "will dance in ecstasy with him" (συγκορυβαντιῶντα). After hearing the speech Sokrates says, in response to Phaidros' ecstatic questions, that he didn't really understand much of it but followed Phaidros' lead and "joined in his Bacchic frenzy" (συνεβάκχευα, 234d). These first references to Corybantic or Bacchic rapture, i.e., to irrational enthusiasm for Lysias' speech, are obviously ironical.

In spite of the impression the speech has made on him, Sokrates says, 235c, that he has heard better on the subject somewhere else—he does not quite remember where. Perhaps it was from "Sappho the fair" (who was notoriously dark and homely) or "Anakreon the wise" (who was notoriously given to love, not wisdom), "or perhaps from certain prose writers." Anyhow "his breast is now full" of words at least as good as Lysias', and since he himself has no gift for that sort of thing it must be that he has been "filled up like a water jar, from channels outside himself." This flow of inspiration now spills over into Sokrates' own speech on love. It is preceded in all due solemnity by an invocation of the Muses, 237a, marked by a learned parenthesis on the origin of their epithet "tuneful" (λίγειαι). A short time later, at the end of the first section of the speech, Sokrates pauses to ask Phaidros whether he does not seem to be "divinely inspired" (θεῖον πάθος πεπονθέναι, 238c)—this because he has ended the section with a couple of highly contorted, sophistically shaped sentences. He ascribes his eloquence to the "divine spot" where they are sitting, and asks Phaidros not to be surprised if in the further course of the speech he becomes entirely "Nymph-mad" (νυμφόληπτος), since he is now close to uttering dithyrambs (238d).

Again the references to inspiration are ironical; Sokrates' speech so far has shown only the most external, puerile evidences of being inspired. When he pauses again, he is "already uttering epic verses, no longer dithyrambs" (241e), and goodness knows what he will say if he actually goes on to praise the nonlover: he will be "possessed by the Nymphs, raving for all to see" (ὑπὸ τῶν Νυμφῶν . . . σαφῶς ἐνθουσιάσω). No, he has said enough; he will depart. But his famous "sign" intervenes before he can do so: "Just as I was about to cross the river, the spirit (δαιμόνιον), my accustomed sign, came to me—it's always restraining me from something I am about to do—and I seemed to hear a voice on the spot, forbidding me to leave until I have made expiation: for I have been guilty of some sin against the divine" (242b–c). And he goes on to say that he is a sort of prophet or seer (μάντις), not a very good one, but good enough for his own purposes; so he now understands what his sin (ἁμάρτημα) was, indeed he was disturbed and upset while he was still delivering the speech, "for you know, my friend, the soul has some mantic capacity also."

This is a curious passage. Ordinarily we would not identify Sokrates' "sign" with prophecy or inspiration, since its activity (according to Plato) was always negative. But here Plato has gone out of his way to indicate the mantic gifts of the soul, and to emphasize the ideas of sin (ἡμαρτηκότα; ἁμάρτημα; cf. ἀμβλακών in the quotation from Ibykos, 242d) and expiation, purification (ἀφοσιώσωμαι). We would normally associate these terms with cases like that of Orestes or Oidipous, not with the rationalistic Sokrates. But in this case Sokrates has indeed been guilty of a major sin (that all this is half-playful, or that the first speech was a purely literary device employed for a deliberate purpose, is irrelevant here). He has sinned against the first guideline for the representation of gods that was laid down in the *Republic* (2.379c), that god is good and the cause of good only; for "love is a god or something divine" (242e), yet Sokrates has made a speech predicated on the assumption that love is evil. It was a stupid speech, as stupid as Lysias', putting on airs to impress silly mortals. So Sokrates must purify himself (*καθήρα-σθαι*, 243a), and he knows an ancient means of purification, a *καθαρμὸς ἀρχαῖος*, for the purpose.

We shall consider the "ancient purification" in a moment. First, observe that Plato has maintained, in fact sharpened, his focus on sin and pollution. It does not seem to have been noticed, in this connection, how closely this passage is linked, in idea and in phrasing, with what Sokrates says at the beginning of his second speech about the first two varieties of god-sent madness, the mantic and the purificatory. The prophetesses at Delphi and Dodona have wrought many a blessing for mankind, and the Sibyls and others, through their divinely inspired prophecies, "have set many people on the right path for the future" (244b), i.e., have saved them from fatal errors. The second form of madness is at least as significant: "Then also most pernicious illnesses and sufferings have arisen in some of our families as a result of ancient crimes of bloodshed which called for vengeance. Often in such cases madness has intervened and, through prophetic utterances, has found a way of deliverance for those in need, having recourse to prayers and services to the gods; whence by means of purifications and initiations (*καθαρμῶν τε καὶ τελετῶν τυχοῦσα*) it has restored the sufferer to health then and thereafter, securing release from his pressing ills for the man who goes mad and is possessed in the right way" (244d–e).

Sokrates' condition at the moment when he makes his "palinode" (243a) has analogies with both these beneficent kinds of madness. His soul had played the mantic role even while he was reciting the speech, and now he offers the recantation of his pernicious doctrine to Eros, the god of love himself—in other words, the long second speech is a kind of prayer and purification, a *katharmos*.

What kind of "madness" is it, then, that dictates the palinode? It partakes of both the mantic and the purificatory. But Plato explicitly cites Stesichoros as the model for his recantation, and he takes pains to emphasize that Stesichoros derived his true insight into the cause of his blinding from still another source: the Muses. He recognized the truth ἅτε μουσικὸς ὤν (243a), "inasmuch as he was a devotee of the Muses." This point is driven home by the contrast with Homer; for Homer too was blind (so said the common tradition) but did *not* recognize the cause. That is, Homer also traduced Helen (by alluding to her adulterous flight to Troy with Paris), but he failed to perceive the truth because he was not μουσικός, and therefore remained blind for life. (This distinction between Homer and Stesichoros will be of further assistance to us a little later.)

A last covert reference to inspiration in the first part of the dialogue, before Sokrates' big speech, calls for our notice. As he is preparing the way for his reversal of position, Sokrates blames his first speech on Phaidros, calling it *"your* speech, which through my mouth bewitched by you was spoken" (242d–e). I have left the words in their original order so as to bring out their deliberate ambiguity. The order as it stands leaves it undetermined which way the phrase "by you" faces. Are we to hear "bewitched by you" or "by you was spoken"? Both. Sokrates' mouth was bewitched by Phaidros, and as a result the speech was spoken through his mouth by Phaidros. Sokrates was merely the pipe, the channel, through which this (spurious) inspiration flowed. Plato is playing with one image for inspiration, as a flow of liquid through a conduit (the poet): a conception which was mentioned in the *Ion* and will be mentioned again in the *Laws*. We recall that earlier, Sokrates proclaimed that his breast was full; he had been "filled like a water jar, from channels outside himself" (235c). A little later, 238d and 241e, there were hints that the (false) inspiration he displayed in the speech stemmed from the Nymphs, although his invocation at 237a had been to the Muses. All these hints and surmises are neither here nor there, now that Phaidros is unmasked as the real source—if that intimation were not the most ironical of all. It is useless to speculate on the origin of "inspirations" that bring no truth.

In Sokrates' second speech, on the other hand, the Muses do bring true inspiration—not because they are invoked, for this time Sokrates does not even mention them; but the idea is hinted at, as in a rebus, in the attribution of the speech to "Stesichoros, son of Euphemos, man of Himera" (244a). Stesichoros is literally "he who stations or halts a chorus"—as the "divine chorus" (247a) of the souls traversing the heaven, or at least the immortal members of it, come to a halt (ἔστησαν, 247b) on the back of heaven to view the "place beyond heaven," the realm of the Forms. Euphemos is "he who speaks well," i.e., speaks words of good omen—as Sokrates is now speaking well, i.e., reverently and auspiciously, of love. And Himera is, for this fancy, the City of Passion (ἵμερος, "longing, craving"). Thus the speech is the vehicle of a philosophical vision, animated by reverence for the gods and inspired by love.

True inspiration, as exemplified in Sokrates' second speech, partakes of and is linked with all four varieties of divine "madness." They are not really separate phenomena; rather they are refractions of the same supreme truth through four different prisms, so to speak, as part of the gods' ministrations to men. The important thing is that they are all divine and therefore separated *toto caelo* from what men are able to do by their own powers, when they are "in their senses" (note between 244b and 245a σωφρονοῦσαι, ἐμφρόνων, σωφροσύνης, ἐκ τέχνης, σωφρονοῦντος). But "divine" here is very close to "philosophical." Philosophy is the craving for that high truth which is concealed behind the visible earth and the visible heavens, and the "wing" that lifts the soul up high enough to see it (246dff.) is warmed and strengthened by love. Love, then, is the philosophical impulse *par excellence*, and the soul that has no share of it will not rise. But the other three kinds of "madness" have some communion with truth also, and of them the Muses' variety is the highest.

This high position of the Muses—the real Muses—helps to explain a passage which is otherwise distressingly opaque. The souls, each following the god to which it is most akin, join in the great mythical journey through the heavens, led by Zeus (246e–248b). Some of them manage to "stand on the back of heaven" (247b) and see the place beyond, but most of them faint by the wayside, grow heavy, and fall back to earth (248c); and each of them is then born into a level and a way of life commensurate with what it has seen. There are nine of these levels of incarnation. The soul which has seen the most of the truth—i.e., of the Forms—is born into one who will be "a lover of wisdom and beauty, or one devoted to the Muses and to love" (φιλοσόφου ἢ φιλοκάλου ἢ μουσικοῦ τινος καὶ ἐρωτικοῦ, 248d). The equation of the Muses' inspiration with that of love, and of that in turn with philosophy ("lover of wisdom"), is complete.

From here the slope goes steeply downward: second level, lawful king or official; third, politician or financier; fourth, one who works hard at physical exercise or the healing of the body; fifth, prophet or purifier; sixth, "one given to poetry or some other form of imitation"; seventh, craftsman or farmer; eighth, sophist or demagogue; ninth, tyrant. The low position of the poet and painter ("some other form of imitation"), just above the sophist and the tyrant, is incomprehensible if the passage on the Muses' madness (245a) was a rehabilitation of all poetry, but is quite compatible with their rating in *Republic* 10. The solution is simple, though paradoxical at first sight: 245a did *not* bring a rehabilitation of all poetry but a carefully nuanced appraisal of the true Muses' inspiration, which is equivalent to philosophy. The first level is reserved for philosophers like Plato, and perhaps a handful of "Musical" poets. Homer and the rest of the mimetic poets will cool their heels in the sixth circle.

A negative but valuable confirmation of this reading is available close at hand, at 247c: "But the place beyond heaven has never been hymned properly by any poet here below, and never will be." Since the level of each soul's incarnation is determined by how much of the truth—i.e., the Ideas—it has seen in its heavenly journey, it is clear that hardly a poet here below (with perhaps an occasional exception like Stesichoros) has ever seen much, if anything, of that truth.

From the other side, the positive side, we observe that it is the philosopher's soul, winged by love, that experiences inspiration (ἐνθου-σιασμός), 249c–d: "and he, rising above all human concerns and coming close to the divine, is chided by the many as a madman but is in fact, though they are not aware of it, full of god" (ἐνθουσιάζων δὲ λέληθεν τοὺς πολλούς; cf. ἐνθουσιῶντες, 253a; τὸν ἔνθεον φίλον, 255b). Thus ἐνθουσιασμός (the word has not been used in the dialogue up to this moment) is now appropriated to describe the true possession of the loving and learning soul by god; it is no longer available to describe a merely literary inspiration, except in irony (cf. 263d, referring to Sokrates' first speech).

The merely mimetic poet, then, is left without any claim to real inspiration by gods *or* Muses. There is no reason for surprise at this harsh verdict. Most readers of the *Phaidros* have been seduced by Plato's mellow mood and the expansive tone of 245a into thinking that he has now forgiven the poets and renewed their old accreditation as inspired creatures. Not a bit of it. The mimetic poet—and that term still embraces all the major poets, especially Homer—is as far from "the king and the truth" (*Republic* 10.597e) as ever. Nothing that he is or knows or does can lift him out of the sixth circle to equal rank with the lover or the philosopher—unless someday he should begin to learn, and then gradually to climb the ladder of incarnations. But that climb would have to be made with the burgeoning "wing" of Philosophy, warmed and guided by Love. There is no literary road to the top.

The verdict is not only harsh, it is dismaying from another point of view. If Homer and all the mimetic poets are excluded from the first circle, what is left? What good poetry—poetically good poetry—belongs there? I am afraid we shall have to say: very little. Stesichoros' *Palinode* apparently qualifies for admission, but we cannot be sure how many of his other poems showed an awareness of the true nature of god: certainly not the original poem on Helen. (Only meager fragments of Stesichoros remain to us.) Pindar? Perhaps a few poems: the first Pythian, maybe, or the second Olympian. Simonides? Not very much, considering his pessimism and his talent for θρῆνοι, for rousing tears. Some of Solon, especially where he says that the woes of the Athenians do not come from the gods but from themselves. As for the tragedians, obviously they cannot rise above the level of their source and inspiration, Homer. Not much will survive Plato's test, and what does survive will not necessarily be of high quality, because the test is not poetic quality but doctrinal soundness.

Much that is poetically excellent will be excluded, then; and contrariwise much that is poetically mediocre may be included. Plato is quite aware of these consequences. He had alluded to them in *Republic* 607a: we admit that Homer is the greatest poet of all, qua poet; but we shall only admit hymns and enkomia (songs in praise of good men) into our city. At 3.398a–b he had been equally frank: we shall employ the "drier, less enjoyable poet and storyteller because of his utility to us" (ὠφελίας ἕνεκα)—the one who will follow our guidelines and help us bring up the Guards as exemplars of virtue.

If we turn back to our master passage at *Phaidros* 245a with these points in mind, and consider again the statement that the Muses' madness "educates the oncoming generation by giving luster to countless deeds of the men of old," I submit that what we are required to think of is not the "great" Greek literature we know from the tradition, with its array of stellar names, but those humbler, "drier but more useful" ἐγκώμια which Plato had admitted to his Republic and will admit again to the state of the *Laws* (801e; cf. 829c, 947c). By holding up the great deeds of the forefathers before the admiring eyes of the young, they will stir them to emulation—that is their "utility"—and at the same time they will illustrate the eternal principle that the good man is happy, in this life and after death.

But we have passed over another candidate for inclusion in Plato's restricted list. We said that Sokrates' second speech, the long one, could be counted as truly inspired. It is of course not an enkomion but a hymn: "we have played (προσεπαίσαμεν) duly and reverently, a kind of mythical hymn to your master and mine, Eros" (265b). As such, the speech and others like it are eminently fitted to take their place among the hymns and enkomia which will impress the truth about gods and men on the oncoming generation. The fact that it is in prose will in no way derogate from its authority. In the same passage I have just quoted, the hymn to Eros is also called οὐ παντάπασιν ἀπίθανον λόγον, "a not entirely implausible speech." And we may recall that the rubric under which the whole discussion of poetry was carried on in *Republic* 2 and 3 was not ποίησις or μῦθος but λόγος (at beginning and end: 376e, 392c). Again in the *Phaidros* Plato makes it emphatically clear that what he has to say about the composition of λόγοι, and about writing in general, applies equally to poetry and prose (258d, 278c). Another straw in the wind is that three times in the dialogue, at 234e, 236d, and 258b, the word ποιητής, "poet," is used alone for "writer," i.e., writer in prose; another, that Sophokles and Euripides are called on at 268c for corroborative testimony on the principles of speech composition (not the composition of speeches in their plays but of the plays as wholes, comparable to speeches).

The second half of the dialogue, after the big speech, makes it evident that Plato's attention is indeed directed to λόγοι; not so much to philosophical speeches, however, as to rhetorical ones. In the course of this discussion (257cff.), he dispenses a variety of counsels which are not only wise but well informed: he knows exactly what is going on among the rhetorical fraternity (see especially his genial but devastating comments on the mania for dividing and subdividing the parts of a speech, 266dff.). Little though we tend to associate Plato with rhetoric, these observations make sense if we recall his situation around the year 370. It was then a good thirty-five years or more since the poetic afflatus had visited him and impelled him to write poetry. Altogether, poetry was no longer a burning issue with him, except when he was dealing with education, and no poetry of great consequence was then being produced. (It is significant, I think, that when Plato wants to reinforce a point of literary technique, 268c, he appeals to Sophokles and Euripides, who had been dead for a generation). During those same years he had been working with increasing intensity and concentration on other things: reading (the pre-Sokratic philosophers especially), studying, talking, learning, teaching, meditating, and writing—writing prose dialogues. Now, at fifty-five or sixty, he was ready for a new self-examination and self-critique. On the one hand he had to face the question: how could he, the pupil of Sokrates, who had never written a line and who believed so firmly that the only λόγος worth anything is the living dialectic that passes between two souls, justify spending so many years of his life setting down words on paper? And on the other hand how did he propose to distinguish his λόγοι from those that were being written by others all around him?

For the situation had changed drastically since Plato's youth. Then rhetoric had been in the flush of its first vogue, in the sense of the giving of speeches; now it was in its ripe maturity, in the sense of the writing of speeches. Thus Plato the writer of philosophical λόγοι now found himself in competition with the writers of rhetorical λόγοι. In the *Gorgias*, 465cff., he had judged their activity with uncompromising harshness: their "art" was not a proper art, in fact not an art at all, but a low form of flattery catering to the multitude. In the *Phaidros*, to our surprise, in spite of severities on particular points, Plato is ready to discuss seriously the idea of a true, philosophically based rhetoric, and along that line he makes several farsighted yet highly practical suggestions. We shall take note of their relevance to poetry.

At 246c Plato writes: "You would agree, I think, that every λόγος should be composed like a living creature (ζῷον), with its own body, so that it is lacking neither head nor feet but has both middle parts and extremities composed (γεγραμμένα) in proportion to one another and the whole." This principle is obviously applicable to poetry, and Plato so applies it later, at 268c–d: "tragedy is nothing but the structuring of these parts"—various kinds of tragic speeches have been mentioned— "proportionately to one another and the whole." Sophokles and Euripides are invoked as witnesses to this truth, and indeed it has special pertinence to the drama (it is in fact the matrix of Aritotle's "unity of action").

Two words in the passage require further explanation. Ζῷον is originally and properly an animal, or rather any living creature (in the famous apophthegm in Aristotle's *Politics*, 1.1.1253a2, man is a ζῷον πολιτικόν). But it also means, by analogy, a painted representation of a living creature. In conjunction with γεγραμμένα, the suggestion of painting is unavoidable. Γράφειν originally meant "to scratch" or draw in outline, then by extension in one direction, "to paint" (hence the painter is a ζωγράφος), in another, "to write" (since Greek writing was originally done with a sharp point). Thus γεγραμμένα can mean either "written" or "painted." Which of these twin meanings is intended here? Both. We are meant to think both of the natural animal and the painted one, both of writing and painting. It is one of Plato's frequent (and untranslatable) wordplays. But the convergence enforced by the image makes painting the dominant idea—and then we are left to wonder whether the comparison did not originally belong to poetry after all: one more case of *ut pictura poesis*.

The approving reference to Sophokles and Euripides in the matter of tragic structure at 268c–d should not mislead us into thinking that they are cited as examples of the inspired bard. Sophokles and Euripides figure here as distinguished practitioners of the *art* (τέχνη) of tragedy (cf. τὰ τραγικά, 269a). And indeed to understand the relationship of parts to wholes, and how to adjust the ones precisely to the other, seems anything but a function of wild-eyed enthusiasm. We are within the range of what a careful, intelligent craftsman can achieve through art alone (245a).

Not that art and inspiration, or logic and inspiration, are incompatible with each other. The complementary processes of inductive and deductive reasoning (or, Collection and Division) are said at 265d–e to provide the only sound basis for the handling of material in speeches; but the first of this pair of methods was presented at 249b–c as constituting our "recollection" (ἀνάμνησις) of the Forms we had once seen in our heavenly journey. Thus the reasoning labor of the soul, working its way carefully from particulars to universals, is sister to the "erotic" drive which lifted the soul to the transcendental vision: it is its down-to-earth, everyday, nonmythical counterpart.

Finally, the ironical, depreciatory account of writing, near the end of the *Phaidros* (274b–278b), arguing that nothing written can be taken very seriously and that the only true λόγοι are those written in the soul, is explicitly applied at 278b–c to prose speeches (Lysias is taken as the representative), poetry (Homer), and written laws (Solon). There is no reference to philosophical λόγοι, but they are included by implication. If we listen carefully we can detect Plato admitting to us, with a discreet smile, that his writing of dialogues is a form of play: a serious form of play, to "remind" (ὑπομνῆσαι) himself and those who will follow him of the truth (276d). If Plato is willing to place his own artistic product so low, why could not poetry occupy a similar position, admittedly humble, but useful? The answer is, it could, if it were able and willing to be winged by "love"—philosophy—and rise toward the vision of the Forms. But that possibility was remote when Plato wrote the *Phaidros*; so remote that when he casts about him for a man who might follow that road the one he hits on is not a poet but the rhetor and speech-writer Isokrates. Poetry is no longer a major force to be contended with, a major enemy. Plato views it with diminished hostility, but also diminished interest.

Philebos, Timaios

THE DIALOGUES between *Phaidros* and *Laws* offer only minor supplements and corrections to what Plato has said about poetry up to this point.[1]

The *Philebos* is not concerned with poetry directly, but its treatment of the various kinds of pleasure and pain brings with it a discussion of the mixed pleasures (pleasures mixed with pain) that attend on the drama (48aff.). The discussion is heavily weighted in the direction of comedy and the envy ($\phi\theta\acute{o}\nu o\varsigma$) which Plato considers to be its root. Tragedy is mentioned only summarily at the beginning (the paradox that its spectators enjoy and weep, $\chi\alpha\acute{\iota}\varrho o\nu\tau\varepsilon\varsigma$ $\varkappa\lambda\acute{\alpha}\omega\sigma\iota$, at the same time) and again near the end of the passage. Here, at 50b, we find the interesting remark that mixtures of pleasure and pain are found "not only in plays but in the entire tragedy and comedy of life." It is startling to find Plato hinting that all the world's a stage; one would have welcomed some development of the idea, but none is forthcoming. Again, a tantalizing list of painful feelings is given at 50b (repeated from 47e with only one minor change in order): "anger and longing and lamentation and fear and passionate desire and rivalry and envy and others of that kind." Does this not suggest an ampler tally of tragic feelings than the pity and fear to which Plato had limited himself in *Republic* 10 (and to which Aristotle will limit himself in the *Poetics*)? Once more there is no clarification. In any case the passage shows us Plato, to our surprise, as a thoughtful and not unsympathetic observer of the drama—the actual drama of his time.

The *Timaios* begins with a self-proclaimed summary of the *Republic*, at least of those portions that deal with the selection and early training of the Guards. We are not concerned to account for the glaring omissions in this summary (for example, Plato's criticisms of the poets are not men-

1. Else did not include in this account any consideration of the passages in the *Sophist* (esp. 232e–242b and 264a–266d) which, while they do not explicitly discuss the poet, deal with his analogues the painter and the sophist as imitators, counterfeitors, artificers of shams that look like the truth. For these passages and their relation to *Republic* 10, see *Structure* 26–31.

tioned). It is of some interest to us to note that Sokrates, likening the description of the ideal state in the *Republic* to a "beautiful creature," whether painted or alive but in repose, expresses a desire to hear an account of its trials and exploits as it contests with others (19b–c). He would not trust himself to laud (ἐγκωμιάσαι, d2) it adequately, nor does he think that either past or present poets could manage it. The "mimetic tribe" imitates best the people and the actions it is familiar with from its own upringing; what lies outside that is hard for it to imitate well in deeds, and even harder in words. This is like what Plato says in the *Republic* (604e), that the virtuous and self-possessed man is hard for the mimetic, i.e. dramatic, poet to imitate, and for the audience in the theater to understand when he is imitated, because that sort of attitude is outside their experience. We need only add that a laudation of the kind desired by Sokrates would be one of the *enkomia* which he admits to the state in *Republic* 10 (607a).

The *Timaios* is significant for Plato's view of poetry in another, indirect way. In this dialogue the metaphor of *mimesis*, replica-making, takes on cosmic stature and importance. At 28a, the δημιουργός or Cosmic Craftsman, "looking to" (βλέπων) that which is eternally the same—the perfect world of the Forms—uses it as his model (τοιούτῳ τινι προσχρώμενος παραδείγματι); the world-soul which he creates is an image of it (εἴκων, 29b; ἄγαλμα, 37c); time is an image of eternity, or "imitates" eternity (38a, 39e). The δημιουργός has carried out his work thus far in the likeness of what he was reproducing (ἀπείργαστο εἰς ὁμοιότητα ᾧπερ ἀπεικάζετο 39e); the minor gods created by him "imitate" his procedure in turn (44d), fashioning the world we see around us. Again the thought of the dialogue lies outside our sphere of interest, but its message is clear: "imitation" is not necessarily a low form of activity, since it lies at the origin of the world. Actually it seems certain that in Plato's thinking the relation between ordinary reality and Forms was more and more recast in the image of copy and model: mimesis replaces *methexis*, "participation," as the master metaphor.[2] This is a natural extension of the propensity we have already noticed in the *Republic*, to formulate the relationship between the worlds of Being and Becoming in visual terms. The cosmos as a work of art and its maker the supreme

2. For an analysis of the vocabulary of the relation of Forms and particulars through the Platonic corpus, see W. D. Ross, *Plato's Theory of Ideas* (Oxford 1951) 228ff.

artist: this vision of the *Timaios* represents a curious inversion, a kind of victory of art over dialectic. Seeing has finally won out over talking, thinking, and arguing. Wilamowitz had good reason to choose as motto for the third "book" of his *Platon*, on Plato's old age, the Goethian apophthegm "Alles Vergängliche ist nur ein Gleichnis."[3]

Laws

POETRY HAS an important place in the education and in the festivals of Plato's "second best city" (*Laws* 5.739a, 7.807b), but discussion of the subject in the longest and last of the dialogues does not in fact add much to what we have already gleaned from its predecessors, especially the *Republic*.[4] Over against the stringent restriction of poetry in the ideal state, however, Plato's new dispensation appears rather more lenient. Poetry is fundamental to education as a constituent of μουσική, the art whereby the impulse to "leap and bound and dance and frolic" (2.653e) common to all young animals is, in the human species alone, disciplined into an apprehension of rhythm and melody. And since early education consists of "drawing and leading children to the rule which has been pronounced right by the voice of the law" (659d), it is essential that the music, dance, and poetry through which they receive instruction express only the qualities of the good life and the character of the good man, in order to inculcate appropriate habits of body and mind (653aff., 7.798d). Festivals have a similar educative function, not only providing relief from the hardship and toils of life, but also giving citizens a way to "correct their habits" (ἵν᾽ ἐπανορθῶνται τὰς τροφάς, 653d) through periodic reinforcement.[5]

For this purpose, as for schooling, Plato is careful to distinguish what is useful from what gives pleasure, what people need from what they crave. The Athenian interlocutor of the *Laws* allows only the pleasure of

3. Ulrich von Wilamowitz-Moellendorff, *Platon* I² (Berlin 1920) 535. The phrase begins the famous concluding chorus of *Faust*, Part 2.

4. In the absence of a draft or extensive notes on the *Laws* by Else, the editor has undertaken to complete the survey of Plato's views on poetry and is solely responsible for the contents of this section.

5. For the text and its interpretation, see Glenn R. Morrow, *Plato's Cretan City: A Historical Interpretation of the Laws* (Princeton 1960) 353, with n. 193.

the wisest and best of men to carry weight in judging music (658e–659a); poets must teach not what will please the masses, but the difficult truth that justice and pleasure fully coincide (660e–664c). Otherwise, poetry will provide only the base pleasure associated with "untrue opinion" (668a). Indeed, the Athenian believes that he has witnessed the degeneration of music in his own city through the desire of its practitioners, "ignorant of what is right and legitimate in the realms of the Muses," merely to give pleasure to the hearer, "whether high or low" (3.700d–e). This change in turn he makes responsible for the general rise of license (701a–b). In prescribing for the festivals of the new city, he makes it amply clear that the closest supervision of the performances will be required.

The *Laws*, then, does not reopen the frontal attacks on Homer and tragedy of earlier dialogues,[6] but it does propose to regulate all literature through an apparatus of censorship (6.764cff., 7.798eff.; 8.829cff.). Comedy, far from being excluded, is treated as essential, "since one cannot know the serious apart from the burlesque, or any contrary apart from its contrary" (7.816d). One who aspires to goodness must not lapse into the ludicrous through ignorance; but he may not deliberately imitate it, either, so that all comic representations are to be given by slaves or hired aliens (816e). Tragedy, as the composition of serious (σπουδαῖοι) and inspired (θεῖοι) poets (817a), must be regulated even more strictly. Plato recognizes the tragedians as his rivals when he has the Athenian say, "We ourselves are authors of a tragedy, the finest and noblest one we know how to make; indeed, our whole state has been constructed as an imitation (μίμησις) of the finest and noblest life, and that we assert most earnestly is the truest tragedy" (817b). Only if the magistrates find that a tragedian's sentiments are compatible with the teachings of the state, or even an improvement on them, will they grant him a chorus (817d).[7]

6. There are, however, incidental criticisms akin to those of earlier dialogues against, e.g., "Homer or Tyrtaios or some other poet" guilty of setting down in his verse bad precepts for living (9.858e) or "poets and any perverse myth-peddlars" who teach that the gods indulge in larceny and robbery (12.941b).

7. Morrow (above, n. 5) 375–376 points out that the procedure proposed here is, at least formally, quite similar to that followed in Athens; and Plato explicitly allows the possibility that some tragedies might be found acceptable to the magistrates. At the same time, however, Plato takes for granted that the tragedians will say "things for the most part entirely opposed" to his own teachings, and it

These passages suggest not so much that Plato has resolved the conflict between poetry and philosophy as that he has made an accommodation to the emotional power of poetry (and music and dance) for the purpose of harnessing it as a positive social force in the city of the *Laws*. Indeed, where Plato allows the larger theoretical issues surrounding poetry to surface, the contradictions loom larger than ever. This is particularly true of the passage in Book 4 (719c–d) in which Plato's great themes of inspiration and imitation are brought together for the first and last time.

Inspiration is depicted here as elsewhere as rendering the poet a passive instrument, bereft of judgment (οὐκ ἔμφρων), opening his verses as freely as a fountain spews water. But since his art consists of imitation (τῆς τέχνης οὔσης μιμήσεως), he must constantly contradict himself since he imitates characters of all sorts without knowing which of their views may be true and which false. If all of these utterances are inspired, with no regard for or clue to their truth, then inspiration is a strange and hollow thing. There can be no question of the Muses' deliberately deceiving the poet (as in the proem to Hesiod's *Theogony*), but inspiration here apparently amounts to no more than a certain persuasiveness or plausibility in imitation. In Book 2, on the other hand, Plato is aware that poems written without possession by the Muses will not only be flat and dull but will risk a dangerous inappropriateness of language, melody, or rhythm: "The Muses indeed would never make the grave mistake of setting masculine language to a feminine scale or melody or wedding tune, or of joining postures worthy of free men to rhythms fit only for slaves," or be guilty of any other such error (669c). In Book 8 Plato is content to allow the verse of men of proven worth and noble character to be sung "even if it has no real musical quality" (829d). Plato here treats the inspiration of the Muses as adding mere aesthetic pleasure to the song, and he unhesitatingly chooses right doctrine over pleasure: "No other citizen shall presume, without authorization by the curators, to sing an unauthorized song, even if its notes are more ravishing than those of Thamyras and Orpheus themselves" (829d–e).

These contradictions point not only to the intractability of the problems raised by Plato's approach to poetry but also to the seeming lack of

---

does not appear likely that tragedy as we know it could have played any very central part in the state of the *Laws*.

any systematic effort on his part to resolve the outstanding issues. Plato's quarrel with the poets was from the beginning related to education and politics, and as time passed poetry as such grew less rather than more central to his interests.[8] In the *Laws* Plato writes as a poet as well as a philosopher. Because he alone can claim to be both, he alone can claim to represent the truth with sufficient clarity to supplant the traditional poetry of Greece.

8. Cf. *Structure* 67: "The fact is that, generally speaking, poetry bulked less and less large in Plato's eyes with the passing years. There were no more poets in the grand style in the fourth century, in Athens or anywhere else in Greece, to inherit or to claim the mantle of Homer, Aischylos, Sophokles, Euripides. Poetry had relapsed into being what it has been in Western culture ever since, except in a few favored times and places: a pabulum for primary education and/or a tolerated special activity for small groups of *literati*."

PART 2

Aristotle's Theory of Literature

4

The Date of the *Poetics*

THE DATES OF composition of classical works are often hard to establish, and in many cases the result is only of limited, technical interest. The date of the *Poetics*, on the other hand, *if* it can be established, is potentially a matter of great, indeed commanding importance for understanding Aristotle's theory of literature.

The periods of Aristotle's life are well known and very clearly marked:

1. Youth in Makedonia, 384–367 B.C. (ages 0–17).
2. Study and teaching in Plato's Akademy, 367–347 (ages 17–37).
3. *Wanderjahre* in the Troad, Lesbos, and Makedonia, 347–335 (ages 37–49).
4. Second period in Athens, 335–323 (ages 49–61).
5. Withdrawal to Chalkis, and death, 323–322 (ages 61–62).

What Aristotle did and learned during his youth in Makedonia is not known to us from any direct testimony. We can only conjecture that as a doctor's son he had access to a good education of Ionic type (certainly including Homer and other epics, probably some elegiac, iambic, and lyric poetry, possibly some acquaintance with medical and scientific texts). It is surely not very venturesome to conjecture further that he may have imbibed during that early period the admiration, not to say worship, of Homer which stands out so dramatically in the *Poetics*.

Aristotle's sojourn in the Akademy, covering almost one half of his productive life, brought an enormous expansion and enrichment of his character and interests and the production of an astounding number of important writings. For some years—obviously with Plato's permission, more likely with his active encouragement—he taught the Akademy's course in rhetoric; he played a leading role in the wide-ranging debates within the school on every possible subject; he became an inveterate, a passionate theatergoer; and he read everything he could get his hands on, especially—perhaps—dramas.

The years in Atarneus, Assos, Mytilene, Mieza, and Pella initiated his lifelong friendship and collaboration with Theophrastos; opened up for him the teeming world of nature (if we can speak of such a polymath as having a scientific specialty, it was surely marine biology, beginning with his studies in the waters around Mytilene); and introduced him for the first time to practical problems in politics (Hermeias, Philip) and education (Alexander).

The second period in Athens is the outward, though perhaps not the inward, apogee of his career. This was the time when it all "came together." He was now *il maestro de color che sanno*: internationally renowned lecturer, teacher, author, researcher, and organizer of research— of the collection of 158 constitutions of Greek and other cities, the records of the Pythian games, and the musical and dramatic contests at Athens. He updated, revised, and augmented his previous studies in logic, metaphysics, physics, biology, psychology, politics, ethics, rhetoric—and on and on.

Aristotle's forty-odd years of intellectual labor produced an *oeuvre* of truly staggering scope and diversity. Now, where in this densely packed roster of achievement does the *Poetics* belong?

I cannot find that this question has often been seriously posed, not to say seriously answered. So far as any attention has been paid to it, the prevailing tendency has been to date the *Poetics* to the second Athenian period, on the ground—normally unspoken—that treatises (the "akroamatic" works; very roughly, the present Aristotelian corpus) belong there, the Akademy period being reserved mainly for the published works, chiefly dialogues.[1] The *Poetics* would then be the fruit of ripe maturity, a distillation of many years of meditation and research on literature.

But these assumptions have been undermined, on the one hand, by increasing masses of evidence which show that large portions of the akroamatic works go back to the Akademy period, while on the other hand the *Poetics* itself, to a dispassionate eye, reveals many youthful traits: splendid insights mingled with audacious generalizations and generous inconsistencies, all poured out with the enthusiasm of youth.

---

1. Augusto Rostagni, *Aristotele, Poetica*[2] (Turin 1945) xx–xxxi, attempts to justify the traditional dating after 335. Else's early dating is shared by Ingemar Düring, *Aristoteles* (Heidelberg 1966) 50, 162–164.

There are, however, more objective reasons for dating the work to the Akademy period and to a relatively early time within that period: around 360–355. The most important of these reasons have to do with the intimate closeness of the *Poetics* to Plato.

It has always been acknowledged, in principle, that the *Poetics* is a reply to Plato's attacks on poetry, but for some reason it has not been recognized that the most natural time for such a reply is the period when Aristotle was in direct, day-to-day contact with Plato and when the questions raised by his attack were being vigorously debated in the school. There is in fact reason to think that both Plato and Aristotle took part in the debates, and perhaps that we can find traces of their mutual poste and riposte. I suggested elsewhere that the first part of Book 10 of the *Republic* is a response by Plato, in the late 360s, to ideas broached by Aristotle in the *Poetics* or some early version of it.[2] This debate would have been at its height just then, and at several places in *Republic* 10 we seem to catch echoes of the fray:

1. At the very beginning of the book, 595aff., Plato seems to be accepting an identification of poetry with mimetic poetry *as such*, which was not so clearly arrived at, or not so clearly stated, in Book 3. This discontinuity is more easily explained if Aristotle's definition of poetry as μίμησις *tout court* had intervened and changed the *données* of the discussion. The same point is involved in Plato's call, 595c, for a new generic definition of mimesis itself: μίμησις ὅλως ὅτι ποτ᾽ ἐστίν; cf. *Poetics* 1.47a16, μίμησεις τὸ σύνολον, and 4.48b4, ὅλως (the general causes that "begot" poetry).

2. At 603c, with a special intra-Akademic form of quotation (φαμέν, "we say"),[3] Plato refers to Aristotle's definition (2.48a1) of the objects of imitation as πράττοντας, "persons acting, performing an action."

3. In the same sentence, the πράττοντες are said to perform βιαίους ἢ ἑκουσίας πράξεις, "forced or voluntary actions"—a coded and not very friendly allusion to Aristotle's concept of the tragic action caused by hamartia—and Plato's next phrase, καὶ ἐκ τοῦ πράττειν ἢ εὖ οἰομένους ἢ κακῶς πεπραγέναι, "and as a result of their acting, thinking that they have fared either well or ill," issues an ulti-

---

2. See *Structure* esp. 55–57.
3. On this use of "we," see Werner Jaeger, *Aristotle*[2] (Oxford 1948) 171.

mate challenge. Good and ill fortune (faring) are the poles between which the tragic action swings, according to Aristotle; in other words, for him they are key structural features of tragedy. But Plato, true to his Sokratic faith that nothing evil can befall the good man, will not allow them to be anything more than illusion, mere thinking.

4. *Τὴν ἡδυσμένην Μοῦσαν*, "the honeyed Muse," 607a, is a malicious reference to *ἡδυσμένῳ λόγῳ* ("sweetened language," language given an extra, adventitious charm by the addition of verse and song) in Aristotle's definition of tragedy, 6.49b25, and beyond that to the *οἰκεία ἡδονή*, the "peculiar pleasure," which Aristotle puts forward as the end of tragedy.

5. In the same vein, the invitation or rather challenge at 607d, "Let poetry's champions, those of them who are not (themselves) poetical, but poetry-lovers (*ὅσοι μὴ ποιητικοί, φιλοποιηταὶ δέ*), show that poetry is not only pleasurable (*ἡδεῖα*) but useful to societies and human life in general," is a coded message laid at Aristotle's door: he has talked about pleasure, now let him talk about social utility as well.

I have put these passages from Plato first, to suggest that the debate over poetry in the Akademy was indeed a two-way affair. But they also have a more general interest. Taken individually, no one of them is particularly telling; taken together, they show Plato reacting to several key points in Aristotle's doctrine: the preeminence of action, the ethical problems involved in the good man's fall, the central place of pleasure as the goal of poetry. Each of these positions represented a threat to a deeply held conviction of Plato's: that the crucial thing in human life is not action but souls; that no plausible reason can be alleged for the fall of a good man, even one who is less than perfectly virtuous; that pleasure in any ordinary sense is not and cannot be the goal of life.

Here the battle lines are drawn sharply and, one would think, unambiguously; one is the more surprised to find that Plato does not develop any of these points in a major way in *Republic* 10. His thinking is in other directions—directions prefigured, for example, in the *Sophist*. In another part of the field, however, Aristotle's position not only does not represent a threat to Plato, but consolidates and extends one of Plato's own theses. I mean what is said in the *Poetics* about the unity of poems, in chapter 8 and elsewhere. The reference to Plato is virtually guaranteed by a particularly striking metaphor, the likening of a beautiful poem to a beautiful ζῷον, 7.50b34ff. (cf. 23.59a20–21). Whether Aristotle has in mind here a living animal or a picture of an animal (ζῷον could mean either), any reader or hearer of the *Poetics* would be irresistibly reminded of a famous passage of the *Phaidros*, 264c, where Plato demands that πᾶς λόγος, "every utterance," have the unity and wholeness of a ζῷον, with head and feet and everything thereto appertaining. "Every utterance" includes poems, though it denotes primarily speeches, discourses; Plato makes the inclusion certain by what he says later, at *Phaidros* 268c–269a, about the unity and wholeness of tragedies, with explicit reference to Sophokles and Euripides.

These passages bring us to a second range of phenomena which favor an early date for the *Poetics*: its affiliations with the *Rhetoric* and other Aristotelian works which are known or plausibly conjectured to be early, in whole or in part—above all, the *Topics* and *Analytics*.

The *Rhetoric* has particularly close relationships with the *Phaidros* on one side and the *Poetics* on the other. On the one hand it carries out (though with significant alterations and modifications) the program for a new, scientifically based rhetoric which Plato calls for in the *Phaidros* (268–272); on the other it is very closely linked with the *Poetics*, especially in its theory of the emotions and its treatment of style. Cross-references in the two works run in both directions and virtually assure that they were developed at the same time and in close mutual rapport.

A similar relationship, though less close in detail, obtains between the *Poetics* and the *Topics* and *Analytics* (also the *Categories*). All these works (including the *Rhetoric*) are "logical," λογικά, in Aristotle's sense: dealing with aspects of λόγος, reasoned utterance. In particular, as we shall see, when he says that poetry "tells, speaks of" universals (9.51b7, μᾶλλον τὰ καθόλου . . . λέγει: i.e., it does so more than history), he is identifying a trait which affiliates it to a certain extent with the reasoning arts.

Other signs of early date are of miscellaneous character and not very significant individually; cumulatively they carry some weight. Thus most of the Aristotelian treatises (πραγματεῖαι, "treatments": i.e., of given subject matters) begin with a survey of previous theories and investigation to indicate what has been done and what remains to be done (showing, in many cases, that Aristotle himself is the culmination of the development). Nothing of this in the *Poetics*; it begins with a series of *diaireseis*, "divisions," of the mimetic arts (chapters 1–3) which are Platonic in their general inspiration though often un-Platonic in their procedures and results.

Similarly, several technical terms which are characteristic of Aristotle's mature terminology and might be expected to turn up in a discussion of literature are missing in the *Poetics*: e.g., μορφή, "form," and ὕλη, "material"; δύναμις, "potentiality," and ἐνέργεια, "actuality, realization"; ἐντελέχεια, "full reality," complete realization of a goal, a τέλος; and συλλογισμός, "syllogism." On the other hand, the *Poetics* does have several words which seem to be characteristically early: μᾶλλον, "rather"; ὁμοίως, "similarly, equally"; and δύναμις, in the sense of "power, ability."

Finally, Walter Burkert has called attention to a piece of evidence which is interesting and, I think, persuasive because it is quite independent of either ideology or linguistic usage.[4] Two passages in the *Rhetoric*—with side connections to the *Poetics*—refer to Aristotle's concrete experiences of the theater, and these can be dated with confidence to some time before 350.

This varied array of evidence makes it, not certain to be sure, but highly probable that the *Poetics* or its basic stock—in any case a substantial portion of the work—dates from before 350, and probably nearer 360.

From this dating, and the evidence supporting it, flow several important corollaries:

1. The *Poetics* itself gives evidence of varied and extensive reading, but the likelihood of its being based on comprehensive scholarly research, at so early a date, is slight indeed. The Pythian and Athenian catalogues—not to speak of the 158 constitutions—were still in the distant future. Moreover, the probability of any reliable documentary evidence for literary events before the fifth century is dim enough; and that of Aristotle's having found his way to it before he was thirty is dimmer still.

2. Efforts to base a complete Aristotelian system of the arts, or even an interpretation of the *Poetics*, on concepts like Form and Matter, Potentiality and Actualization, or the Four Causes, come to grief on the plain fact that there is not so much as a whisper of these things in the treatise. Aristotle had not yet drawn them into his thinking on literature, and the few scattered allusions to such matters in other works do not cohere to form a theory but suggest that he

---

4. "Aristoteles im Theater: Zur Datierung des 3. Buchs der 'Rhetorik' und der 'Poetik,'" *MH* 32 (1975) 67–72.

never again thought about the problem in a systematic way, after the *Poetics*.

3. Looking at the same evidence from another angle, we observe that although many of the theses propounded in the *Poetics* have great power and originality, the questions to which they respond are from first to last Platonic questions. Without the challenge of Plato's attack on the poets, Aristotle would surely not have been stimulated to this depth and vigor of response; and in fact he never responded so again. Nature, the cosmos, the polis, biology, the human organism and its moral life, gave him more than enough problems to chew on for the rest of his life; poetry, no longer a living issue, became only a topic for documentation and research after Plato passed from the scene.

To sum up: Nothing in Aristotle's previous education or subsequent experience, outside the Akademy, could have impelled him to take up the cudgels in defense of poetry. It was the immediate shock of Plato's attack on all that he held most holy—above all, Homer—that engendered the *Poetics*. He had the materials for a defense ready in his mind; it was only a question of organizing them.

5
Mimesis

Background of the Concept

Μίμησις, "imitation," is clearly the centerpiece of Aristotle's poetic theory, but it is by no means immediately clear what he means by it—except that he cannot mean simply "copying," as the word itself might suggest. Aristotle himself is partly to blame for this ambiguous state of affairs. Instead of propounding an entirely new descriptive term for poetry, he has taken over Plato's concept of μίμησις—itself already complex and devious to a degree—and then given it a 180-degree turn, so that it ends up meaning almost exactly the opposite of what Plato had meant by it. And Aristotle does not come out and tell us frankly what he is doing. But surely we must acquit him of any deliberate intention to deceive. The context within which he was operating, in the Akademy, defined the issue quite precisely: everybody around him would know what he was up to and what was at stake. Moreover it is very likely—I would say almost certain—that he had led off his response to Plato with a public discussion of the leading issues, in the dialogue *On Poets*. And finally, the pupil's respect for the master might naturally lead him to tone down his response by clothing it in the relatively objective terms of scientific discourse. Whatever the reasons, Aristotle does not make a frontal attack on Plato's concept of μίμησις, but bores at it from within.

In our discussion of mimesis in Plato (p. 26), we noted that in fifth-century Athens, μιμεῖσθαι and μίμησις had developed the broad sense of "imitation" in any of various contexts and that this was presumably the accepted meaning of μίμησις there at the time Plato wrote *Republic* 3. But in 3.392dff. Plato reverts to something much closer to the original sense, "impersonation, performance" (of a dramatic or quasi-dramatic role), and he feels obliged to explain it with care and in great detail. (Had that meaning grown dim in Athens by the 370s?) His purpose in reviving this special sense of mimesis is to point out the danger to his young Guards, not from any dramatic poet, but from Homer. Homer does not merely present his characters; by his use of direct speech he pretends that he *is* those characters and tries to make us believe that they, not he, are speaking—all this to gain entrance to the Guards' unguarded souls and pave the way for variousness, confusion, and loss of moral standards. The absurdity, from our point of view, of this charge against Homer may blind us to its deadly seriousness. For Plato, Homer is the archenemy, the supreme enchanter, who seduces otherwise rational people into accepting the tragic view of life as true. The tragic poets only follow the lead he gave (in the *Iliad*, of course).

Now, how does Aristotle go about refuting this intensely personal, subjectivist view of poetry and of Homer in particular? In a word, he does not refute it; he ignores it and substitutes for it a wholly impersonal, objectivist view of the poet—Homer above all—as a *maker of structures*. "Imitation" so defined becomes the closest neighbor to creation: not out of nothing—no Greek ever believed in creation *ex nihilo*—but out of carefully observed "universal" human tendencies to thought and action.

Aristotle says nothing about these preliminary matters in the *Poetics*. He does, however, speculate at the beginning of chapter 4 on the basic causes which gave rise to poetry, and thinks it "stands to reason" (ἐοίκασι, 48b4) that they were the universal human tendency to imitate (here "imitate" visibly refers to copying, mimicry of behavior) and our natural predilection for rhythm and melody. And he emphasizes there, in conscious opposition to Plato's elitist view of human nature, that imitation stems basically from the desire to know, *which all men have*. Thus we are authorized to consider poetry, qua imitation, human activity and poets our natural allies in being human.

The Divisions of Mimesis

CHAPTERS 1–3 of the *Poetics* offer a series of discriminations of mimesis according to its media (chapter 1), its objects (chapter 2), and its methods (chapter 3). This procedure has its roots in the Platonic method of *diairesis*, bilateral division, exemplified especially in the *Sophist* and *Politikos*; but Aristotle's handling of it is so different in both concept and execution as to make it in effect a new, distinctively Aristotelian method.

Let us first be clear what it is that Aristotle is dividing. He does not quite say outright, at the beginning, that all poetry is mimetic or, what comes to the same thing, that only mimetic poetry is poetry; but the indications are there from the start. The μῦθοι, the "plots," turn up in the second line of the treatise; and only mimetic poems have plots. Again, the beginning of the actual argument, 47a13ff., is a seemingly informal list of poetic genres: epic, tragedy, comedy, dithyramb, and "most flute and lyre music"—an introduction (ἐπαγωγή), though it is not called so here. But Aristotle says at once, "These are all in point of fact imitative processes in their totality" (τὸ σύνολον), a totality which we are left to infer is the genus poetry. And at 1.47b13ff., in a long footnote which Aristotle has dragged in by the the the heels, we have the significant phrase κατὰ τὴν μίμησιν ποιητάς, "poets in accordance with, by virtue of their imitating" (b15; cf. 9.51b28–29).

Thus poetry and μίμησις are identical or practically identical after all. Indeed the identification goes so far as to deny Empedokles—a poet whom Aristotle especially admired as "Homeric" and a master of poetic style—the very title of poet because he is not an imitator in Aristotle's sense but only a φυσιολόγος, a writer on Nature (47b19). Youthful absolutism could go no farther. If Empedokles is excluded from the company of poets in spite of his drama(s) of the cosmos and the soul, it is clear that Hesiod, Theognis, Parmenides, and many others will never reach the gate of the compound.

With these prolegomena out of the way, we are ready to consider Aristotle's differentiations.

By the media: ῥυθμός, λόγος, ἁρμονία (rhythm, speech, melody) and their combinations, 1.47a18–b29

THE MASTER PRINCIPLE of this chapter—unrecognized, misrepresented, overlaid by interpolations in the text and by generations of commentators—is the bilateral division between imitative arts using melody and rhythm only (instrumental music: 47a23–26) and imitative arts using speech and rhythm only (the "nameless art," 47a28–b24) followed by those which use all three media (b24–28). This division is prefigured by the one between visual and vocal arts, 47a18–20, and exactly matched in chapter 3, where we shall find two antithetical methods and a mixture of the two. Chapter 2, on the other hand, offers only the antithetical classes "serious" and "low-down, no-good." Aristotle's scheme has no room for tragicomedy or for any mixed class of objects.

The trail of Aristotle's bilateral division in chapter 1 has been obscured by three factors: (1) misapprehension of the part played by rhythm in his scheme; (2) the apparent vagueness and indefiniteness of the "nameless art"; and (3) misunderstandings as to the length and purport of the long sentence 47a18–b22(23), especially its interjected footnote, b13–20. And points 1 and 3 have been further complicated by intrusions into the text partly caused by these very misapprehensions. (No doubt confusion has also been promoted by a feeling that the first limb of Aristotle's disjunction, instrumental music, is too unliterary to have a full place here.)

To take up the three points in order:

(1) It has been assumed—without question, so far as I can see—that the three media are free and equal, in the sense that each can serve as medium alone or in combination with either of the others or with both of the others. Thus there are seven possibilities in all: three with one medium, three combinations of two, and one combination of three. But this tidy scheme is nonsense. No mimetic art known to Aristotle ever operated with rhythm alone or entirely *without* rhythm, so that four of the seven alleged posts are empty: the only real possibilities are melody with rhythm (the first limb of our *diairesis*), speech with rhythm (the other limb), and speech *and* melody with rhythm (the mixed class).

The reason for the error, aside from inattention to the facts of Greek artistic life in the classical period, is that scholars have read the pronoun τούτοις, "with these," in 47a22, as referring to all three media, whereas actually it means "with these latter ones (speech and melody) either separately or mixed."

This error, once committed, seems to have drawn another after it, for the text actually contains almost three lines which claim a place for rhythm alone in this sequence: 47a26–28, "and just by rhythm itself those (the rhythms) of dancers make their imitation, without melody; for these (dancers) by means of their patterned rhythms imitate both characters and sufferings (or experiences or emotions: πάθη) and actions." The syntax of the sentence is unexceptionable in an independent statement, but it will not fit into Aristotle's sentence; testimony thereto are two Renaissance emendations and a series of pullings and haulings ever since.[1] And the statement, if it refers to anything, seems to refer to the

---

1. The text translated here is that of the chief MSS: αὐτῷ δὲ τῷ ῥυθμῷ μι-μοῦνται χωρὶς ἁρμονίας οἱ τῶν ὀρχηστῶν: καὶ γὰρ οὗτοι διὰ τῶν σχημα-τιζομένων ῥυθμῶν μιμοῦνται καὶ ἤθη καὶ πάθη καὶ πράξεις. The emendations (in the first clause) μιμεῖται for μιμοῦνται and ἡ for οἱ, found in a fifteenth-century MS, do not make the sentence any more natural a part of the construc-

pantomimes of the Roman Imperial period—though even they were nor-
mally accompanied by music—rather than anything known to Aristotle.

(2) Similar infelicities have attended the second half of Aristotle's long
sentence (it is in fact unconscionably long, stretching from a18 to
b22[23]). The chief problem of interpretation here is to assign content
and identity to Aristotle's seemingly amorphous "nameless art," 47b9.
(Unfortunately Kassel has admitted into his text at this point a pair of
emendations from Lobel which destroy Aristotle's syntax and his argu-
ment by doubling the number of arts.)[2] The nameless art is one which
operates with prose discourses (λόγοι), "bare" (i.e., of music) *or* with
verses (μέτρα) similarly bare, or—here follows, at a great distance (b20–
21), a final possibility—with a mixture of "all kinds of verse" (ἅπαντα
τὰ μέτρα), likewise bare.

Aristotle specifies the kind of thing he has in mind under prose with-
out music: mimes and Sokratic dialogues. Here he touches close upon
Plato, and we know that in the dialogue *On Poets* he said that Plato's
style was "(halfway) between prose and poetry"; but the mere inclusion
of Sokratic dialogues under the nameless art, *alongside* the mime, shows
sufficiently that Aristotle was aware of his master's poetic achievement.
As for imitations in verse without music, epic of course belongs here (the
actual word was inserted in the text at 47a28, by somebody who had lost
the thread of Aristotle's sentence). But the second part of the disjunction
is purely hypothetical: 47b11–13, "if somebody *should* make his imita-
tion by means of trimeters or elegiacs or some others of such verses"—in
other words, nobody has done it so far. And the final extension to "all
kinds of verse" is equally hypothetical except that Chairemon has actu-
ally produced a *Kentaur*.[3]

Now, what reality, if any, lurks behind this phantom, the nameless art?

---

tion. Deletion of μιμοῦνται, favored by many recent editors, appears to heal the
construction but still leaves a real inconsistency in the logic of the passage, since
the introduction of dancing here interrupts the clearly stated antithesis of instru-
mental music on the one hand and unaccompanied recitation on the other. For
details, see *Argument* 33–36.

2. Rudolf Kassel's Oxford text (1965) prints καὶ ἥ for MSS ἥ at 1447a29 and
ἀνώνυμοι τυγχάνουσι for Bernays' ⟨ἀνώνυμος⟩ τυγχάνουσα at b9. The effect is
to make two "nameless arts," one in prose (λόγοις ψιλοῖς) and the other in verse
(τοῖς μέτροις).

3. This was, in all probability, a dramatic poem, most likely a satyr play. See
Argument 58–60.

Unless Aristotle is playing—a thing most unlike him—he seems to be calling attention to a possibility that was still open in his time, of mounting a new mimetic art in verse without music, to form a pendant to the mimes and Sokratic dialogues. If so, the challenge was not taken up— except that as Aristotle himself points out (18.56a29–30), the tragedians ever since Agathon had been composing ἐμβόλιμα, textually indifferent *intermezzi*, in lieu of real choral odes, so that the plays were essentially reduced to their dialogue parts; and we know from the papyrus texts that New Comedy did the same. Thus the new experiment Aristotle was suggesting (if that is what he is doing here) almost came off; but the combined force of tradition and inanition left tragedy too weak to try the venture head-on.

(3) It remains to retrace the full course of Aristotle's inordinately long sentence, beginning at 47a18:

For as certain people imitate many things, making replicas by means of colors (some through art, some through mere practical experience), whereas other people do it with the voice, so among the aforementioned arts (the complex of musical-poetic arts) all make the imitation by means of rhythm, speech, and melody, but with these (latter two) either separately or mixed together: for example, flute- and lyre-playing using melody and rhythm alone—and any others which are like them in capacity, e.g., the art of the panpipes [And just by rhythm itself those (the rhythms) of dancers make their imitations, without melody; for these (dancers) by means of their patterned rhythms imitate both characters and sufferings and actions.]; but the other art (using) either prose utterances bare (of music) or verses (bare of music), and either mixing these (the verses) together or using one particular class of verses—an art which happens to be nameless up to now; for we could not even give a common name to the mimes of Sophron and Xenarchos and the Sokratic dialogues, nor (could we) if someone should make his imitation in trimeters or elegiacs or some of the other verses of that kind; except people do attach the word *making* to the verse and speak of elegy-makers and of others as epic-makers, not on the basis of their being poets by virtue of imitation, but giving them a common name in accordance with the verse; for even if they set forth some medical or scientific (physical) topic in verses, that is the customary name for them; yet Homer and Empedokles have nothing in common *except* the verse, hence it is proper to call the one a poet but the

other a nature-writer rather than a poet, and similarly also if some-
one should mix all the verses in making his imitation, as Chairemon
made a *Kentaur* [a mixed recitation] out of all the kinds of verses
[and he should be called a poet].[4]

Two things, it seems to me, appear from this endless sentence: (1) Aris-
totle's stylistic sense either was in abeyance or yielded to his earnest
desire to set forth his *diairesis* in total completeness; but (2) that yielded
to an even more urgent desire: to establish that poetry is imitation.
However we interpret these signs, they seem to point to youth.

But what *is* imitation? So far we have learned very little about it. The
more significant indications are still to come.

By objects: human beings in action, 2.48a1–18

CHAPTER 2 begins with the affirmation that imitators—i.e., the poets—
imitate men acting, in action. Plato, who notes and returns to Aristotle's
theory at *Republic* 10.603c4ff., understands this assertion and under-
lines it by putting the participle first in his sentence, even at the cost
of a violent hyperbaton: πράττοντας, φαμέν, ἀνθρώπους μιμεῖται ἡ
μιμητικὴ βιαίους ἢ ἑκουσίας πράξεις, "mimetic poetry imitates human
beings doing forced or voluntary actions." Aristotle's emphasis on action
is worth noting for its originality. In *Republic* 3.392dff., the key passage
for this subject, nothing is said about action; the talk is entirely of
speech. We are told at 392c and again at 394c that what the poets talk
about has already been dealt with; all that remains to be discussed is
how they say it.

Aristotle himself underlines his emphasis on action by an amendment
and enlargement of his original formulation, first in the definition of
tragedy (6.49b24ff.), and then at 6.50a16ff., ἡ γὰρ τραγῳδία μίμησίς
ἐστιν οὐκ ἀνθρώπων ἀλλὰ πράξεως καὶ βίου καὶ εὐδαιμονίας, "for
tragedy is an imitation not of persons but of an action, a life, a happi-
ness."[5] Πρᾶξις here has not the connotation of mere activeness, stirring

---

4. In this translation, as elsewhere in this book, material in square brackets
represents interpolation into Aristotle's original text; material in parentheses is
explanatory and added by the translator.

5. Almost all MSS read βίου καὶ εὐδαιμονίας καὶ ἡ κακοδαιμονία ἐν πράξει
ἐστίν. Kassel brackets after βίου, but Else regards καὶ εὐδαιμονίας as genuine,
arguing that the interpolation after it of καὶ εὐδαιμονία καὶ κακοδαιμονία κτλ.,

about, nor does it refer to physical action. From its parent word, the verb
πράττειν, it has in it the notion of a moral or intellectual *program* aimed
at a goal; and the goal of human life is happiness, εὐδαιμονία. The
tragic action, in particular, swings in an arc between the two poles of
happiness and unhappiness; in fact it is measured by that arc (7.51a11–
15). Action in this sense is what the plot, ὁ μῦθος, imitates, and "the plot
is the principle (of motion) and as it were the soul of tragedy" (6.50a38–
39). The centrality of the poetic action in Aristotle's theory will occupy
us again in these pages. It is not the same thing as the general importance
of action in human life, any more than βίον in 6.50a17 means life in
general or εὐδαιμονίας happiness. What is central in tragedy is *an* ac-
tion, *a* life (career), *a* happiness.

The next point in the argument in chapter 2 is 48a1–2, ἀνάγκη δὲ
τούτους ἢ σπουδαίους ἢ φαύλους εἶναι, "and (since) these (the persons
acting) must necessarily be either morally superior or inferior (no-
good)." Aristotle's justification of this "necessity" has been widely misin-
terpreted: 48a2–3, τὰ γὰρ ἤθη σχεδὸν ἀεὶ τούτοις ἀκολουθεῖ μόνοις,
"for (definite) characters pretty much always follow (or attach to) these
alone." The error has consisted in referring τούτοις, "these," to the
σπουδαῖοι and φαῦλοι (i.e., to the division between them), whereas
actually it refers to πράττοντες: it is *men acting* who practically always
develop fixed characters. The misinterpretation inspired and then was
fostered by the spurious next clause, a3–4, κακίᾳ γὰρ καὶ ἀρετῇ τὰ ἤθη
διαφέρουσι πάντες, "for in vice and virtue of character (lit., as to their
characters) all men differ," which substitutes a trivial moral platitude for
Aristotle's carefully worded phrase. But he cannot be absolved from all
blame, for he does not show why the necessary development of character
necessarily turns up just these two kinds of people.

The sentence resumes at a4, ἤτοι βελτίονας ἢ καθ' ἡμᾶς ἢ χείρονας,
"persons either better or worse than average. . . ." Here a main verb has
to be restored (not just understood), to govern the accusatives, and obvi-
ously it should be μιμοῦνται, "they imitate," to match μιμοῦνται in a1.
It may well have been displaced by the following phrase, a5, ἢ καὶ
τοιούτους, "or also"—note the *also*—"as such" (i.e., like average peo-
ple). This is the first of three short phrases—the second is a6, Διονύσιος
δὲ ὁμοίους εἴκαζεν, "and Dionysios painted men like (ourselves)," and

---

later simplified by haplography, best accounts for the received text. See *Argu-
ment* 254–255 and p. 114 below.

there is a similar remark about Kleophon in a12—all referring to a third class of poetic object, the average man. This third group has a dubious existence at best. Aristotle's genuine theory seems to have no room for either an intermediate class *or* a mixed class combining the other two; and what poetic genre would imitate it? If the three phrases are from Aristotle, they must be subsequent additions representing an amendment to the theory, perhaps stemming from further thought about the need for the tragic hero to be "like" us so that he can inspire fear and pity (see 13.53a5–6, and cf. 15.54b8–15). But the references to Dionysios and Kleophon are troublesome, especially the latter, and altogether it is more likely that these are interpolations from a later reader who thought that Aristotle had or ought to have a third class, to match chapters 1 and 3. It should be noted that at a15 only two classes of object are suggested for dithyramb and nome, represented by Timotheus and Philoxenos respectively, and that at a18 the distinction between tragedy and comedy is said to "fall exactly in (on) the differential between those better and worse than average" (χείρους and βελτίους, repeating a4 to the letter). Finally, we shall see that in chapter 4 the dichotomy is maintained from beginning to end.

If we seek a larger reason why Aristotle holds—or originally held—strictly to his dichotomy between σπουδαῖοι and φαῦλοι, the answer must be that the distinction was fundamental in the Greek aristocratic code, beginning with Homer. It would be strange if Aristotle had not imbibed it early in his pre-Athenian education; and as Jaeger says, his heart remained true to the old ideal. He would have found in a work such as Arthur Miller's *Death of a Salesman* an intolerable mixture of genres and attitudes.

By methods: τὸ ὡς ἕκαστα τούτων μιμήσαιτο ἄν τις, *"how one can imitate each of these," 3.48a19–25*

THIS IS the most important of the differentiations; in other words, Aristotle's order is climactic. In his eyes, all poetry aspires to the condition of drama: we shall see the story spread out over time in chapter 4. Plato had centered his attack here, on μίμησις in the specifically dramatic sense of impersonation (we are speaking, as always, of *Republic* 3), and Aristotle counters by making μίμησις—but in his new objective version—the heart of his defense.

This time, for a reason we shall come to in a moment, the mixed category is mentioned first, followed by the two pure methods, narrative (a22–23) and dramatic (a23–24). But the text dealing with the first category has suffered a serious deformation. The mixed method should be described in two alternating phrases, of which the first is intact: (μιμεῖσθαι ἔστιν) ὁτὲ μὲν ἀπαγγέλλοντα, "(it is possible to imitate) at certain times by narrating." This should be balanced by a second phrase saying that "at other times" (ὁτὲ δέ) the dramatic mode is used. But no balancing ὁτὲ δέ appears, and health cannot be restored to the sentence simply by substituting ὁτὲ δέ for ἤ, "or," because the phrase which follows, ἢ ἕτερόν τι γιγνόμενον, "or becoming something different," is radically false to Aristotle's conception of the dramatic mode.

We are not far enough into the *Poetics* to document this rejection fully: all we can do at the moment is to repeat our earlier statement that for Aristotle μίμησις—of which the dramatic mode is the purest form—is an act of construction. Poets do not "become" anybody or anything; they build. The phrase we are objecting to is Platonic, not Aristotelian, and it has a specific form of origin in Book 3 of the *Republic*. At 393a, after introducing the three modes—the same as Aristotle's: narrative, dramatic, and mixed—Plato describes the mixed mode in a most peculiar way. Taking up Homer first, because he has him most on his mind (and Aristotle follows suit for the same reason), he says that in his narrative passages Homer speaks in his own person throughout and does not try to make us think ὡς ἄλλος τις ὁ λέγων ἢ αὐτός, "that the speaker is *someone other* than himself," though elsewhere, e.g., in the speech of the old priest Chryses in *Iliad* 1.17–21, 37–40, ὥσπερ αὐτὸς ὢν ὁ Χρύσης λέγει, "he speaks as (if) being Chryses himself."

Plato's picture is so fantastically unlike anything *we* can see in Homer that we tend to discount it, even to dismiss it from our minds. But it is desperately important to him; and it is the idea summarized in ἢ ἕτερόν τι γιγνόμενον. The phrase has displaced whatever Aristotle wrote; I have suggested ὁτὲ δὲ ἦθός τι εἰσάγοντα, "but at other times bringing on (onstage) some character."[6] This is based on a phrase in 24.60a9–11 which speaks precisely of Homer, though there cannot be any warrant for the exact wording.

Here again, then, we find an interpolator at work; and this time the inspiration is clearly Platonic. Meanwhile, the sentence goes on to sketch the narrative and pure dramatic modes. They can best be considered together: 3.48a22–24, ἢ (μιμεῖσθαι ἔστιν) ὡς τὸν αὐτὸν καὶ μὴ μεταβάλλοντα, ἢ πάντας ὡς πράττοντας καὶ ἐνεργοῦντας τοὺς μιμου-

6. *Argument* 95.

μένους, "or (it is possible to imitate) in the way that the same person (does it), not changing; or in the way that all the imitators (do it) by acting and energizing." Strange expressions; but this time our task will be to interpret and justify them, not to question them.

The image which lurks behind these curious phrases is that of a total potential cast of imitators made up of the poet and his characters. Of this total cast, the narrative poet alone ("the same person") does the imitating throughout, without a change of cast, i.e., not shifting to the characters; whereas in the dramatic mode all the imitators do the imitating by "acting and energizing": i.e., the characters do it themselves, without the poet.

However quaint this idea may seem to us, it can be shown that it turns up in a number of places in later antiquity;[7] and at least we have to admire Aristotle's originality in projecting it. He has gotten as far away from Plato's subjectivist scheme as anyone very well could. Our only complaint must be that he has clothed his idea in language of such Delphic brevity and ambiguity. But surely this idea too was originally put forward in the dialogue *On Poets*.

THE SECTION on comedy at the end of chapter 3, 48a29–b2, will occupy us later. Its authenticity is not above suspicion, and so therefore is that of the intervening passage a24–29, which seems to have been written solely to provide a transition to it, via the word δρᾶμα (δρά-ματα). This transitional passage contains various crudities and infe-licities, such as the remark that Sophokles is "the same imitator" as Homer, but its emphasis on δρᾶμα and the verb δρᾶν (participle δρῶντας, "doing," a29, anticipating δρώντων in the definition of tragedy, 6.49b26), *is* apposite to Aristotle's theory. Δρᾶμα (δράματα) appears several times later in the *Poetics*; even more significant are the derivative form δραματικός, "dramatic," 4.48b35, 23.59a19, and the compound δραματοποιήσας, "by composing as a drama, in dramatic form," 4.48b37. These two words appear within two lines of each other in chapter 4, in the discussion of Homer. There cannot be much doubt, to my mind, that Aristotle invented this generic application of δρᾶμα to designate dramatic form; there is no trace of it in Plato, even in the famous passage at the end of the *Symposion*, 223d. (Dorian plays were indeed called δράματα—though not for the reason alleged at 3.48b1— but only comedies; the Dorians had no tragedies.) It remained for the

7. See *Argument* 98–99.

novus homo from Makedonia to perceive the identity of "drama" as a single genus, a form.

On the other hand it is no accident that Aristotle perceived this form in Homer above all. It was precisely Homer the dramatist—though he did not call him that—whom Plato feared most urgently. Indeed the careful reader of the *Republic* and *Poetics* may already have remarked the curious fact that for both men the storm center of the debate over tragedy is not the tragedians but Homer. Another feature of this complex question must be reserved for treatment later in this book: that Plato objected not merely to Homer's dramatic talents but to his tragic message (in the *Iliad*). Meanwhile it should be noticed that the peculiar view of drama embodied in chapter 3 of the *Poetics*, 48a23–24—that the imitation is carried on by the persons of the drama themselves, "acting" as if without intervention from the poet—will be incorporated directly into the analysis of tragedy in chapter 6. It is the dramatic persons who must necessarily be seen (in some sense or other) and heard, 49b31–34; who necessarily have this or that kind of character and thought, b37–38; etc. Drama belongs to the doers.

One more question awaits us before we leave the three differentiations of μίμησις. Are we to conceive of them as three independent overlays, so to speak, on the same grid, or are they cumulative, each making further discriminations within the boundaries previously laid down? Aristotle seems to intend the latter: 2.48a7–8, "each of the *aforesaid* imitations will have these differentiae"; 3.48a19, "And *further*, a third differentiation of these is . . . ," where "these" presumably refers to the arts just mentioned in chapter 2. Chapters 1–3 would then represent a progressive narrowing of focus: e.g., epic would be that species (subgenus?) of the "nameless art" which (1) operates with one kind of verses, (2) imitating serious or superior persons, (3) by means of the mixed mode. The last differentia would be the smallest and the most definitive.

The procedure certainly has a kinship with Platonic *diairesis* as exemplified in *Sophist* and *Politikos*, but there are conspicuous differences. Plato begins with one class or genus marked by a familiar name (e.g., τέχνη, *Soph.* 219a; θηρευτική (τέχνη), hunting (art), 221d), and proceeds (218e–226e) by successive bilateral divisions of it and its "right-hand halves" in a single line down to the *infima species* (ἄτομον εἶδος, 229d). Aristotle's scheme, though bilateral within each stage of differentiation, starts over again each time, with media, objects, and methods, and these are in each case plural, not singular.

There can be no question, to my mind, that Aristotle intended to apply this kind of scheme to the classification of poetry; but there *is* a question how far he has indeed applied it and how far the application is effective. He begins with something that certainly was not a common, accepted idea: Plato's concept of μίμησις in *Republic* 3, and then proceeds, as we have seen, to turn it inside out. In chapter 1 he sets up, with some insistence, a wholly unfamiliar new category, the "nameless art"—and then makes no further use of it in the *Poetics*. The substantial thing in chapter 2 is the dichotomy tragedy–comedy (which is explicitly marked as standing exactly on the dividing line: ἐν αὐτῇ δὲ τῇ διαφορᾷ, "in the differentia itself," 48a16), but chapter 3 pays no explicit heed to that discrimination. In the end, from chapter 4 on, the real entities that remain to be dealt with are the old familiar genres: epic, tragedy, and comedy. Nevertheless all is not quite lost. The crucial discrimination, that between drama and nondrama, emerges at the climactic place which Aristotle had reserved for it, in chapter 3—even though later, by a triumphant non sequitur, Homer will stand forth as the consummate dramatist.

It seems likely enough that this procedure is meant as an improvement on Plato's, and indeed it recalls a famous passage on classification in the *Parts of Animals*, 1.3.643b10ff., which makes two main points obviously in criticism of Plato: (1) one has to start with large, well-established, commonly recognized classes, e.g., in biology, with Birds and Fishes, and (2) more than one principle of division is needed. I think we may assume that Aristotle intended to follow these principles in *Poetics* 1–3; but how well has he succeeded? With respect to the first principle, not very well, or only in very approximate fashion. Μίμησις was not a commonly recognized generic character of all Poetry when Plato began; it was only a notion put forward by him (in *Republic* 3) for one division of the class, and Aristotle altered it fundamentally in adopting it as the generic character. Or again, the "nameless art," as a single entity, was not a generally accepted category but a special intuition of Aristotle's. In these cases we find Aristotle seeing things that had not been seen before and insisting on his perceptions with the enthusiastic radicalism of youth. On the other point, meanwhile, the need for multiple criteria, he is the calm-eyed observer of reality. Both these persons are Aristotle.

A further observation seems in order here concerning the general character and tenor of chapters 1–3. Their compression and angularity are noteworthy even in a work as compressed and difficult as the *Poetics*—in fact especially noteworthy just at the beginning. Aristotle is introducing here a radically new method of classification, as against the Platonic *diairesis*; a radically changed, indeed inverted, conception of μίμησις as against Plato's (we are speaking, as always, of *Republic* 3); and, potentially at least, a radically changed evaluation of Homer. Yet he does not say or even hint that he is doing any of these revolutionary things. All is masked by a pose of scientific—i.e., logical—objectivity. Why does he proceed in this apparently disingenuous way?

No doubt we may assume that much of what is missing in these lecture notes (for that is what we are dealing with) was explicated in oral statements and subsequent discussions. But I think we must also assume that the basic groundwork for the new theory—how much of it, we cannot tell—was laid in the public dialogue *On Poets*. Without going as far as Rostagni in this direction,[8] we can surely suppose that Aristotle set forth there the main points of difference between himself and Plato with respect to method and the concept of μίμησις. Otherwise his brevity in the lecture script would only propagate confusion.

As for the text of chapters 1–3, we have alleged, and tried to suggest evidence for, interpolations. What is the source and date of these intrusions (as distinguished from additions by Aristotle himself, like the long footnote in chapter 1)? The question is a ticklish one and does not, strictly speaking, fall within the purview of this book, but a general preliminary point can be made which may be useful to bear in mind when we come to further phenomena of this kind—as we shall: there is no assurance that all of them come from the same time or the same source. Some, e.g., the passage on the Dorian claims to the invention of comedy, 3.48a29–b2, have a contemporary, fourth-century air and may have originated with Aristotle's own school (the Lykeion, in his second Athenian period); others, like the remarks on dancing and the intermediate class of objects, in chapters 1 and 2, perhaps smack of the first or second century A.D.; while the phrase "becoming something different," in chapter 3, is clearly Platonic in inspiration. In other words the interpolations have a heterogeneous rather than a uniform character.

The difficulty in solving these problems is that we know nothing—even less than for the other akroamatic works—about the transmission of the *Poetics* text between the time it left Aristotle's hand and the fifteenth century A.D., when the chief extant Greek manuscript, *A*, turned up in Italy. There are a few negative indications. We have no firm evidence, in the form of direct quotations or unmistakable allusions, that

8. Augusto Rostagni, "Il dialogo aristotelico Περὶ ποιητῶν," RFIC 4 (1926) 433–470, 5 (1927) 145–173.

the *Poetics* text (as distinguished from possible percolation of leading ideas) was actually seen by anybody between the fourth century B.C. and the fourth A.D.; no commentary was ever written on it in antiquity; and the text that finally came to light in *A* (late tenth century A.D.) did not appear in association with other Aristotelian writings as such but as part of a bundle of rhetorical works, some by Aristotle, some by others. It looks as though the *Poetics* text had a precarious, isolated existence in antiquity, known to very few people. Thus the interpolations we have found, if they come from those blank centuries, are of very uncertain provenience. (In Byzantine times, on the other hand, the work *was* known to some and exerted a modest influence.)

6

The Development of Poetry

HAVING ESTABLISHED his classificatory grid, Aristotle proceeds in chapter 4 to justify it by a sketch of the development of poetry from the beginning up to a point which, for tragedy, is marked by Aischylos and Sophokles. To call this sketch a "history" would prejudice the case from two different angles of approach: (1) from Aristotle's own point of view, since he insists (9.51b5–7) that history deals "more" with particulars, whereas poetry deals more with universals; and (2) from our point of view, because we tend to assume that the writing of history is based on systematic research, whereas there is no evidence and no likelihood that chapter 4 is based on such research.

The very first sentence of the chapter should have sounded a warning in this regard: 48b4ff., "It stands to reason (ἐοίκασι, it is likely) that two natural causes gave birth to (γεννῆσαι) poetry." Ἐοίκασι embodies the principle of probability, τὸ εἰκός, which lies near the heart of Aristotle's theory not only in poetics but in rhetoric. In fact it is a rhetorical principle in origin, embedded in that discipline from the beginning. The application here is not specifically rhetorical, but it does mean that this point of origin for poetry was not suggested to Aristotle by research but by reason, by its probability.

Clearly the first of the two "begetting" causes is the human instinct for imitation (48b5–8), but there has been a considerable debate over the second cause. Is it the pleasure that all men take in imitations (b8–9, τὸ χαίρειν τοῖς μιμήμασι πάντας), or the natural gift for melody and rhythm (b20–21)? Careful reading of the chapter points to the latter; for what is sketched here as a historical development is the unfolding over time of the three differentiations of μίμησις. The human animal is predisposed by his nature to imitate, and his modes of imitation are shaped by his native gift for melody and rhythm. The first improvisations (b23–24) embody the basic dichotomy between serious and trivial (b25–26, σεμνότεροι = σπουδαῖοι; εὐτελέστεροι = φαῦλοι). This dichotomy remains fundamental throughout, as does the drive to imitate; the media, meanwhile, change to match the course of the development.

The passage b9–19 is a long footnote (cf. 1.47b13–23) tracing the imitative drive and the pleasure all men take in imitations to the universal human desire for knowledge. This is connected with the famous opening words of the *Metaphysics*, as a part of Aristotle's polemic against Plato's intellectual elitism (learning is most pleasurable not only to philosophers but to "the others" as well, 48b13–15). The reference to graphic images or replicas (εἰκόνας, b11 and 15), including "those of the most despised creatures, and of corpses" (b12), is interesting from still another point of view, suggesting that Aristotle had perhaps begun studies of animal (and human?) physiology even in his Akademy period. In any case the close textual parallels between this passage and the one we have already cited from the *Parts of Animals* seem to show Aristotle launching out into biological studies (as distinguished from Platonic exercises in classification) even before he left Athens.

After this gesture toward the ultimate sources of poetry, Aristotle begins his story at the stage of improvisation (ἐκ τῶν αὐτοσχεδιασμάτων, 48b23–24). Obviously these impromptu performances are thought of as springing directly from the primitive mimetic impulse, with little or no mediation from art. The concept of "oral composition," so familiar to us from the studies of Milman Parry and others, is already implied here, but at a stage considerably antedating Homer; Aristotle, if challenged, would perhaps minimize its value as against the later stages. The beginnings are important but unimpressive.

More significant but equally unobtrusive is the mention of hymns and enkomia, which are paired with the improvised ψόγοι, invectives, at 48b27. The verb which governs them (b25, ἐμιμοῦντο, "they were imitating," imperfect tense) indicates that these activities *are* the improvisational performances out of which poetry was "begotten" (b23, ἐγέννησαν, aorist, echoing γεννῆσαι, b4). The mention of invectives may remind us of what Plato says at *Philebos* 48a–c about jealousy (φθόνος) as the root comic impulse; the hymns and enkomia will certainly remind us of *Republic* 10.607a, where precisely these genres are selected for exclusive admission to the ideal state. Aristotle is saying in effect—and surely the implication is deliberate—that Plato's preferred poetic forms are hopelessly primitive: they belong to the earliest stirrings of the mimetic impulse, not to anything further up the line of poetic evolution.

Two points need to be stressed vigorously at this point and throughout our account of Aristotle's "history" of poetry: (1) in art and thought (even if not in biology) Aristotle is an evolutionist; and (2) he firmly believes that the most important thing about artistic or intellectual evolution is not what goes into it but what comes out of it—not the ἀρχή but the τέλος. Both these attitudes are different enough from those that prevail nowadays to call for explication.

Aristotle's evolutionism has a pattern which is most clearly stated at the end of the *Sophistic Refutations* (33.183b17–34), i.e., at the end of the *Topics* (and of the whole Organon), where it is assumed that the beginning (ἀρχή) of anything (e.g., any art) is small and hard to discern, but mighty in potential. Those who follow, working as if in a line of succession, advance it little by little until it attains some magnitude. A similar schema is implied in Book A of the *Metaphysics*, and John J. Keaney claimed to have found another in the *Constitution of the Athenians*.[1]

Now, why is Aristotle an evolutionist in the arts of culture but not in nature? The answer must lie in the phenomenal rapidity of change in Greek cultural history, a rapidity so great that the attentive eye could discover evidences of it on all sides; perceptible change in natural species takes such a very long time—centuries or millennia—that even an observer as keen as Aristotle could miss it. (Darwin would not have noticed it either, if he had not been confronted all of a sudden by the startling evidence of the Galapagos species.) At any rate Aristotle has detected evidence for changes in poetry over time. But we need not suppose that there was a great deal of evidence, or that Aristotle acquired his knowledge of it through elaborate, carefully organized research. He knew from his schema that there must have been a process of development toward a τέλος, and he knew what that τέλος was: the final unfolding of μίμησις in the dramatists, especially Sophokles.

A second point: Aristotle's attention is focused throughout on the end of the story, not the beginning. Understanding this fact is vital and will help us over several difficulties in the text. The only caveat is that Homer's position—interpolated into a sequence in which he does not really belong—causes problems at several places.

Very well, the process begins with the simultaneous production ("begetting") out of improvisations, of two parallel branches of poetry, higher and lower, serious and trivial. Neither of these branches was de-

---

1. "The Structure of Aristotle's *Athenaion Politeia*," HSCP 67 (1963) 115–146.

rived from the other. Aristotle is convinced that they have coexisted throughout all time, in the improvisational stage and thereafter, because they spring from and represent the two perennially existing classes of human beings, *σπουδαῖοι* and *φαῦλοι*. Their distinctness is a permanent feature of the story, as it is of the human scene.

The first development away from improvisations toward art was a parallel one for the two categories and led in each case to a twofold result (48b28–33): (1) the adoption of a suitable verse form, and (2) the emergence of poets in place of improvisers. But the poets, at this early stage, were still tied very closely to their respective verse forms: they were still just makers of verses rather than real poets, i.e., makers of plots. That forward step was reserved for Homer. The early development already shows a reciprocal relationship between form and what is expressed by form; but what was expressed by the form at this stage was not so much the objects represented—the "serious" or "trivial" persons—as the method or mode. The essential difference was that between narrative and action. Since Aristotle does not make his point clear just here we must draw on other passages in the *Poetics* to explain it.

On the serious side the matter is relatively simple. Every Greek knew that hymns and enkomia dilated at length on the "aretalogy," the great deeds, of gods and heroes: in other words, that they went in heavily for narrative. Hence the "heroic" verse (i.e., dactylic hexameter) was adopted for this function as a result of experiment (*ἀπὸ τῆς πείρας*, 24.59b32), because it is the slowest (*στασιμώτατον*, "most stationary," b34) and weightiest of the verses—and, Aristotle adds, for that reason also the most receptive of exotic words and metaphors (by "metaphors" he means above all the long, leisurely Homeric similes). Thus the primary reason for settling on heroic verse was its suitability for the *longueurs* of epic narrative. But *ὀγκωδέστατον*, "weightiest, most majestic," shows that the other aspect was also present to Aristotle's mind.

So far so good (the latent inconsistency will not emerge until we get to Homer). On the comic side, however, things were not quite so simple. The word *ἴαμβος* has two distinct though interrelated meanings: (1) with respect to verse form it denotes the syllabic sequence short–long (actually the basic *μέτρον* of the trimeter, etc., is ˘ ¯ ˘ ¯); and (2) with respect to ethos or spirit it denotes, or rather connotes, unbridled personal satire, vilification—what was called *ψόγοι* at 48b27.[2] Aristotle has

2. See Martin L. West, *Studies in Greek Elegy and Iambus* (Berlin 1974) 22–39.

no patience at all with this side of the comic spirit (the ἰαμβικὴ ἰδέα, 5.49b8) and does his best to get it out of the story as early as possible. His strategy for doing this is interesting. At 3.48b31–32 he comments that iambic verse "came (in)" as the appropriate vehicle for personal attacks: "That in fact is why it is called ἰαμβεῖον (= iambic trimeter) today, because it was in this verse that they vilified (ἰάμβιζον) each other." Although the satirical idea is certainly present in ἰάμβιζον, the clue to Aristotle's thinking here may be in the word ἀλλήλους, "each other": he may have thought that iambic verse was used initially because of its suitability for exchange of speeches, for conversation, and then later acquired its other meaning from its early use, because those exchanges were satirical.

This seemingly wayward interpretation seems to be recommended by the later passage in chapter 4, 49a23–27, where Aristotle is accounting for the adoption of iambic as the standard verse of *tragic* dialogue—an entirely different situation from the earlier one—by the fact or alleged fact that it is "the most speakable (μάλιστα λεκτικόν) of the verses." We are left to choose whether Aristotle has deliberately offered different and incompatible explanations of the same event in the two different contexts, or whether he has tried to modulate between the two in the earlier situation.

This latter solution may be recommended by the three lines of text 48b28–30. The interpretation offered above about the "coming" of iambic verse sprang over these lines and attached that development to the primitive ψόγοι. But the three intervening lines may represent an attempt (subsequently added by Aristotle?) to mediate: "From those before Homer, indeed, we cannot cite any such poem (any ψόγος), but it stands to reason (εἰκὸς δέ) that there were many; beginning with Homer we *can* (cite some): e.g., his *Margites* and poems of that kind." "Of that kind" is deplorably vague. Does it mean ψόγοι? Hardly, since the *Margites* is cited just below (48b38) as a poem which was *not* one (and in fact we know that it did not attack an individual but ridiculed a type, that of the learned or pretentious idiot; also, that it contained iambic trimeters in—apparently—random mixture with hexameters). If Aristotle did write the three lines in question, he is guilty of a barefaced equivocation: the *Margites* used iambics because it was a ψόγος, but it was not a ψόγος, or else the text conceals some incomplete or halfhearted attempt to reconcile the opposites.

However we interpret this passage, it represents the end of the primitive stage (τῶν παλαιῶν, "of the ancients," b33). Higher and lower branches of poetry now have their respective poets—and Homer stands at the door. His coming is the sign of a new era, that of *protodrama* on both levels. To begin with, we must recognize that the comic side of the account has had primacy in the discussion since line 27 ("first composing ψόγοι as others did ... "). Hence b34 starts off by righting the balance: "And just as Homer was also most a poet in the serious line (for he alone not only composed well but made dramatic imitations), so also he first sketched out the forms of comedy by dramatizing not vituperation but the laughable."

Here several points demand attention. "Most a poet" means "most a dramatist," as expounded at 24.60a5–11: not to "compete," occupy the stage oneself, but to bring on characters after a minimum of prefatory matter; and Homer "alone of the poets" (i.e., the epic poets) understood this. These are not the only places in the *Poetics* where the epithets "first" and "only" are attached to Homer. The significance of this procedure for Aristotle's view of epic will concern us later; meanwhile we note only that Homer has a decided edge on his rivals from his first appearance. He is *unicus inter impares*.

"The forms of comedy" involve the dramatization of the ludicrous rather than personal denigration. We must realize that the motive for inserting this definition of "comedy" at such an early stage is to exclude the other kind, that of Aristophanes and his acknowledged predecessor Archilochos, from the story. Both positively and negatively, Aristotle's procedure here is governed by preconceived ideas rather than any recognizable facts; and in the case of the *Margites* his youthful enthusiasm for his god-among-poets, Homer, has dulled his critical sense; for the man who perceived that the Epic Cycle was not genuinely Homeric (though perhaps that was a later insight) should have perceived that the *Margites* was not by Homer either. The decisive thing is that Aristotle wanted it to be genuine because it prefigured the right kind of comedy.

The case of Archilochos is essentially of the same kind, but even more damaging to Aristotle's credit as a historian. Archilochos undeniably existed and was a great poet, but he has no place in Aristotle's "history," either before or after Homer, because he was a writer of ψόγοι at a time when that kind of thing was outmoded, *passé*, according to Aristotle's schema.

At this point we move into the third period, in which Homer's achievements provide the chief model. Aristotle has just said, 48b38–49a2, that the *Margites* "stands in the same relation (proportion: ἀνάλογον, b38) to the comedies as the *Iliad* does to the tragedies."³ But when he proceeds to say, 49a2ff., "And when tragedy and comedy had just appeared (παραφανείσης) . . . ," it has for some reason not been apparent to the commentators that this refers to their appearance *in Homer*. That manifestation was what galvanized "those who were in motion (ὁρμῶντες, a3) toward each kind of poetry" to become comic instead of iambic and tragic instead of epic poets, "because these forms were larger (μείζω, a6) and more impressive than the others."

This statement makes very little sense by historical standards, ancient or modern, but Aristotle is committed to it. What he means is that what impressed the writers of heroic and iambic verses was not the *Iliad* or the *Margites* as such but the forms implicit in them: dramatic imitation of heroic characters and of the ludicrous. These forms were not completely realized in *Iliad* or *Margites*; they were embodied in them as ideas, models still to be realized, and that is what exerted such a powerful attraction on the epic and iambic poets. The entelechic pull of the idea, the form (τὰ σχήματα, 49a6), is for Aristotle the most potent influence in the realm of art.

This orientation forward toward the future culmination of the process rather than backward toward its beginnings is the most important thing about chapter 4, and especially important just here. Failure to observe it has led to a whole series of misunderstandings of the next passage, all the way from a7 to a28. (Incidentally, we must note that the focus of interest shifts back again at a7, from comedy to tragedy; the further story of comedy, so far as Aristotle deals with it at all, is deferred to chapter 5.)

"Well then, a review of the question whether already tragedy is adequate to the forms (τοῖς εἴδεσιν) or not—(a question) which is (properly) judged both in itself and in relation to the theater audiences—is another story." Here misinterpretation has fixed on the word ἤδη, "already" (a7), which was thought to date the question to Aristotle's own time: "whether tragedy is adequate to the forms *by now*." The concluding phrase ἄλλος λόγος, "another story," then hangs in the air, for Aristotle regularly uses it to point to a question which will be discussed at a later time, but there is no such discussion in the *Poetics*. There is, how-

---

3. Omitting καὶ ἡ Ὀδύσσεια, a reference to the *Odyssey* that Else regarded as interpolated both here and at 26.62b9–10 (see Appendix 2, nos. 11 and 43). To cite the *Odyssey* as a model for tragedy stands in sharp contrast to what Aristotle says about the affinity of its plot to comedy at 13.53a31–36; see below, p. 181.

ever, another discussion later on, in chapter 26, about epic and tragedy, on the question whether tragedy as distinguished from epic is adequate to the forms. The reason for that final review is that tragedy has been praised more highly throughout the *Poetics*; the situation here is similar and naturally suggests the question whether "even" (ἤδη) tragedy—tragedy, to come to it; tragedy, to go no further—deserves this praise.

Well, says Aristotle, however that may be, "in any case (δ' οὖν) tragedy, having sprung from an improvisational beginning . . . , was augmented little by little as they (the poets) developed so much of it as was becoming visible; and after going through a number of changes, it did arrive at its natural end (a15, ἐπαύσατο ἐπεὶ ἔσχε τὴν αὐτῆς φύσιν, "it stopped when it had acquired its own (full) nature").

I have left out some troublesome clauses which have led the commentators, mesmerized by the mention in them of dithyramb and phallic (?) songs, to ignore the real bearing of Aristotle's sentence and to fix all their attention on the beginning rather than the end of the story. Unfortunately, consideration of this passage must begin with the disquieting thought that it may be an interpolation in Aristotle's text. It is at the very least a parenthesis without any organic link to the text which surrounds it. Lines 49a9–13 run like this: "In any case tragedy did grow out of an improvisational beginning, it and comedy, the one from those who used to lead off the dithyramb (ἀπὸ τῶν ἐξαρχόντων τὸν διθύραμβον), the other from those who led the phallic songs (?) which still remain customary in many cities." That the improvisational beginnings were dithyrambic and phallic respectively is a purely incidental piece of information unless it were shown that these modes had some special significance for the future of tragedy and comedy; but no such showing is made. On the contrary, it can be argued that they interrupt the continuity of Aristotle's narrative, garble his chronology, and give rise to large problems of interpretation in their own right.

For tragedy, let us take it as proven that Aristotle's movement is forward at this point, toward the culmination in Aischylos and Sophokles. But then what is the point of mentioning the dithyramb songs at this stage in the development? We have already had one improvisational beginning, from the hymns and enkomia. Is this a second improvisational stage, and if so, what is it doing here? It is at least equally plausible that Aristotle recognized only one such stage, the original one, and that now, having inserted Homer in the development as an inspiration to all future tragic poets, he had no use for another.

On the comic side, the "phallic songs" provide no surer footing; indeed the very name may be a mirage. Editions of the *Poetics* since the Renaissance have dutifully and mechanically printed τὰ φαλλικά, "the phallic (songs)," at 49a11–12, without revealing—even Kassel's 1965 Oxford text does not make it clear—that this reading is found in one fifteenth-century manuscript only, the heavily interpolated Parisinus 2038. Τὰ φαλλικά is purely and simply a Renaissance conjecture; what the other manuscripts give, without exception, is the nonexistent word φαυλ(λ)ικά. The Parisinus 2038 may be given credit for trying to make sense of this nonsense, but its reading cannot be accepted as a genuine piece of tradition. We just do not know what Aristotle wrote here—if he wrote these lines at all; perhaps simply τὰ φαῦλα, "the low-class (performances)," in concert with 48b26, τῶν φαύλων.

The upshot of this discussion is unsatisfactory at best. Lines 49a10–13 cannot be definitively declared spurious; if, on the other hand, Aristotle wrote them, we cannot be sure what he meant by them. But there is no doubt about the bearing of the main sentence, at a13: "(In any case, having come from an improvisational beginning, . . .) it (tragedy) was augmented little by little as they (the poets) developed so much of it as was becoming visible; and after going through many changes it stopped when it had achieved its own (full) nature." The subject throughout is tragedy; comedy's turn will come later. The explicit statement of the subject, ἡ τραγῳδία, a14–15, is therefore otiose, or would be but for the parenthesis a10–13. In other words, if those lines are a later addition, so is ἡ τραγῳδία, and its presence here tends to strengthen our doubt concerning the parenthesis. The two phrases stand or fall together.

Now, if they have both been added, who is more likely to have added them, Aristotle or a later annotator? The answer to this question depends in turn on whether we think the dithyramb and the phallic (?) songs are intended to represent a second improvisational stage separate from the first. It seems evident that they are so intended—dithyrambs are not obviously identical with hymns and enkomia, or phallic (?) songs with ψόγοι—and thus it seems very unlikely that Aristotle was the author. He would have had no good motive for duplicating improvisational stages, or for slowing the forward thrust of his sentence for the sake of a pair of purely antiquarian references. Why should he go back to primitive phenomena of the seventh and/or sixth century at a time when according to his own schema Homer's example was already transforming epic poets into tragedians and iambic poets into comedians? A later annotator, on the other hand, could have been a simple, literal-minded fellow who missed the point of Aristotle's sentence, thought—like his modern congeners—that the "improvisational beginning" was a new one, and therefore helpfully filled in the missing genre names according to his lights.

No certainty can be attained here. The only point I would insist on is that the sentence begins at γενομένη δ' οὖν, 49a9, and summarizes the whole stretch of Aristotle's history from the primitive beginnings, 48b22, to the final culmination, 49a15—all this in response to the question promulgated in a7–9, whether even tragedy is "adequate to the forms."

It remains to point out that even if we accept the passage as Aristotle's own, it does not say much of what commentators have imputed to it. Very significantly, for example, it says nothing about Dionysos. This observation may appear heretical. Since Nietzsche (whose *Birth of Tragedy* has exercised a tidal pull of influence on everybody ever since), it has been an article of faith with classical scholars as well as the general literate public that tragedy began as a Dionysiac presentation. This universal agreement rests on two foundations: (1) the indubitable fact that tragedy was first performed (i.e., officially performed) at a festival of Dionysos, the City or Greater Dionysia in Athens under the tyrant Peisistratos around the year 534, and (2) the fact (open, as we have seen, to question) that Aristotle speaks of the dithyramb. But neither of these facts proves that tragedy was originally Dionysiac. Its introduction into Peisistratos's new festival was an act of *Religionspolitik* in favor of the popular god Dionysos but proves nothing as to its original character or function. And Aristotle's testimony is even less immediately usable. The operative question is not what the dithyramb was in the sixth century but what he thought it was; and there is nothing to prove that he thought it was Dionysiac. The dithyramb had in fact ceased to be Dionysiac long before Aristotle's time; what remained was a longish choral poem of predominantly narrative cast. That is what Plato had in mind at *Republic* 3.394c, and we need not assume that Aristotle had anything more in mind. A longish poem of predominantly narrative cast would serve perfectly well as foil and background for Homer's achievement as Aristotle saw it: the creation of dramatic imitations of serious subjects. The Dionysian note in these speculations (for they are all speculations, from first to last) is Nietzsche's contribution to the witches' brew, not Aristotle's, although it is based on the reference to dithyramb in the *Poetics*.

Who, then, did Aristotle think were the original "leaders-off" of the dithyramb, and what did he think was the date of these performances? Nothing is certain here, but it seems arguable that a clue can be found in the tradition about the activities of Arion, the kitharode in Korinth in the early sixth century. From a statement of Herodotos about the dithyramb, it seems to emerge that Arion (1) stationed the chorus in one place, (2) gave it a fixed text to sing, and (3) gave the text a name, i.e., a title. Aristotle, then, may have thought of Arion's chorus as successor to the original "leaders-off" of the improvised dithyramb, who were therefore its chorus.[4]

Before we proceed, we should mention another curious fact: that Thespis is not mentioned in Aristotle's sketch. Thespis was the cornerstone of the Athenian tradition about early tragedy, and we might be tempted to wonder whether he has been omitted deliberately here, out of bias. But Themistios, a learned and reliable Aristotelian of the fourth century A.D., quotes Aristotle as saying, presumably in the dialogue *On Poets*, "In the beginning the chorus used to sing to the gods as it entered; then Thespis introduced a prologue and a set speech (ῥῆσις)." This seems to imply the scheme of development which has been accepted as standard by most modern expositors of the history of the drama: tragedy was originally a choral performance (dithyramb?), then Thespis introduced the first actor (himself) and the first spoken verses. This is perfectly consonant with the phrase in the *Poetics*, 49a13–14, "as they developed so much of it as was becoming visible." Thespis would then be the most important follower of Homer, for having actually introduced dramatic form into tragedy. But it remains puzzling that he is not mentioned here.

We now turn to the final stage, the attainment of tragedy's "nature." This sentence, like the last one, is clogged with at least one interpolation; in this case the result is that the sentence is effectively torn apart and its structure cannot be discerned at all. We must therefore begin with the structure. The καί which leads off at 49a15 is epexegetic ("And," "Namely"), and the sentence which follows has two main parts, the first (a15–18, τότε τῶν ὑποκριτῶν πλῆθος . . . παρεσκεύασεν) relating the decisive contributions of Aischylos to the development, the other (a21–24, τό τε μέτρον . . . τὸ οἰκεῖον μέτρον εὗρε) specifying the metrical consequences of Aischylos's achievement. These two parts of the sentence are yoked together by an unobtrusive but effective pair of coordinate particles τε . . . τε, which signify that the two sets of events are of equal rank.

These two coordinate clauses have to do with the victory of speech (over song) under Aischylos and the consequent adoption of iambic verse

---

4. These paragraphs reiterate views which Else developed at greater length in *The Origin and Early Form of Greek Tragedy* (Cambridge, Mass. 1965).

as the vehicle for tragic dialogue. That is the essential pair of events to which Aristotle addresses himself. Whatever else is in the sentence is at best secondary, *Beiwerk*; but in this case the *Beiwerk* (a18–21, τρεῖς δὲ . . . ἀπεσεμνύνθη) has covered over and obscured the main structure.

The first half of Aristotle's sentence reports three decisive acts of Aischylos: he (1) increased the number of actors, (2) diminished the choral parts, and (3) made the dialogue take on the leading role. The second half relates the result: a17f., τὸν λόγον πρωταγωνιστεῖν παρεσκεύασεν, "when speech came in (i.e., gained primacy), the very nature (of the genre; or, of speech itself) discovered the appropriate verse form." Following this Aristotle explains why it was the appropriate form. Nothing in this scenario speaks to dignity or seriousness in tragedy—that was inherent in it from the beginning (48b24–27)—or to its dramatic quality—Homer had added that aspect. What remained to be discovered and/or emphasized was speech: the presentation of tragic action through the medium of language made to sound like conversation. (Cf. 49a26–27: we speak more iambics than any other kind of verse ἐν τῇ διαλέκτῳ τῇ πρὸς ἀλλήλους, "in our conversation with one another.")

Into this strict diairetic pattern, having to do only with speech and verse form, some other ingredients have been incorporated—whether by one hand or more than one, is not clear; but this time it is relatively clear that the hand was not Aristotle's. The ascription of the third actor and scene-painting to Sophokles (49a18), although a bit ragged in phrasing and only marginally related to the point about the predominance of dialogue and the change in meter, is not decisive against the passage. The next sentence—if it is a sentence—shows a preoccupation with loftiness and grandeur that is quite out of keeping with Aristotle's argument. In a distressingly oblique construction, it emphasizes these qualities thrice over: 49a19–21, ἔτι δὲ τὸ μέγεθος, "and furthermore (Aischylos added?) the grandeur"; ἐκ μικρῶν μύθων καὶ λέξεως γελοίας, "out of trivial (small) stories and comic diction" (construction uncertain, but the parallel form of the two phrases recommends a qualitative rather than a quantitative interpretation of μικρῶν); and διὰ τὸ ἐκ σατυρικοῦ μεταβαλεῖν ὀψὲ ἀπεσεμνύνθη, "on account of having changed out of satyr(-drama?) it acquired (tragic) solemnity late."

This is an aspect of tragedy that Aristotle chose not to emphasize in the *Poetics*. He used the term μέγεθος, to go no further, to characterize tragedy's "bulk," not its "loftiness" (49b25, 51a11). In any case, the last of the clauses just quoted may give a clue how this passage came to rest in the *Poetics*. Aristotle's genuine text says that when Aischylos brought about the primacy of speech, the verse changed from (trochaic) tetrameter to iambic (trimeter): 49a22ff., at first they used tetrameter "because the poetic form was satyr-like and more dance-like," διὰ τὸ σατυρικὴν καὶ ὀρχηστικωτέραν εἶναι τὴν ποίησιν, "but when speech (λέξις) came in, its very nature found the appropriate verse; for the iambic is of all verses the one most suited to speech." The ποίησις which had been "satyr-like and more dance-like" was the song medium used by the chorus; the word does not say or imply that the chorus was composed of satyrs or that "its diction was ludicrous." In the added text this stylistic concept has been changed into a genre designation: tragedy "changed out of satyr(-play) and acquired solemnity late."

The difference in conception is clear. Aristotle is thinking of a stylistic and linguistic shift within an established genre, from a predominance of song-and-dance to a predominance of speech; the writer of the other lines—stimulated, it would appear, by the word σατυρικήν in a22—is thinking of a substantive, last-minute change of genre from a comic or quasi-comic form, satyr drama, to the high seriousness of tragedy. Such a crossing over from one side of Aristotle's serious–trivial dichotomy to the other is not permitted by his system at any stage.

Who, then, imported these divergent views into Aristotle's story, and was it the same person or persons as in the case of the dithyramb and the phallic (?) songs? A speculation or two on these questions will be found in Chapter 10.

The narrative ends, 49a28–30, with a reference to "numbers of episodes, and the way the other particular adornments are said to have been added. Let us consider that all that has been said; for it would be, would it not? a considerable job to go through it in detail." These are not the words of a man oppressed by *or* rejoicing in an accumulated mass of research material. Aristotle has intuited a main line of development from the primitive improvisations to Aischylos and Sophokles, *et voilá tout; cela suffit.* He is interested in the idea, the "universals," not the particulars. In other words, he is not a historian. Wilamowitz said long ago, in a famous *ex cathedra* pronouncement, that in this matter we are bound by Aristotle's facts but not by his ideas.[5] But the fact is that in Aristotle's "history" of poetry there are hardly any facts, only ideas. (Even Homer is an idea.)

We must add to this inventory another passage where the historical

---

5. Ulrich von Wilamowitz-Moellendorff, *Euripides Herakles* I [*Einleitung in die griechische Tragödie*] (Berlin 1889) 49.

relation between epic and tragedy is touched on: 5.49b9ff., "Well then, epic followed tragedy up to the point of being a sizable imitation of serious matters in verse; but in its having its verse single (free of music) and being narrative, there they differ." This crisp, straightforward sentence has been strangely distorted and misrepresented. In the first place, "followed" obviously does not mean that epic came later than tragedy. It means that it *followed in the train* of the higher genre (the way a "follower," an ἀκόλουθος, accompanies a king) on the upward progress which was outlined in chapter 4, but managed to go only so far along that way. How far, is indicated in the ensuing pregnant words: μέτρῳ μεγάλη μίμησις εἶναι σπουδαίων, "to be, with verse (as medium), a sizable imitation of serious subjects." Epic and tragedy, then, differ in the manner specified; they also differ with respect to length (49b12, ἔτι δὲ τῷ μήκει), but we shall leave that point to future discussion. What is clear without further preliminaries is that epic achieved an honorable place in the development but never caught up with the leader of the procession, tragedy. If this seems incompatible with the superlative praise which Aristotle showers on Homer on every occasion, the answer is that in an important sense Homer is not an epic poet but a dramatist. He is a unique phenomenon in his genre, a poet outside the normal rules. His genre is, ultimately, second-rate; *he* is supreme among poets.

7

The "Parts" of Tragedy

Plot (μῦθος) and Action (πρᾶξις)

HAVING FINISHED his "history" of poetry (so far as he intends to write one) with a glance at comedy, 5.49a32–b9, a preliminary statement of the likenesses and differences between epic and tragedy, 49b9–20, and a summary indication that epic and comedy will be discussed later, 6.49b21–22, Aristotle draws up a balance sheet of what we have learned about tragedy so far. This definition is drawn, he says, from the preceding chapters: b22–24, περὶ δὲ τραγῳδίας λέγωμεν ἀναλαβόντες αυτῆς ἐκ τῶν εἰρημένων τὸν γινόμενον ὅρον τῆς οὐσίας, "But let us talk about tragedy by gathering up from the things that have been said the definition of its essence which was in process of development (γινό-μενον)." The particular reference is to chapter 4, thus confirming—if it needed confirmation—that what the "history" presented was the discriminations of poetry (from chapters 1–3) as a development spread over time. Γινόμενον, "becoming," is even an echo of 49a13–14, ὅσον ἐγίγνετο φανερὸν αὐτῆς, "so much of it (tragedy) as was becoming visible"; for any process of becoming, γένεσις, is not a coming-into-being of something that was not there before but a progressive uncovering of an essence, a form, that was there all the time.

The definition of tragedy does indeed turn out to be "gathered up" from what was said before, with two exceptions: the notion of a "complete" (τελείας, b25) action and that of katharsis, b27–28, which we shall take up in Chapter 11.

Tragedy, then, is a μίμησις, an "imitation." Have we really learned by now what Aristotle means by "imitation"? Hardly. Qualifications and refinements will continue to be made throughout most of the treatment of tragedy, especially the discussion of plot (μῦθος); but even the most important point, the heaven-wide difference between Aristotle's concept of μίμησις and Plato's, has hardly been established up to now except by indirection. A hint of it was given at 3.48a21–22 and again at 4.48b35–36, where Aristotle speaks of Homer's dramatic or quasi-dra-

matic method, and δρῶντας, 3.48a29, if genuine, may be intended to
foreshadow the crucial word δρώντων in the definition, 6.49b26. A
further unobtrusive but useful indication is in μίμησις itself. The verbal
suffix -σις (= English -ing in verbal nouns) is everywhere treated as fully
active by Aristotle. Μίμησις is therefore not just "imitation" in the sense
of a product, but "imitating" in the sense of a process, an activity, and
τραγῳδία throughout the *Poetics* should be taken as a shorthand equiva-
lent of ἡ τῆς τραγῳδίας ποίησις, 1.47a13–14: "the *making* of tragedy,"
i.e., the art of tragedy in action.

Tragedy, then, is "an imitating of an *action*," a πρᾶξις. We can note at
once here a significant change in wording, an implicit correction of the
first sentence of chapter 2: tragedy is not after all an imitation of people
acting, but of an action. The point is made explicit at 6.50a16–17. But
what does it mean; what *is* an action, in this context? This is a complex
question whose answer will take time and care. We need not spend time,
however, laboring the point that action is a primary concept in Aristotle's
view of life—not only the moral life of men but all life. Character and
thought are all very well, but—to use a vulgar but expressive modern-
ism—action is the payoff. An awareness of this principle is at the root of
the interpolations that have obscured the passage 6.50a17–19, of which
more later.

Πρᾶξις ("doing," verbal noun from πράττειν) has in it the connota-
tion of *purposeful* action, striving toward a goal or a destination. Now
we know in general terms the goal of the σπουδαῖοι, the heroes of
Homer and tragedy. It is called from one point of view ἀρετή—oh, how
misleadingly rendered "virtue" in English!—and, from another, εὐδαι-
μονία, "happiness." From the point of view of the heroes these two goals
are one. Ἀρετή, "excellence," *is* "happiness," the end for which they
live, fight, suffer, and die. To be supremely excellent in the warrior's
virtues, and to be recognized for them—that is the goal of Achilleus,
Aias, Herakles, Philoktetes, and all the rest. Σπουδαίας, "serious," in
the definition of tragedy (b24) has that connotation strongly; but
τελείας, "complete" (b24), adds something else, something that was not
said before.

From the Homeric hero's point of view, ἀρετή is the superior concept;
from Aristotle's, εὐδαιμονία. Happiness is the goal for which all men—
all serious human beings—strive, and the tragic action, if it is really to
represent human life fairly, has to present the full reach of that striving,
up to the point of success or failure. But Aristotle stretches it still farther,
to make it a total swing from one opposite pole, happiness or unhappi-

ness, to the other (7.51a13–14). The reasons for this requirement are partly aesthetic, partly psychological, i.e., emotional; we shall have more to say about it hereafter under both headings.

Very well, the tragic action is to be (for let us be clear about one thing: the *Poetics* offers not merely descriptions of what tragedy is but prescriptions of what it should be)—is to be both serious, involving the ultimate aims of human life, and complete, showing them spread over a scale from total realization to total failure. It is also required to be of a certain size (49b25): large enough with respect to time for the requisite shift-to-the-opposite to appear plausible or necessary within its limits (7.51a11–15).

Next, tragedy is presented through "sweetened or highly flavored discourse (ἡδυσμένῳ λόγῳ 49b25), with each of its species separately in the parts of the play," which, as Aristotle proceeds to explain, means that the body of the play is divided between spoken verses, μέτρα, and song, μέλος.

"Sweetened" (adorned, embellished) betrays one of Aristotle's less attractive prejudices, namely that the external garb of poetry, whether spoken verses or song, is merely an adventitious attraction, a concession to the audience. Plato, understanding Aristotle perfectly and using the epithet ἡδυσμένος as a reproach, warns (*Republic* 10.607a) that the ἡδυσμένη Μοῦσα, if not severely curbed, will undermine the polity in states and individual souls.

The climax and centerpiece of the definition, 49b26, δρώντων καὶ οὐ δι' ἀπαγγελίας, "with (the characters) *doing* (it), not through narration," has already been sufficiently explained. It remains to be seen how this central concept serves as anchor point for the deductions that follow, concerning the "parts" of tragedy. The reader needs only to be reminded that these are parts not of tragedy as a finished product but of the ongoing activity of making tragedy: the art of tragedy-making *in actu*.

As we approach the first of the six "parts," the μῦθος, a brief orientation seems in order. *Μῦθος* as Aristotle defines it for his purpose here (6.50a4–5; cf. a15) is not "myth" in the prevailing sense of that word either in his time or in ours—a traditional story which may or may not be true. It is a fact that Greek heroic legends normally had some basis in history. But for Aristotle—unlike Plato—the historicity of the μῦθος is not an issue. He is well aware that the tragic poets mostly dramatized the traditional stories (9.51b15–16), and he is prepared to accept that practice, though with a pointed suggestion that they "need not stick to them at all costs" (b23–25). The point is that whether the plot outline is taken from tradition or not, the poet must perform his task "well" (καλῶς, 14.53b25–26), and his essential task is one of construction, not copying.

We shall have to ask, eventually, how μίμησις could get so far from its obvious native meaning and still be used as a serious aesthetic term. For the moment let us content ourselves with scrutinizing the word μῦθος. Aristotle has just said that poetry (poetic composition, ποίησις) imitates action, and that which imitates the action, he says later (6.50a3–4), is the μῦθος. We find ourselves here at the intersection of four concepts: μίμησις, ποίησις (represented here by its species τραγῳδίας ποίησις), μῦθος, πρᾶξις. The interrelations of this tetrad constitute the central core of the Aristotelian poetic system: a system of great subtlety and originality, very little indebted to any previous ideas, even Plato's, except as a starting point.

As an English equivalent of μῦθος I have chosen the old-fashioned word "plot," because it suggests something consciously made by the poet, and the central paradox in Aristotle's nest of paradoxes is that the poet is an "imitator" by virtue of being a maker. But what *is* the tragic plot, and what is it made of? Our first clue is the phrase which Aristotle offers at 6.50a4–5 as the specific definition of μῦθος: it is the σύνθεσις τῶν πραγμάτων, the "composing of the events." With regular substitution of σύστασις, "structuring," for σύνθεσις, the phrase recurs a number of times in the *Poetics* as Aristotle's preferred periphrasis for μῦθος, to emphasize the poet's active role in "imitation."

The plot, then, is an ordered structur(ing) of events. As an ordered structure it has three general properties (the special properties of *tragic* plots will occupy us in due course): unity, logical sequence, and determinate size (length). But these are not really separate characteristics, they are three aspects of the same thing; we can most efficiently group them under the heading of unity. We have now, in fact, arrived at the famous "unity of action"; for Aristotle holds that unity of plot depends on the fact that the plot is the representation of action (πρᾶξις) which is "single and a whole," 8.51a31–32; cf. 7.50b23–24. Actually, μῦθος and πρᾶξις are so closely identified that either word can be used for the other in our further discussion.

The most striking expression in Aristotle's treatment of unity of plot or action (chapters 7 and 8) is his comparison of a unified μῦθος to a beautiful ζῷον, an animal, 7.50b34ff; cf. 23.59a20. The point ostensibly at issue in these lines is size (length, μέγεθος, b36), but the operative criterion is whether the size is such as to reveal, not conceal, the unity, τὸ ἓν καὶ τὸ ὅλον, "the one and the whole," 7.51a1–2. In any case, whether the animal Aristotle has in mind is a real, live creature or only a painted one (the context seems to favor the former, though ζῷον could mean either; see above, p. 57), the comparison reminds us forcibly of Plato's demand in the *Phaidros*, 264c, that πάντα λόγον, any discourse (potentially including poetry as well), ὥσπερ ζῷον συνιστάναι σῶμά τι ἔχοντα αὐτὸν αὑτοῦ, κτλ., ὥστε . . . μέσα τε ἔχειν καὶ ἄκρα, πρέποντα ἀλλήλοις κτλ., "be *fitted together* (be a σύστασις) like a creature having a certain body of its own, so that . . . it has both middle parts and outer parts, drawn to suit (fit) one another and the whole." But there is an even more explicit reference to tragedy at *Phaidros* 268d: Sophokles and Euripides would laugh at anyone who thinks that tragedy is anything else than τὴν τούτων σύστασιν πρέπουσαν ἀλλήλοις τὲ καὶ τῷ ὅλῳ συνισταμένην, "the *structuring together* of these things fitting(ly) to one another and the whole"—where "these things" are speeches of varying lengths and tenors.

There cannot be any doubt, I think, that the *Poetics* is quoting and responding to these requirements set forth in the *Phaidros*. What was laid down there for speeches *and* tragedy is applied specifically to tragedy by Aristotle, but with a difference. For Plato, the elements which constituted tragedy when properly fitted together were just speeches: "very long . . . or very short, tearful, or fearful and threatening, or whatever" (*Phaidros* 268c). In Aristotle's scheme, as we shall soon see, they are characteristic utterances or actions of certain kinds of men, and thereby bound together in a coherent structure. The σύστασις τῶν πραγμάτων is a firmer and more substantive unity than Plato's clusters of speeches.

This tighter unity is already visible in chapter 7 in what is said about "whole," "beginning," "middle," and "end." These middles and ends no longer have the vagueness of Plato's "middle and outer parts," but are very precisely defined in abstract terms as parts of a necessary sequence (50b27–31). These logical sequences (the reason why I call them "logical" will appear presently) are the very heart of Aristotle's theory. They are given a quasi-mathematical definition here; chapter 9 will flesh it out.

The most original part of this theory, and one by which Aristotle appears to set particular store (7.50b34–51a15), is the concept of proper size or length (μέγεθος, b36, a12, 15; μῆκος, a6) of poems. To survey it will necessitate a glance back at 5.49b12–16. We observed (p. 102) how epic "followed" tragedy up to the point of being "a large-scale imitation of serious things in verse," but differed in having its verse unmixed (with song) and in being narrative. "Furthermore, with respect to its length the one (tragedy) strives as much as possible to exist during a single day, or to varying but little (in length), while the epic is indeterminate with respect to its time." Aristotle is referring to the real time or length of epic and tragedy respectively, not to that Renaissance will-o'-the-wisp, the "dramatic" or alleged time of the action in terms of clock hours or calendar days.[1] This interpretation is confirmed by the end of chapter 7, 51a3–15, where the ὅρος τοῦ μεγέθους, the limit of length of the tragic μῦθος, clearly refers to actual length of performance (or of reading), not to the indeterminate duration of the action in terms of an alleged "internal" time span.

It must be added that the passage in chapter 5 has not previously been applied to interpretation of the one in chapter 7, or vice versa, just because the former was thought to be concerned only with "dramatic" time while the latter clearly meant real time. Later utterances in the *Poetics* about both tragedy and epic make clear that we are in the presence of a considered theory about the length of poems. Its crucial point is the longer or shorter space of time within which the poem is experienced by the listener or reader; for in this context, provided the general laws of poetic composition are equally observed, the long, drawn-out experience is more "diluted," the shorter one more concentrated: 26.62a18-b3, Ἔτι (sc. ἡ τραγῳδία διαφέρει) τῷ ἐν ἐλάττονι μήκει τὸ τέλος τῆς μιμήσεως εἶναι, "Furthermore (tragedy differs, is superior to epic) by virtue of the fact that the end of the imitation is (comes) in less length." For as Aristotle goes on to say, "the more concentrated is more pleasurable than what is mixed with an abundance of time" (b1–2), and to illustrate his point graphically he imagines the *Oidipous* of Sophokles spun out to the length of the *Iliad*.

In this case, less is better. Chapter 26 assumes that tragedies are shorter than epics, and the same is implied in chapter 24, 59b17ff. There Aristotle recalls the norm (ὅρος) of length that was set up for tragedy at 7.51a5ff.—that the whole structure be εὐσύνοπτον or εὐμνημόνευτον, easily seeable or rememberable *as a whole* in one synoptic experience— and he suggests that this aim could be achieved if epics were shorter than the "ancient" ones. Details of this suggestion, and of the difficulties it involves, belong in our discussion of Homer and the epic. At the moment it is more profitable to note the stricter formulation at 5.49b12–14: the difference between epic and tragedy with respect to length is not simply

1. For a detailed discussion of this point, see *Argument* 207–219.

that the one is longer and the other shorter, but that tragedy has an effective limit or norm while epic has not (ἀόριστος τῷ χρόνῳ). The limit can be defined externally, as it is there (one circuit of the sun), or internally as in chapter 7 (that length within which a plausible or necessary shift can take place from happiness to unhappiness or the reverse); either way, tragedy follows it, epic does not—though Homer will turn out to be an exception to this as he is to almost all rules.

Are the unity, logical sequence, and restricted length attributes of the plot, or of the action which the plot imitates? The question is really otiose since, as we have already said, plot and action are in a very real sense overlapping, if not identical things for Aristotle. Their practical identity is especially plain at the end of chapter 8, 51a30–35, where he is summarizing and emphasizing his precept of unity; and it is equally plain there that logical sequence is the effective test of unity, as limited length is its visible or audible sign. Unity, length, and sequence are in fact, as we said before, three aspects of a single entity, and that entity can be called either μῦθος or πρᾶξις depending on one's angle of approach.

But we need to take a closer look at the *components* of the plot or action: the "parts" (μέρη, μόρια, 8.51a32, 33, 35) out of which it is constructed. Aristotle indicates in his transition at the beginning of chapter 9 that the quality or character of the parts is a matter of prime importance; but the connection has mostly been overlooked. He says, 51a36–38, Φανερὸν δὲ ἐκ τῶν εἰρημένων καὶ ὅτι οὐ τὸ τὰ γενόμενα λέγειν, τοῦτο ποιητοῦ ἔργον ἐστίν, ἀλλ' οἷα ἂν γένοιτο καὶ τὰ δυνατὰ κατὰ τὸ εἰκὸς ἢ τὸ ἀναγκαῖον, "It is also obvious from what has been said that it is not the poet's job to relate what has happened but what *could* happen, i.e., the things that are possible according to probability or necessity." The point of connection is that only "parts" which are probable or necessary can be fitted together (συνεστάναι, 51a32–33) to make a whole in the tight fashion called for at the end of chapter 8. But what does Aristotle actually mean by "probability or necessity," and what is the relation of the two concepts to each other?

It is not hard to give a general answer to the first of these questions; the second one is not often asked and even less often answered. The general direction we must go is marked out in Aristotle's contrast between poetry and history, 9.51b5–11: poetry "tells" τὰ καθόλου, "universals"; history, τὰ καθ' ἕκαστα, "particulars." Aristotle hastens to explain what he means in this context: b8–11, ἔστιν δὲ καθόλου μέν, τῷ ποίῳ τὰ ποῖα ἄττα συμβαίνει λέγειν ἢ πράττειν κατὰ τὸ εἰκὸς ἢ τὸ ἀναγκαῖον . . . , τὸ δὲ καθ' ἕκαστον, τί 'Αλκιβιάδης ἔπραξεν ἢ τί ἔπαθεν, " 'Universal' means what sorts of things a certain kind of man will naturally say or do in accordance with probability or necessity . . . ; the 'particular,' what Alkibiades did or what was done to him." And he goes on (b15) to say that the comic poets have been pursuing the universal for some time, while the tragedians have muddled the account by "sticking to the historical names," τῶν γενομένων ὀνομάτων (the names that have happened). In other words the comedians have been sketching type-characters while the tragedians have felt they were bound to the traditional individual characters of Aias, Oidipous, Klytaimnestra, etc. It is interesting and significant that Aristotle thinks (as he obviously does) that the two arts ought to pursue the same course, the generalizing one, in this matter. We shall return to the question later.

Let us begin our closer study by noticing two points of Greek expression, both of which will turn out to have important corollaries for Aristotle's theory. In the first place, he never says that poetry "imitates" either universals or particulars; rather, he consistently uses the verb λέγειν, "say," "tell," "declare," throughout the passage (9.51a37, b1,4–5,7). The poet is to imitate the *action*; he is to tell, state, the universals. What does this difference in idiom signify? If we remember that the plot/action is a whole made up of parts—a whole which also consists of *transaction*—and that the universals are the parts which make up the whole, we may be on the way to a solution. The universals then appear as relatively simple terms or premises which come together and interact in a necessary or plausible way to constitute an entity of a different order. They are univocal, identified by the differing kinds of men they represent; the action is a complex, individual nexus in which they are absorbed.

Another invention of Aristotle's genius during the Akademy years, the syllogism, shows similar traits. In defining the syllogism (*Analytica Priora* 1.24b18ff.), Aristotle emphasizes the logical necessity by which a conclusion results from premises arranged in determinate patterns: Συλλογισμὸς δέ ἐστι λόγος ἐν ᾧ τεθέντων τινῶν ἕτερόν τι τῶν κειμένων ἐξ ἀνάγκης συμβαίνει τῷ ταῦτα εἶναι, " 'Syllogism' is a statement in which, when certain things are assumed, something other than the things assumed follows necessarily by virtue of their being (so)." Similarly, a tragic action synthesizes from the acts and speeches of its characters what necessity (or probability) dictates, by virtue of the acts, speeches, and characters being what they are.

The chronology of Aristotle's works offers no impediment to the idea that his thinking about logical structures may have contributed to his thinking about poetic structures, or that they may have influenced each other. Most of the logical works (the so-called Organon) were composed during the Akademy period, when Aristotle was also thinking hard about poetry. And he was not the man, at any time of life, to confine his thought within strict departmental boundaries.

The possibility of a cross-influence between Aristotle's logic and his poetic theory is certainly compatible with the generally logical, rational cast of that theory; it may also be recommended, if only to a minor degree, by the use of the word συμβαίνει in 51b8. It "befalls" the certain kind of man to say or do certain kinds of things; but there can be no question of this being a purely accidental "befalling." The accidental sense of συμβαίνειν is certainly found in the *Poetics*, e.g., at 8.51a17: πολλὰ καὶ ἄπειρα τῷ ἑνὶ συμβαίνει, ἐξ ὧν ἐνίων οὐδέν ἐστιν ἕν, "Many, in fact unlimited, things happen to the individual, from some of which there is no unity." The "happening" that is involved in a poetic universal cannot be of this haphazard kind, if the nexus of unity is to be achieved. It must partake of necessity, a necessity similar to that which binds the premises of the syllogism together to make a conclusion.

Of course it is not the case that the universals which make up the tragic action are bound together by the same necessity as binds the premises of the syllogism. Human life at its best is not as tidy as mathematics (which provided the model for the syllogism). Its native principle is not necessity but τὸ ὡς ἐπὶ τὸ πολύ, "the by-and-large, for-the-most-part"; its actions and reactions are not certain but *tend* to develop in such-and-such ways. Aristotle's term for this contingent truth makes up the other half of his standing formula in the *Poetics*: κατὰ τὸ εἰκὸς ἢ τὸ ἀναγκαῖον, "according to probability or necessity."

Τὸ εἰκός, "probability," comes from a totally different quarter of the Greek horizon, rhetoric; it was in fact the hallmark and heart's-blood of rhetoric from its earliest beginnings in Sicily (early fifth century). This part of the formula, then, looks away from the strict rules of scientific proof to the looser gait of persuasion in Greek assemblies and courts of law. "Probability" natively means *plausibility*: that which an ordinary man in a law court or an assembly can be made to believe is reasonable. Indeed most Greeks got whatever training they had in the arts of argument and judgment, down to the fourth century, from rhetoric. And this connection too was readily at hand to Aristotle at just this time. Most of his *Rhetoric* was written in the Akademy period, and in very close proximity to the *Poetics*. Poetic and rhetoric had been sister-arts in Athens since the late fifth century; he developed them concurrently and borrowed much from each art into the other.

Once more we see Aristotle the realist at work. He wants to give his poetic universal a higher status than that of mere accident or tendency, but he will not claim true, absolute necessity for it. In spite of his idealization of both epic and tragedy, he mediates. "Probability or necessity" only hints at a variation toward the upper side.

If the analogy with the syllogism holds good, a corollary of uncommon importance and suggestiveness also holds good: that the action, though made up of universals, is an individual creation. And this implies a further corollary, that each plot/action—each version of the Oidipous story, let us say—is an individual composition, independent of and different from all the others in the same way (but only to the same degree?) that each syllogism is individual and different from all others.

It may seem anachronistic to ascribe such a modern idea as individuality to Aristotle. He harps constantly on generality, universality, not individuality; but there is warrant for thinking that our inference may have been present to his mind even though he does not emphasize it. The first evidence is on view in chapter 9, in what he says about possibility. The term is introduced at the very beginning of the chapter, 51a37–38. The poet's job is to "tell what could happen (might happen), that is, the things that are possible according to probability or necessity." Here τὰ δυνατά (τὸ δυνατόν) is an alternative formulation of οἷα ἂν γένοιτο. But this sense of possibility has to be distinguished carefully from the ordinary sense, where the possible is defined by the actual (τὰ γενόμενα, "the things that have happened," 51a36–37, b4, 17–18, 29–30). What has happened before could obviously (we tend to think) happen again: i.e., it is possible.

Aristotle's attack on this mistaken idea takes up a good part of chapter 9; the famous contrast between poetry and history is introduced mainly in order to counter it. After stating the difference between universals and particulars, he goes on to say, 51b11–16, that the point has now become clear as between comedy and tragedy: the comedians construct their plots on the principle of probability (διὰ τῶν εἰκότων, b13) while the tragedians "stick to the names that have happened" (see above, p. 110). Aristotle explains this as due to false reasoning, a paralogism: b16–19, αἴτιον δ' ὅτι πιθανόν ἐστι τὸ δυνατόν, τὰ μὲν οὖν μὴ γενόμενα οὔπω πιστεύομεν εἶναι δυνατά, τὰ δὲ γενόμενα φανερόν (sc. πιστεύομεν εἶναι) ὅτι δυνατά. οὐ γὰρ ἂν ἐγένετο, εἰ ἦν ἀδύνατα, "The reason is that the possible is persuasive (believable); so then, the things that have not happened we do not yet (or, not quite) believe to be possible, but it is evident (we believe) that the things that have happened *are* possible; for (we say) they would not have happened if they were impossible."

The root fallacy in this paralogism is the unwarranted assumption that possibility and actuality are identical, so that what is real (e.g., has happened) must also be "possible." Aristotle attacks this assumption in the second key passage, with the zest for paradox which is so characteristic of him: 51b29–32, Κἂν ἄρα συμβῇ γενόμενα ποιεῖν, οὐθὲν ἧττον ποιητής ἐστι, τῶν γὰρ γενομένων ἔνια οὐδὲν κωλύει τοιαῦτα εἶναι οἷα ἂν εἰκὸς γενέσθαι καί δυνατὰ γενέσθαί, καθ᾽ ὅ ἐιεῖνος αὐτῶν ποιητής ἐστιν, "Even, then, if it befalls him to make poetry out of actual events (to "make" things that have happened), he is nonetheless a poet; for nothing prevents *some* of the things that have happened from being the kinds of things that might probably happen, i.e., being possible to happen; (which is the principle) by which he is their maker." Here the bold statement that *some* actual events can be "probable" and "possible" in Aristotle's sense proves that not all of them are so, however much most people (the "we" of πιστεύομεν, b17) think they are.

Another paradox comes to the surface here (and only here): that the poet is a creator (a ποιητής, a maker) just where he brings the universals to life most faithfully. This is at the same time the heart of Aristotle's defense of poetry against Plato. The poet is not an impersonator, deceiving us by pretending to be Agamemnon, Achilleus, and the rest; he is the maker, the creator of these characters just by virtue of observing and depicting the universal tendencies of human nature. He creates, in fact, as Nature creates, out of respect for what *can be*, what is "possible to happen" in accordance with probability or necessity.

It may be said that this is too romantic: that Aristotle shows no awareness of or sympathy for any idea so Promethean. But this is not quite true. To be sure, he does not use the modern lingo of creativity. But he does insinuate that the tragic poets should follow the example of Agathon, who invented both the incidents and the names in his *Antheus*, 9.51b21–23; he calls on the poet, whether he has decided to invent (εὑρίσκειν, "find") his plot or use the "transmitted ones" (τοῖς παραδεδομένοις), to do it "artistically" (καλῶς, "well"), 14.53b25–26; and his advice to the dramatist, again whether his plots are "preformed" (πεποιημένους) or he is making them himself, is first to "lay them out in general terms," ἐκτίθεσθαι καθόλου, 17.55a34ff.

This last instruction may seem to negate our thesis that the plot is an

individual construction; on the contrary, it reinforces it. We did not say
that the persons, or their speeches and actions which make up the plot,
were individual, only that the total plot/action was so. And what would
be the point of a plot outline of the Iphigeneia story if this plot were
identical with every other version? Its function is surely to safeguard the
integrity of the poet's construction.

It must be admitted that Aristotle does not dwell on the individuality
of the poet's creation; it is an inference we draw from what he says about
the poet as maker of plots. Aristotle himself was much more concerned
to emphasize the universality of the elements that make up the plot,
because that was the way to maintain, against Plato, that the poet pos-
sessed a genuine art based on knowledge (knowledge is only of
universals; on that Plato and Aristotle agree).

Something remains to be said about the relative ratings of the parts of
tragedy at 6.50a15–39, all of them adduced in order to enforce the
primacy of plot over the others. The text of the first argument, 50a16–
23, has suffered some deformation from an intruded note. The beginning
is preserved intact in the Greek manuscript tradition: ἡ γὰρ τραγῳδία
μίμησίς ἐστιν οὐκ ἀνθρώπων ἀλλὰ πράξεως καὶ βίου καὶ εὐδαιμονίας,
"For tragedy is an imitation not of persons but of an action, a life, a
happiness." A following note, beginning ἡ εὐδαιμονία καὶ ἡ
κακοδαιμονία ἐν πράξει ἐστὶν, "Happiness and unhappiness are (is) in
action," etc., appears to have been conflated with, in fact telescoped into,
our sentence, and this has caused confusion because the added matter is
clearly gnomic, concerned with Life and Happiness in the large, while
the genuine part speaks directly to the tragic structure: a particular ac-
tion, life, career, etc.

These singular nouns, if I am not mistaken, strongly support our iden-
tification of the plot/action as a unique, individual happening. But this
happening originates in the dramatic characters (strictly speaking, in the
character of the characters); and it is worth noting that they are the
subject of the verbs that follow, a19–22: εἰσὶν δὲ κατὰ μὲν τὰ ἤθη ποιοί
τινες, κατὰ δὲ τὰς πράξεις εὐδαίμονες ἢ τοὐναντίον, οὔκουν ὅπως τὰ
ἤθη μιμήσωνται πράττουσιν, ἀλλὰ τὰ ἤθη συμπεριλαμβάνουσιν διὰ
τὰς πράξεις, "They are this or that kind of people in accordance with
their characters, but they are happy or the opposite in accordance with
their actions; so they do not act in order that they may imitate their
characters, but they pick up their characters along with (their actions)
for the sake of the actions."

Unfortunately this statement is incomplete in one very important particular. What the dramatic persons do, and why, could not be more clearly stated; what happens to them (according to the Greek idiom, ὅ τι πάσχουσιν, "what they suffer, undergo") is not even mentioned. To take the *Oidipous*, since Aristotle obviously considered it the best possible drama: everything that Oidipous *does* in the play—taking charge of the situation, sending Kreon to Delphoi, making the great proclamation, summoning Teiresias, etc., etc.—is accounted for, since it all flows from his character; what has happened to Oidipous before the play begins— that he has been marked out to kill his father and marry his mother—is not accounted for, cannot be accounted for, by anything in Aristotle's canon. In his book there is no universal named Destiny or Fate or The Gods. About why these things happened to Oidipous, Aristotle is totally silent. Was he unaware of the question? We shall consider that, and other matters related to it, in due course.

The other arguments which Aristotle musters for the supremacy of plot carry less weight and need not detain us long. When he says, 50a23–29, that a tragedy cannot exist without an action but can exist without characters—"in fact we have seen a good many such plays lately"—he makes it plain that (1) fourth-century tragedy went in heavily for melodrama in which the characters were "flat," but (2) he had never seen an important class of twentieth-century plays in which there is no plot but only characters—many of them flat, besides—stewing in their own juice.

The references to τὸ τῆς τραγῳδίας ἔργον, "the work of tragedy," 50a30–31, and to "the greatest means by which tragedy affects the soul," namely peripeties and recognitions, a33–35, must be dealt with later because they are aspects of what I call the tragic side of the tragic plot (see below, p. 144). Finally, the fact—if it is a fact—that young poets master style and character portrayal before they do plot construction, is a "sign" (σημεῖον, a35), of Aristotle's point rather than an inherent characteristic of the art.

So much for the general aspects of the tragic plot. We could go on at once to its specifically tragic aspects; but although this might seem the logical course, there are tactical considerations which make it preferable to deal with the other "parts" of tragedy (i.e., as ever, of the art of making tragedy) first. The main reason is that Aristotle himself proceeds in this order, reserving the tragic side of tragedy for separate treatment beginning at 9.52a1. We shall therefore reserve that side for our Chapters 10 and 11.

8

The "Parts" of Tragedy
Character (ἦθος) and Thought (διάνοια)

CHARACTER AND THOUGHT will be treated together in this chapter, as they are in chapter 6 of the *Poetics*, because (1) they jointly constitute and determine those "universal" acts and speeches which make up the total plot/action, and (2) Aristotle obviously had some trouble defining and distinguishing them.

Some general prolegomena will be necessary. First and most important, we must be constantly on our guard against a deep-seated modern prejudice ("prejudice" in its root sense of a judgment before the fact). We, with our rooted perception of the autonomous individual as the ultimate source of all acts and decisions, naturally assume that Aristotle understands ἦθος, at least, in the same way; but he does not. Both concepts are objectively determined, to mean a set of acts or utterances which are significantly related to the dramatic person; but neither issues from any secret, unitary source inside that person.

Confusion on this point has been at the root of many misunderstandings of Aristotle. It has misled John Jones, for example, to the absurd statement that there is no such thing as the tragic hero in the *Poetics*.[1] What Jones means is something quite different: there is no intimate, inward personality of modern type at the core of Aristotle's ἦθος. Jones speaks (p. 31) of "the now settled habit in which we see action issuing from a solitary focus of consciousness—secret, inward, interesting"; of "our ceaseless, animating consideration of the state of affairs 'inside' him who acts"; and he denies that this is what Aristotle means by "character." Jones is quite right if he is only saying that Aristotle did not perceive Oidipous or Aias as a unitary personality in the modern sense. Many classical scholars had found such personalities in Sophokleian characters, but the younger Wilamowitz blew that presumption out of the wa-

---

1. *On Aristotle and Greek Tragedy* (Oxford 1962) esp. 11–62.

ter sixty years ago, and his refutation has not really been refuted.[2] Actually, two misconceptions are at work here, the first overlaid on the second: one pertaining to Aristotle, the other to Sophokles and the other classical poets. What we must recognize for Aristotle at least is that ἦθος in his theory refers to a certain kind of man, not an individual, as the center and source of actions, and that διάνοια from the beginning has to do with generalizations about human life, not the perceptions of a unique individual.

A second caveat is equally necessary. When we speak of "thought" in connection with a drama, we usually mean the poet's thought (assuming, incidentally, that it issues from the same kind of unitary source as "character"). We must resign ourselves to the fact that there is no such heading in Aristotle's canon. In his view, poets do not think, they build, or at most they think about what they are building. "Thought," with him, is really reserved for the dramatic characters. They think in this or that way, and the utterances of their thought constitute an important part of the drama, the part we may call rhetorical.

Aristotle's definitions of character and thought are on view in two passages in chapter 6, 50a5–7 and 50b4–12, with a supplement for διάνοια in chapter 19, 56a33–b8. What emerges from a careful examination of these three passages is that thought, relatively speaking, is a simpler and more straightforward concept than character. Aristotle is careful to emphasize in each of the passages that thought has to do with speeches and speaking. This is but natural, since—as Aristotle also takes pains to emphasize, 19.56a34–36—its native home and center is rhetoric. Rhetoric is the sphere of deliberate effort to achieve something through speech(es). (Note the appearance of forms of παρασκευάζειν, a technical term whose connotation is "to produce consciously, by use of art," four times in eight lines, 56a37, 38, b4, 6). In the case of tragedy, it is an effort by the characters to persuade each other. This is a serious undertaking, calling for an art, not just a knack acquired through experience. But two points which we should think obvious are not explicitly mentioned by Aristotle: the role of the poet in all this, and its relationship to character.

It is indeed obvious that the dramatic persons' speeches are written for them by the poet, but this fact is not explicitly mentioned by Aris-

2. Tycho von Wilamowitz-Moellendorff, *Die dramatische Technik des Sophokles* (Berlin 1917).

totle, only implied at 19.56a34–36: "Let the (problems, procedures) connected with thought be sought (*κείσθω*, lit. let them be stored up) in our *Rhetoric*; for this is more a particular concern of that discipline." Clearly the persons who are to consult the *Rhetoric* are the poets, not the characters. For more specific guidance we are tempted to go back to what was said in chapter 9 about universals: "to what kind of man it naturally falls (*συμβαίνει*) to say or do what kinds of thing." But that turns out to be no help. Thought is said, in three places, 6.40a6–7, 50b11–12, and 19.56a37–38, to involve proofs and refutations and/or the statement of general views (although the word *καθόλου* appears only at 50b12, it is surely to be understood in the other places also); but it is not suggested that such arguments and statements can come only from a certain kind of character—a generalizing type of man, let us say. On the contrary, the whole thrust of the *Rhetoric*, and of the art of rhetoric in general, is that any intelligent person can learn to do these things.

Moreover, Aristotle makes it clear that he wants somehow to separate thought from character. Unfortunately it is precisely here that the difficulty I spoke of emerges. The very first mention of character, 6.50a5–6, though it does not tell us much, does say that character is "that (factor) in accordance with which we say that the persons acting are of this or that (moral) kind (*ποιούς τινας*)," and no such statement is ever made about thought. At 50b6–8 Aristotle seems to be talking more specifically—if we could be sure what he is saying. A contrast is made there between the political and the rhetorical art: *οἱ μὲν γὰρ ἀρχαῖοι πολιτικῶς ἐποίουν λέγοντας, οἱ δὲ νῦν ῥητορικῶς*, "For the old (poets) made (their characters) speak (lit. composed them speaking) politically, but those nowadays rhetorically." We might paraphrase the two adverbs as "like citizens" and "like conscious speech-makers." That is to say, "politically" does not mean what we now designate by that word, but suggests rather the straightforward speech of a man facing real issues of public moment; by contrast, speaking "rhetorically" would suggest an elaborate display based on the rules of the rhetorical art, speeches in short "by the book," not according to the dictates of one's own character.[3] The contrast then seems (I emphasize "seems") tolerably clear.

3. In *Argument* 265–271, Else argued for a version of the view put forward by Johannes Vahlen, *Aristotelis de arte poetica liber*[3] (Leipzig 1885) 124–125, that *πολιτικῶς* here means much the same as *ἠθικῶς*, i.e., according to the character of the speaker. The present formulation is closer to that of Carl Brandstaetter, "De notionum *πολιτικὸς* et *σοφιστὴς* usu rhetorico," *Leipziger Studien* 15 (1893) 145–146.

Sophokles' characters, e.g., Aias, Antigone, or Oidipous, speak as we would expect Aias, Antigone, or Oidipous to speak, whereas Euripides' Hekabe cross-questioning Helen in the *Trojan Women,* or Medeia debating with Jason, or Theseus arguing the case for democracy in the *Suppliants,* speaks like an accomplished trial-lawyer or a seasoned speaker in the Athenian assembly rather than like an aged, defeated queen of Troy, a fierce Kolchian princess, or a prehistoric king of Athens. Moreover these speakers have a strong family resemblance to each other. It appears that rhetoric exerts an impersonal sway, subjecting the "characters" to a strictly intellectual, nonmoral discipline and thereby stripping them of character.

This, by the way, is the clue we need to the "characterless tragedies" which Aristotle mentioned earlier (50a25; see above, p. 115). They are simply rhetorical tragedies; the uncompromising statement, which has put many scholars off, is just an example of the drastic emphasis which Aristotle—the young Aristotle—often likes to employ.

Aristotle himself gives color to the distinction between thought and character by defining ἦθος, the second time around (50b8–9), as "that kind of thing which makes the (character's) choice (προαίρεσις) clear, what moral quality it has"; whereas διάνοια is defined here essentially as it was before (at 50a6–7), without any reference to moral choice, as something present whenever speakers "undertake to prove that something is or is not (the case) or place a general statement on view" (50b11–12).

Thus Aristotle is clearly trying to distinguish character from thought as moral versus nonmoral. On the other hand, in the very passage which we have been studying, another potential distinction between them seems to be cancelled. It is plausible that thought can be expressed only through speech whereas character can be revealed by speech *or* action, and in fact exactly that is said about character at 15.54a18: ἐὰν ποιῇ φανερὸν ὁ λόγος ἢ ἡ πρᾶξις προαίρεσίν τινα. But our passage seems determined to erase that option by subsuming character *and* thought under the faculty of speech, and thus in fact under thought: 50b4–5, "Third (in rank) is thought; this is the capacity (τὸ δύνασθαι) to say what is relevant (τὰ ἐνόντα καὶ τὰ ἁρμόττοντα, the things that are in [the subject] and appropriate)." Here the category of relevance is perhaps meant to pertain more to rhetoric and appropriateness than to the "political" art; but the distinction cannot be made exclusive. In any case it cannot be denied that both "parts" are here subsumed under speech. The passage bristles with references to speech and speeches: 50b5, λέγειν;

b6, ἐπὶ τῶν λόγων; b7, λέγοντας; b10, τῶν λόγων; b10, ὁ λέγων. This plethora of indicators makes it possible that the phrase in b8–9 ("that kind of thing which reveals the moral choice") also refers to speeches rather than actions. But in that case Aristotle is guilty of a confusion, if not a contradiction: in subsuming both character and thought under thought, he has threatened to denature the former and has made the latter one of its own species.

Confusion is evident in Aristotle's treatment of character and thought no matter how we read the text. No doubt the root of the trouble is, as A. M. Dale says,[4] that he has imported the category of Thought straight out of rhetoric into the *Poetics*, without adaptation and without thinking sufficiently about the differences between the two arts. Character is also a factor in rhetoric, as the *Rhetoric* (1.2.1356a1–13) tells us; only there it means the deliberate projection of a certain character—a good one— by the speaker. Now, in terms of the *Poetics*, is this character or thought? It seems to partake of both, since it has to do with character but smacks of contrivance. We must conclude, at least tentatively, that Aristotle has not given sufficient thought to the difference between actual persons in a courtroom and fictive persons in a play; and this neglect seems conso- nant with his realistic—naively realistic?—view of the dramatic persons as independent of the poet: he seems to treat them as if they were real people. (It is also consonant with our dating of the *Poetics* to a period when Aristotle was actively at work on rhetoric, so that it could influ- ence or, it may be, get in the way of his poetics.)

There is one other reference to nonmoral speeches: 6.50b10–11, "Those speeches do not have ἦθος in which there is nothing at all that the speaker chooses or rejects." But we know from the *Rhetoric* (3.16.1417a19) that these are scientific or mathematical discourses: not ones, then, that would be likely to fall under the heading of thought in poetry.

We are left with a confused, unsatisfactory rendering of the distinction between character and thought—a skewed distribution stemming from their very different origins in traditional ethics on the one hand and rhetoric on the other. Concretely, the skewing reflects the disparity be- tween the classical drama—especially Sophokles—which Aristotle read and most admired while he was in the Akademy, and the wildly rhetori-

4. "Ethos and Dianoia: 'Character' and 'Thought' in Aristotle's *Poetics*," *AUMLA* no. 11 (September 1959) 3–16 = *Collected Papers* (Cambridge 1969) 139–155.

cal theater which was flourishing all around him in Athens in the 360s and 350s. Aristotle found no real common denominator between these two kinds of "tragedy," and he never managed to provide one.

Another set of prescriptions for ἦθος, or rather τὰ ἤθη, "the characters," is to be found in chapter 15.[5] These are connected with the plot/action rather than with thought and are correspondingly less intimately related to speech(es). Four requirements are formulated here.

1. *Goodness*: 54a17, ὅπως χρηστὰ ᾖ, "that they be good." It is under this rubric that Aristotle says, "They (the characters) will have character if their speech or action makes clear some moral choice, whatever it may be, and good (character) if a good (choice)." He then adds that goodness goes by classes: a20–22, "there is (such a thing as) a good woman or a slave, and yet I think we can say (ἴσως) (that) one of these (classes) is inferior and the other, as a whole, no good." Commentary would be superfluous.

2. *Appropriateness*: a22–24, "It is possible (for a character to be) brave, but it is not appropriate for a woman to be brave in that way, or clever." The special point of "in that way" (οὕτως) eludes us, but the general point is clear enough (the inappropriate cleverness was that of Melanippe "the clever," mentioned below at 54a31).

3. *Likeness*: 54a24, τὸ ὅμοιον. This trait is not defined just here, but Aristotle makes it clear later in the chapter, in a passage which we shall consider in a moment, that it means likeness to the average norm of humanity.

4. *Consistency or Uniformity*: 54a26, τὸ ὁμαλόν. This one is not defined either, but the citation of Euripides' *Iphigeneia at Aulis* (a31–33) makes it sufficiently clear. Whether Aristotle's drastic statement of the discrepancy—"the girl supplicating (for her life, *Iphigeneia* 1211–1252) has no resemblance to the later one (offering up her life for her country, 1368–1401)"—is correct is another matter. The really intriguing question is whether either speech (for it is obvious that Aristotle means the two great speeches) was intended by Euripides as an example of character and not rather of thought. Each is a rhetorical set piece and develops a theme which may ultimately come into conflict with the other: Life is the Sweetest

5. Cf. Ingram Bywater, "On Certain Technical Terms in Aristotle's *Poetics*," *Festschrift Theodor Gomperz* (Vienna 1902) 165.

Thing; My Country, My Country, I Owe Everything to Thee. It
looks as though in this case Aristotle has been inappropriately or
inconsistently severe in his judgment, applying the criterion of
πολιτικῶς λέγειν to a specimen of ῥητορικῶς λέγειν.

There are some signs that these prescriptions in chapter 15 are meant
not only for the leading characters—the hero(in)es—but for all the per-
sons of tragedy. The mention of slaves points that way, and also the
counsel that is given in 54b8–15 on how to reconcile "likeness" with
goodness. The approach here is notably different from that in chapter 2,
although the passage begins in the same vein: 54b8, "Since tragedy is an
imitation of persons better than average, one must imitate the good
portrait-painters; for in fact they, while making (their subjects) 'like' by
rendering their individual looks, paint them handsomer; so also the poet,
in imitating irascible and slack-tempered men and other character traits
of that kind, should make them, while being like (that), good men, as
Homer made Achilleus good and (like)."[6]
The novelty here, over against chapter 2, is that the human average (of
irascibility, slackness, etc.) seems to be taken as the point of departure,
from which the serious artist sets out to *improve* his subjects. That was
not Aristotle's original idea, and the first clause of this sentence (54b8)
seems to indicate that it is not his present idea either. What *is* his idea,
then? Some thoughts on this topic will be presented when we come to
deal with the tragic side of tragedy; for "likeness" is a key concept in
that emotionally charged complex. (We shall also consider later whether
we must recognize two or more stages in Aristotle's thinking about
tragedy.)
Another passage in chapter 15, 54a33–36, reaffirms, if that were re-
quired, the mutual need for necessity or probability in character *and*
plot, ending with the inference (54a37–b2)—if the text we have is cor-
rect—that "the denouements (lit. loosenings) of the plots should result
from the character (of the hero?) itself and not (from miracles, e.g.) the
crane, as in the *Medeia*, or (divine intervention as in) the sailing of the
fleet in *(Iphigeneia) at Aulis*."[7] In connection with this renewed demand

6. "Like" (ὅμοιον) is Else's supplement, first proposed in *Argument* 475–480;
see below, p. 210.
7. Else reads ἐν τῇ ἐν Αὐλίδι for the mss ἐν τῇ Ἰλιάδι, in which there is no
sailing and the only possible referent, Agamemnon's trial of his army (*Iliad*
2.110–206) with the suggestion that they sail away, is also unsuitable either as an
example of divine intervention or as the λύσις of a plot. With Else's reading, the

for "necessity or probability" we may notice the example which Aristotle offers of "unnecessary villainy," at 54a28–29. It is the case of Menelaos's cowardice in the *Orestes*: his failure to come to the rescue of Orestes and his sister after pledging in the most impassioned terms to do so. From this example of unnecessary poltroonery we gather that Aristotle might waive his general requirement of goodness of character if villainy were really necessary to the outcome of the plot.

Chapter 18, 56a1, mentions the "moral," ἡ ἠθική, as one of the four species of tragedy, but the examples are not helpful. At 24.59b9 the same species is attributed to the epic, and at b15 the *Odyssey* is cited as an example. In this case we can take the word to suggest "moral" in the sense of the "double structure" already adduced at 13.53a32–33, where it is pointed out that the *Odyssey* ends in opposite fashion for the better and worse characters. But as Aristotle himself adds, such a structure "belongs more to comedy" (a37); and in later antiquity "ethical" was often more or less equivalent to "comic."

Chapter 25, on "problems," mainly in epic, is altogether eccentric to the main argument of the *Poetics*, but we may just notice two remarks. (1) At 60b33–35, "Sophokles said that he portrayed (composed) people the way one should, but Euripides the way they are." Here the possibility of a third, intermediate class of objects, which we first discussed in connection with chapter 2 (see above, p. 82), does seem to be envisaged. And (2) we can note also that, as in chapter 2 but not in chapter 9, the verb μιμεῖσθαι, "imitate," is attached to these objects at 60b9–11: "One can imitate (things) as they are, or as tradition and common opinion report them, or as they should be." And 61b12–13, "(to make the persons) such as Zeuxis painted"—we remember that he was a realistic painter, without character, 6.50a28–29—"but better; for the model must surpass (the average?)," seems to be drawn from the same circle of ideas.

Aside from these apparently eccentric remarks, as we look back over Aristotle's offerings on character and thought we are struck by the obliquity of stance into which he was driven ("forced" would perhaps be too strong a word). He clearly perceived the difference between Sophokles—his ideal in these matters—and everything from Euripides on. (It is touching to see that Sophokles counts as one of the "ancients,"

reference is to the lost ending of the *Iphigeneia at Aulis*, in which Artemis apparently appeared to announce that she had saved Iphigeneia and to send the fleet on its way with her blessing.

οἱ ἀρχαῖοι, while "those now(adays)" begin with Euripides.) But he cannot quite see a way out of the trap. His sympathies are with the old, but his realism tells him the new is here to stay. And from Aristotle's point of view, in his own time, his perceptions were quite right. If he had lived somewhat earlier, before the end of the fifth century, or a good deal later, in the revived classicism of the second century A.D., he might have achieved a more balanced view of the whole literary enterprise, including the relative positions of character and thought. As it is, the combined forces of his native conservatism and his realistic eye have driven him into a corner. Only his great vigor of mind secured for him a—partial—escape.

9

The "Parts" of Tragedy
Composition in Word (λέξις), Music (μελοποιία),
and Appearance (ὄψις)

AT THIS POINT we cross a major dividing line. Plot, character, and thought constitute, in modern terms, the content of tragedy: 6.50a11, ἃ μιμοῦνται, "(the things) which they (the actors) imitate." Λέξις and μελοποιία are its instruments, a10, οἷς μιμοῦνται, "(the things) with which they imitate"; and ὄψις is the mode, a11, ὡς μιμοῦνται, "how they imitate." Instruments and mode are for Aristotle subservient categories, and he ranks these parts respectively fourth, fifth, and last in importance (50b12–20).

There is not and cannot be any adequate single English equivalent for λέξις. "Language" would be too broad and vague; "diction" is much too restrictive, connoting only the poet's choice of words; "utterance" lacks clear definition in English; "style" includes both too little and too much; and so on. On the whole, we here shall stick to the Greek word.

Λέξις is a verbal noun derived from the root λεγ- (λέγειν, "say," "tell") by means of that verbal suffix -σις (= -ing in English verbal nouns) which we have already noticed in μίμησις and ποίησις. As we said, it retains its active sense in the *Poetics*; so that λέξις denotes not the poet's stock of words or merely his style, but his activity with respect to language, his putting of the poetic content into words. And in fact that meaning is pithily indicated in the phrase τὴν διὰ τῆς ὀνομασίας ἑρμηνείαν, 6.50b13–14, "the conveyance of meaning through words." Unfortunately Aristotle's clear and simple point has been deflected by a series of misunderstandings earlier in chapter 6.

The groundwork for Aristotle's definition was laid in chapter 1. Λέξις is at home in the "nameless art," the one which imitates by means of speech (λόγος) and rhythm alone, while μελοποιία in tragedy represents the arts which use all three media, speech, rhythm, and melody, "in

turn" (κατὰ μέρος, 1.47b28). This distinction is picked up in the defini-
tion of tragedy by the summary phrase ἡδυσμένῳ λόγῳ, "with embel-
lished speech," 6.49b25, some parts in verses, μέτρα, only and others by
song, μέλος, b30–31.

Alas for Aristotle's effort at clarification; he has been obstinately mis-
understood. When he first comes to introduce λέξις as a "part" of
tragedy, at 49b34, he says, λέγω δὲ λέξιν μὲν αὐτὴν τὴν τῶν μέτρων
σύνθεσιν, "I mean by λέξις the composition itself of the verses." His
reference to the preceding remark about μέτρα, in 49b30, could not be
clearer, but modern scholars, by an effort of will, have misunderstood
him to mean merely their versification. Assisting in this travesty has been
the modern determination to read μέτρα as "meters" (abstract), whereas
everywhere in the *Poetics* it means "verses" (concrete). Furthermore it
means spoken verses as against those which are sung; that is implicit in
the root λεγ-. The corollary is that μελοποιία (which Aristotle neglects
to define here, thinking it "totally clear") covers all the lyrical parts of
tragedy, including their text.

"The composition of the verses," then, means supplying the verbal
integument of plot/character/thought. But new misunderstandings inter-
vene when Aristotle comes to his second mention of λέξις, in the evalua-
tive half of chapter 6: 50b12–15, τέταρτον δὲ τῶν μὲν λόγων ἡ λέξις,
λέγω δὲ ὥσπερ πρότερον εἴρηται, λέξιν εἶναι τὴν διὰ τῆς ὀνομασίας
ἑρμηνείαν, ὃ καὶ ἐπὶ τῶν ἐμμέτρων καὶ ἐπὶ τῶν λόγων, ἔχει τὴν αὐτὴν
δύναμιν, "Fourth (in rank) is the verbal expression of the speeches; I
mean (it) (in the same sense) as has been said previously, that λέξις is the
conveyance of meaning through words; which has the same force (mean-
ing) when applied to verses as to speeches." Τῶν μὲν λόγων ἡ λέξις, "the
verbal expression of speeches," is exactly balanced by the phrase in
50b15–16, τῶν δὲ λοιπῶν ἡ μελοποιία, "the song composition of
the remaining (parts)"—the same disjunction we had to begin with in
49b30–31. But there and in 49b35 Aristotle said μέτρων, "verses"; here
(50b12) he has said λόγων, "speeches," and that has caused all the
trouble.

Aristotle took off originally from the dichotomy μέτρα–μέλος,
"verses"–"song," in 49b30–31, and his reference to the verses was ex-
plicit because so close. This time, at 50b12, he comes to λέξις after ten
lines on the content of thought in speeches; so the natural reference here
is to "the expression of the speeches." Then, to avert misunderstanding,
Aristotle takes care to say that it does not matter whether you say

"verses" or "speeches," the meaning is the same; but again his plain meaning has been mistaken.

Λέξις, then, so far as tragedy is concerned, refers to verbal expression only in the spoken parts. The text of the musical parts—if Aristotle paid any attention to it—belongs under μελοποιία. But although this cuts off λέξις from any direct contact with the lyrical parts, another wide sphere of activity is open to it in the various actual and hypothetical species of the "nameless art," including epic, and in the nonmimetic genre of rhetoric. Indeed some of Aristotle's most detailed and original treatments of λέξις are to be found in Book 3 of the *Rhetoric*. Cross-references to the *Poetics* cluster especially thick there, implying that the latter was written first; but the two works belong to the same period, and it would be unwise to rely too much on minor chronological indices.

Rhetoric 3 and *Poetics* not only are close to each other in time; they complement each other, dividing the topic of λέξις between them in an interesting way. Aristotle's outline of basic grammar is assigned to chapter 20 and parts of 21 of the *Poetics*, with a relatively brief discussion of style in 22; *Rhetoric* 3 takes up a number of stylistic topics such as diction, prose rhythm, periodic structure, metaphors and similes, and propriety (τὸ πρέπον). In other words the more fundamental characteristics of language are dealt with in the *Poetics*, with a nod at the special traits of poetic style; the general doctrine of style, that is, of λέξις aimed at producing a determinate effect upon a hearer, is reserved for the *Rhetoric*. This is thoroughly consonant with Aristotle's position on the subject of language. On the one hand, as is generally agreed, his logic is derived from and to a large extent dependent on linguistic categories— i.e., the categories of the Greek language. On the other hand, as a philosopher he is sensitive to and on the whole disapproves of the calculated use of language to win cases, score debating points, and the like. Aristotle speaks from the heart when he says, *Rhetoric* 3.1.1404a1ff., that rhetoric is wholly directed toward δόξα, opinion (i.e., not to ἐπιστήμη, knowledge); that its pursuit is not so much right as "necessary," for it has great power "owing to the depravity of the hearer"; but that in the last analysis this is all φαντασία, imagination, mere fancy: διὸ οὐδεὶς οὕτω γεωμετρεῖν διδάσκει, "Therefore nobody teaches (anybody) to pursue geometry that way." Yet since things are as they are and we have to accept the world as it is, Aristotle is quite ready to formulate principles for the rhetorical use of language, ransack the literature for examples, and so on.

Let us summarize briefly Aristotle's basic view(s) of language. Against the "naturalist" theory that words are likenesses or replicas, ὁμοιώματα, of things, he holds that uttered sounds are conventional tokens, σύμβολα, of the affections, παθήματα (impressions, perceptions, ideas, etc.), in our souls, and written words in turn are tokens of uttered sounds (*De Interpretatione* 1.16a3; cf. ibid. 20). More important for our purpose, however, is Aristotle's theory of the structure of language, leading up to his conception of the λόγος.

A λόγος is not a "word," a vocabulary item, but a statement, a judgment. It cannot consist of less than an ὄνομα, a "name" (noun), and a ῥῆμα, something that is said (ῥῆ-μα, "said-thing") about the noun (predicate). The ῥῆμα may be simply a verb, as in Κλέων βαδίζει, "Kleon walks," and indeed ῥῆμα is the standard Greek word for "verb." Or it may be what we call an adjective, e.g., Κλέων λευκός (ἐστιν), "Kleon (is) white." In this case ἐστιν, "is," can be left to be understood rather than expressed (Greek permits that option with the third person of the verb "to be"), but Aristotle appears to consider that it is and must be understood in all cases, for the verb adds the judgment of existence to the identification of a subject and thus converts a mere utterance, a φάσις ("say-ing"), into a true-or-false judgment, a λόγος. Indeed Aristotle seems to think that Κλέων βαδίζει is a short form of expression for Κλέων βαδίζων (participle) ἐστίν, "Kleon is walking, is (a) walking (person)."

For us the most important feature of Aristotle's theory of language is the close parallel—so close as to be almost an identity—between language as the vehicle of logic and language as the vehicle of expression in rhetoric and poetics. This closeness pertains not to words as such, as tokens or symbols, but to the structure of language, and this in turn has to do with its division into ὀνόματα and ῥήματα. Names properly denote "first substances," πρῶται οὐσίαι as they are called in the *Categories* and *De Interpretatione*; the rest of Aristotle's famous ten categories—Quality, Quantity, Location, etc.—are predicates (κατηγορίαι means "predications") that can be asserted of those primary substances: e.g., "Sokrates is mortal."

The subject–predicate pattern is the nucleus of Aristotle's logic. Thus a definition is a λόγος—e.g., ἄνθρωπος ζῷον (ἐστίν), "(A) man (is) (an) animal"—to which other specifications can be added: ζῷον δίπουν, "two-footed animal," πολιτικὸν ζῷον, "city-making animal," etc. And Aristotle's most highly developed logical instrument, the syllogism, is a structure, a σύνθεσις, of three λόγοι, two premises and a conclusion, so put together that the conclusion follows necessarily from the premises, e.g.:

> If all men are animate beings,
> and if all animate beings are mortal,
> then all men must necessarily be mortal.[1]

Guido Morpurgo-Tagliabue has shown in detail how the list of the "parts" of language in chapter 20 of the *Poetics*, rising from στοιχεῖον ("element," i.e., letter or phoneme) through syllable, connective, noun, verb, and inflection to λόγος, is identical with that in the *De Interpretatione*, except that the *Poetics* omits the logical and substantive aspects of language (e.g., its arbitrary character; the λόγος as a judgment) and sticks exclusively to its linguistic features, those which are significant for its use in expression and persuasion.[2] From these and other phenomena it appears that the order of composition of these works was *Categories* and *De Interpretatione*, then *Poetics*, then *Rhetoric* 3; but again the important thing is that they were written during more or less the same period and reflect the cross-connections between various aspects of Aristotle's intensive thinking about language at that time.

Chapter 21 of the *Poetics* takes up the varieties and variations of the noun—common, dialectal, ornamental, invented, and so on—which are allowable and useful in poetry. By far the most prominent item in Aristotle's catalogue is metaphor, which he classifies as a variety of treatment of the noun but regards as the most important.

Chapter 21 having dealt with diction, chapter 22 at last brings us to what we may fairly call "style." Here Aristotle makes programmatic utterances which he himself summarizes in a simple sentence: "The virtue of λέξις is to be clear but not low (ταπεινή)" (58a18). In Aristotle's eye the basic function of all language, including poetic language, is the communication of meaning on a fairly direct, rational level. Once that is accomplished, it is allowed to seek a certain degree of elevation; but only a certain degree. Essentially the same prescriptions and tolerances are established for rhetoric; the difference is again only one of degree, and degrees of difference are allowed within the field of rhetoric also.

---

1. This example follows Aristotle's formulation at *Prior Analytics* 1.25b37–39 of the type of syllogism traditionally known as "Barbara."
2. *Linguistica e stilistica di Aristotele* (Rome 1967) esp. 29–139.

In other words, Aristotle's view of poetical style is essentially a prosy, rationalistic one. It would be no use suggesting to him that perhaps the real function of poetic language is not to communicate meaning but to suggest, to bemuse, to inspire awe, to lift up or cast down, and so on. Such uses of language belong to an earlier period—Sappho, Pindar, Aischylos—and are far removed from Aristotle's purview. (And anyhow most of them appear in lyric poetry and the lyrical parts of early tragedy—parts which we have said are dealt with by Aristotle, if at all, under μελοποιία, not λέξις.)

Aristotle does allow a "pathetic" or emotional use of language, i.e., its employment to arouse certain feelings, πάθη—pity, fear, anger—in the hearer. But this is a rhetorical category: see *Poetics* 19.56b1; 19.56a34–b8; *Rhetoric* 3.7.1408a16–25. The repeated use of παρασκευάζειν in the *Poetics* passage, as we have already noticed (above, p. 117), emphasizes the contrived, calculated quality of λέξις designed to excite the emotions. We can compare the similar prevalance of forms of this verb at 14.53b7–12, 54a11, where the subject is the production of the pity and fear appropriate to tragedy.

On the whole, however, emotional language betrays what in Aristotle's view is its basic function, in poetry and speech-making alike: to convey meaning clearly, straightforwardly, rationally. Poetry has a license, but only within limits—and rhetoric has one also, within still narrower limits—to heighten, spice, or, as Aristotle puts it in his marvelously expressive epithet ἡδυσμένος (*Poetics* 6.49b25), to "sweeten" language, give it an adventitious flavor and attractiveness. A like notion seems to lurk in the remark about the visual element of tragedy at 14.53b4–7: the effects of fear and pity should come not from the ὄψις but from the plot, the structure of events. It should be so constructed that one shudders and pities merely from hearing the events unfold—ἅπερ ἂν πάθοι τις ἀκούων τὸν τοῦ Οἰδίπου μῦθον, "which is what one would experience on (while) hearing the plot of the *Oidipous*." Μῦθος here is the bare plot outline, before it is given literary form; any other reading is excluded by the context. When all is said and done, both the visual and the verbal integument are extraneous.

The same set of attitudes accounts for the high marks which Aristotle gives to metaphor as a poetic and rhetorical device. It is indeed noteworthy that metaphor is treated at length in both *Rhetoric* 3 and *Poetics* 21; the basic analysis is given in the latter, 57b7–33. In Aristotle's eyes metaphor is an eminently rational, intellectual procedure, a "transfer" (μεταφορά) from genus to species, or species to genus, or species to species, or "by proportion" (κατὰ τὸ ἀνάλογον); the latter involves four terms instead of two.[3] The whole schema gives Aristotle opportunity to indulge his mania for divisions and classifications, and this partially accounts for his enthusiasm for metaphor. It is, he says at 22.59a4–8, "much the greatest thing" in poetic language. It alone is a mark of real talent—i.e., intellectual talent—and cannot be learned from anybody else: τὸ γὰρ εὖ μεταφέρειν τὸ τὸ ὅμοιον θεωρεῖν ἐστιν, "For to do well (at) metaphor is to perceive similarity (lit. the similar)." In other words, finding metaphors is a quasi-philosophical activity (θεωρεῖν is a specifically Platonic, and even more specifically Akademic, term for philosophical contemplation); for similarities are generic, not individual.

Metaphor is not exclusively a poetic or high poetic form. Aristotle emphasizes, *Rhetoric* 3.2.1404b34–35, that it is a natural mode of expression among all classes of people and at all levels of language. It is therefore equally accessible to the speech-maker, and should be a prominent part of his weaponry. Here as everywhere along the range we see a gradual, not a total difference between rhetoric and poetry. Aristotle may say on occasion that poetry is "inspired" (ἔνθεον, *Rhetoric* 3.7.1408b19), but that is a *façon de parler* rather than a serious reference to divine inspiration. Aristotle makes that much clear in the words which introduce the remark, ibid. 13–17, that the orator may indulge in embellished language when he already "has" his auditors and "has set them (properly) raving" (ἐνθουσιάσαι ποιήσῃ); for they themselves talk in such ways when they are in an "inspired" state (ἐνθουσιάζοντες). The context throughout is one of contrivance, deliberate manipulation of the audience by the speaker; the gods have nothing to do with it. The whole passage falls under the rubric of appropriate, timely use of inflated language (e.g., "double nouns," redoubled epithets, foreign words, 11–13): the speaker will be "forgiven" for it (συγγνώμη, sc. ἐστίν, 12) if he already has his hearers well along in that direction.

The *Rhetoric* has a plenitude of interesting observations on λέξις in both speeches and poetry and on the distinctions appropriate to

3. "Metaphor by proportion occurs when the second term is related to the first in the same way as the fourth to the third" (57b16–18), i.e., A:B = C:D. In such metaphors, B is given the name of D. Thus (b20–22), since Ares:shield = Dionysos:cup, a shield may be referred to metaphorically as "Ares' cup" (or a cup as "Dionysos' shield").

each. Appropriateness (τὸ πρέπον, 3.7.1408a10ff.; εὐκαίρως χρῆσθαι, "timely use," b1ff.; τὸ ἁρμόττον, "the fitting," *Poetics* 22.58b15; cf. 59a8–14 on which kinds of words befit the different species of verse) is indeed one of Aristotle's major principles, and one which through the mediation of Horace, Quintilian, and others became an integral part of the classical tradition in poetry, rhetoric, and the arts generally (the affiliated concept of the Mean has an equally long and rich afterlife in classicist ethics). Most of the offenses against good taste which Aristotle catalogues under the heading of ψυχρά, "frigid(ities)," in *Rhetoric* 3.7 are offenses against appropriateness, proportion, moderation (τοῦ μετρίου, "the measured, moderation," 7.1406a16; cf. μέτρον, *Poetics* 22.58b12). Here, as so often, Aristotle figures as spokesman for the robust good sense of classical Greek ethics and aesthetic, incorporated above all in the ancient motto μηδὲν ἄγαν, "nothing too much." Its spirit penetrates everything he says on the use of metaphors, similes, strange words (γλῶτται, 3.3), compound words (διπλὰ ὀνόματα, 3.3), witticisms (ἀσταῖα, 3.10–11), and the various species of oratory (3.12).

One section of *Rhetoric* 3 is not duplicated in the *Poetics*: chapters 8 on prose rhythms and 9 on sentence form (εἰρομένη, "strung-out," 1409a29–35, and κατεστραμμένη, "periodic," a35–b32). Versification, the actual detailed construction of the μέτρα—i.e., the three main ones: hexameters, trimeters, tetrameters—is left to the μετρικοί, the verse specialists; and about sentence form in poetry Aristotle says nothing at all except by remote implication, e.g., that the Homeric similes do sometimes drag on to considerable length. On the other hand, as we have seen, he does have important and worthwhile things to say in the *Poetics* about the spirit and shape of the three main verse forms and their appropriateness to the poetic genres to which they "have come to be fitted" (ἥρμοκεν, 24.59b32): hexameters to epic, 24.59b31–60a5; tetrameters to a "satyr-like, danceable composition" like early tragedy, 4.49a21–23 (cf. *Rhetoric* 3.1408b36–9a1); iambic trimeters to the ψόγοι, 4.48b30–32, *and* to tragedy, 4.49a23–28.

What does it all come to? One is reluctant to ascribe to Aristotle *tout court* the idea that the verbal integument of poetry is simply a necessary evil, but he really leaves us very little choice in this matter. Sensitivity to the special glories of poetic style was, for better or worse, not a strong element in his nature. He knew that there was such a thing as κάλλος ὀνόματος, "beauty of (a) word," since persons whose judgment he respected said so; but it is significant that the reference to it in the *Rhetoric* is just two lines long (3.2.1405b6–8) and that there is no such reference at all in the *Poetics*.[4]

One other factor can perhaps be cited, besides Aristotle's own prosy nature and the demands of rhetoric, for his insensitivity to the sensuous side of poetry, and that is the enormous pull exerted by his logical and dialectical studies in the Akademy. We have referred to the close links which he saw between the logical and dialectical uses of language on the one hand and its mimetic uses on the other, as evidenced by the strict parallel between the list of elements of λόγος in the *De Interpretatione* and chapter 20 of the *Poetics*. But it stands to reason that the intellectual energy required for penetration and creative intervention, or invention, in the new fields of logic, dialectic, and rhetoric was of a higher intensity than that required for exploration in a traditional realm like poetry. The range and vigor of Aristotle's mind is on view everywhere, but logic and rhetoric posed tasks more substantial, demanding more originality, than poetry. In the *Poetics* Aristotle is vindicating the Greek poetic tradition against the aberrations of his master; in the Organon and the *Rhetoric* he is creating new traditions for all time to come.

In turning from λέξις to μελοποιία, I must reiterate that everything Aristotle says about λέξις in either *Poetics* or *Rhetoric* has to do only with spoken words in prose or verse. The phenomena of elevated poetic language which strike us so forcibly in the choruses of tragedy, especially those of Aischylos and Sophokles, are simply not at issue here or anywhere else in Aristotle's work: he ignores them.

We have already established that μελοποιία, "song composition," covers the words *and* music of the musical parts of tragedy, since it and λέξις divide the body of the play between them (6.49b29–31); and we noted how unfortunate it is that Aristotle did not bother to define μελοποιία because "its meaning is entirely plain," b35–36. There is, as a matter of fact, one place where he seems to be caught in an ambiguity. In chapter 1, 47b24–28, after establishing the two sides of his dichotomy, instrumental music (rhythm and melody) and the "nameless art" (rhythm and speech), he comes to the mixed class which uses all three media; but this time, instead of calling them rhythm, speech, and melody, he says ῥυθμῷ

---

4. The references to poetic language at the end of chapter 24 are openly deprecatory: "The poet makes irrationalities hard to see by sweetening (ἡδύνων) them with the other good things" of his art (1460b2–3); his "over-brilliant diction" (ἡ λίαν λαμπρὰ λέξις) conceals both character and thought (b5–6).

καὶ μέλει καὶ μέτρῳ, "rhythm and song and verse." The trouble is that song and verse include rhythm, which therefore ought not to be mentioned alongside them: the triad ought to give way to a dyad. The ambiguity is not serious for the drama, where verse(s) and song alternate cleanly (at least in Aristotle's view), κατὰ μέρος, b28; but it is troublesome for dithyramb and nome, which use the three media "all at once," ἅμα πᾶσιν, ibid. There Aristotle's clean distinction between sung and spoken parts does not hold: the "verses" are sung also. (Actually we know too little about the fourth-century dithyramb to be sure whether or to what extent it still used regular μέτρα—e.g., the hexameter—or just how Aristotle interpreted the situation.) We shall have to say, I think, that Aristotle has the drama chiefly in mind, and so introduces his new triad at the cost of a discrepancy.

The only other place in the *Poetics* where μελοποιία is mentioned at all, even by implication, is a brief passage at the end of chapter 18, 56a25–32. Here Aristotle says that the poet "should consider the chorus one of his actors," that it should be "a part of the whole" (the whole play) and should "work together" (with the poet, toward success in the competition) the way it did with Sophokles, not Euripides. To this he adds that "with the other poets the songs (τὰ ᾀδόμενα) are no more a part of the plot than of another tragedy"; hence, beginning with Agathon, they (the choruses) sang ἐμβόλιμα, intermezzi (lit. "inserted pieces") of uncertain relevance to the particular play. It is clear that Aristotle disapproves of this practice, since he says that at that rate you might as well "transfer a speech, or a whole episode, from one play to another."

These remarks are not made about μελοποιία as such; they seem to bear on the *content* of the choral parts. Nevertheless they are of interest as implying that the songs should be relevant to the play as a whole, and therefore (?) that their expression also is not a matter of complete indifference. But that is all that Aristotle says or implies. Detailed instructions are not given here or anywhere else for the diction of the choral odes. Other lyrical elements such as the arias for actors are not even mentioned in the *Poetics* except in the spurious chapter 12:[5] τὰ ἀπὸ σκηνῆς καὶ κομμοί, "the (arias) from the stage and antiphonal songs."

It should be noted that even these sketchy comments in chapter 18 are

5. Else considered chapter 12, from 52b15 to the end, to be a late and inept addition to the text: see Appendix 2, no. 21, and *Argument* 359–363.

put under the practical heading of success in the competitions. They are a long chalk away from the careful prescriptions in chapter 6 (and 9 and elsewhere) concerning unity and verisimilitude in plot, character, and thought and represent no more than a piece of incidental advice to the poets on how to win in the dramatic competitions. They certainly form no part of Aristotle's main theory or poetic structure.

This is perhaps as good a place as any to say something about Greek lyric (more properly "melic") rhythms and their relationship to our texts of Greek poetry and, indirectly, to Aristotle. The modern misguided practice of calling them "lyric *meters*" has only propagated confusion; although in this matter the moderns have done no more than follow the confusions propagated by the ancients themselves.

We do not know how the lyrical parts of a Greek text, say of a Sophokleian tragedy, looked in Sophokles' own time, that is, how the notes were transcribed; the few Greek musical transcriptions still extant do not antedate the Hellenistic period. Sophokles himself must obviously have had some musical notation for his odes and arias, if only to train his choruses and actors. But were those only private notes for his own use, and what happened to them when the verbal texts began to be transcribed and copied? To make the question concrete: we have said that Aristotle seems to have read all the drama he could get his hands on while in the Akademy; but did those texts include the music? Considering what he says about the growing use of ἐμβόλιμα, *intermezzi*, beginning with Agathon, it looks as though what Aristotle already found available in Athens was merely bare texts like ours. If he found musical notations as well, however, they likely were too sketchy or unclear to command his attention.

In any case, we have no evidence whatever that Aristotle's interest in poetic rhythm extended beyond the regular μέτρα (dactylic hexameter, iambic trimeter, and the like) to the vast, intricate web of lyric rhythms used, for example, in the choral and solo songs of fifth-century drama. It is to his credit that he makes such a clear distinction between λέξις and μελοποιία, but not to his credit that he paid so little attention to the latter. What would Aischylos or Sophokles, or even Euripides, be to us without their great choruses? No matter; for Aristotle, to all practical purposes, they do not exist.

Ὄψις, the last and least of the "parts" of tragedy, suffers from a similar neglect by Aristotle and has been equally misinterpreted. In most of the commentaries it figures as "spectacle": everything about a tragedy which can strike the eye. We think naturally of the *mise-en-scène* and its adornments (including, in the modern indoor theater, lighting); the person who added scene-painting to Aristotle's sketch of the development of tragedy (4.49a18) presumably thought along the same line.[6] But stage decoration played no great role in Greek drama, at least down to the fourth century, and Aristotle has made it quite adequately clear that he has a different meaning in mind.

Ὄψις contains that same active suffix -σις which we found in μίμησις, ποίησις, and λέξις. It therefore means not so much what is seen on the stage, as the making of something visible: "visualizing." And what is it that is made visible? The characters of the drama: ὄψις refers to *their* appearance. That should have been obvious from at least two converging lines of evidence, but the point was missed.

The first mention of ὄψις, at 6.49b31–33, makes it depend on that conception of drama as *enacted* which as we saw (above, p. 80) was the central armature for the derivation of all six "parts" of tragedy; and as we also saw, the characters are the enacters. "Since they perform the imitation by acting/enacting (πράττοντες), first of all the adornment of the(ir) appearance (ὁ τῆς ὄψεως κόσμος) must necessarily be some part of tragedy." "Some part" is deliberately modest, to prepare for the next statement on the subject; but at least it is clear that the appearance which is adorned is that of the dramatic persons, not the stage set; for it is they who do the acting/enacting.

The next statement is at the very end of chapter 6, 50b16–20: "The ὄψις has emotional power, to be sure, but is least artistic and least organic to the poetic art; for the power of tragedy exists even without competition(s) or actors, and the art of the property man is even more decisive for the production of the visual effects (τῶν ὄψεων) than that of the poets." These visual effects (the plural ὄψεων is significant) are the masks and costumes of the players, not the stage set. It is understandable that Aristotle rates this—apparently—external factor lowest of the six "parts," on the very edge of the poetic enterprise; for he insists, not only here but elsewhere, that the power or effect (δύναμις) of tragedy can be experienced through reading alone, without external props.

Yet this is not the whole story either. Aristotle is involved in a paradox here, a conflict between internal and external factors, which seems to have stimulated him to further thought. At the end of chapter 15,

6. For Else's view on the interpolation of 49a18–21, see Appendix 2, no. 13, and *Argument* 166–179.

54b15–18, when he has finished his official treatment of plot and character, he suddenly refers to "offenses against the perceptions which necessarily attend upon the poetic art." He says that "these have been fully (ἱκανῶς, adequately) treated in the published discussions"—almost certainly the three-book dialogue *On Poets*—but a brief observation on the subject is also to be found at the beginning of chapter 17, immediately following the remark at the end of 15:[7] "But one should construct one's plots and work them out in language while keeping them before one's eyes as much as possible (μάλιστα πρὸ ὀμμάτων τιθέμενον)," 55a23. This is explained in the following lines as a matter of the poet's guiding the stage action by a correct intuition of the dramatic characters' whereabouts on and off stage.

Aristotle seems to be struggling with his paradox. The actors onstage are not his real concern, yet as persons in a drama, since they enact the action directly, they have somehow or other an irreducible presence which has to be kept in the poet's mental field of vision, or he may commit some elementary offense against "the perceptions which necessarily attend upon the poetic art." It is to Aristotle's credit that he perceived this necessity even though he may have read more drama in the library than he saw in the theater; but it raises some more general questions to which he gives no answer. In a play which is merely read rather than viewed in a theater, not only ὄψις but μελοποιία comes up short; this effectually deprives the drama of the two "parts" which it has over and above epic; and if those two parts are dispensable, the very structure of his analysis of tragedy is undermined. Moreover a reading of the tragic text *solus*, without the interplay of voices, timbres, and vocal melodies (even in the spoken parts) which characterizes a full dramatization, threatens to curtail or inhibit λέξις as well. Thus a deliberate abstraction from full performance—i.e., Aristotle's insistence that reading can do the job just as well (25.62a12ff.)—begets some highly dubious consequences.

It is important, however, to be clear *why* he insists so on the power of reading. First of all, because that was the way he himself had come to know most of the tragedies from the fifth century. But much more significant is the fact that abstraction—abstraction from the details of tragic character and thought as well as from its visible and audible garment—was Aristotle's chosen way of countering Plato. For Plato, the sensuous

7. Chapter 16 is in Else's view a note by Aristotle that has been arbitrarily inserted into its present place (see Appendix 2, no. 28, and *Argument* 484–485).

garb of tragedy, including the sense that the poet is lurking immediately behind the facade of words, was a primal intuition. Aristotle had no such primal intuition of poetry, but he was intelligent enough to perceive it in Plato and devise a system that would contain and neutralize it—defuse it, so to speak. That is what he is up to in the *Poetics*.

IO

The Tragic Side

Pity (ἔλεος) and Fear (φόβος)

IT IS NOT ENOUGH that the tragic plot/action be beautiful, i.e., have unity, coherent structure, and determinate size; it must also arouse the tragic emotions, pity and fear, and that in certain specified ways.

Aristotle himself makes the transition explicit toward the end of chapter 9: 52a1–3, Ἐπεὶ δὲ οὐ μόνον τελείας ἐστὶ πράξεως ἡ μίμησις ἀλλὰ καὶ φοβερῶν καὶ ἐλεεινῶν. . . , "But since the imitation is not only of a complete action but *also* of fearful and pitiful things. . . ." Moreover he leaves no doubt, here or anywhere else in the *Poetics*, that there are two and just two tragic emotions, fear and pity. Up to now they had been mentioned only in the katharsis clause of the definition of tragedy, 5.49b27–28, but from this point on they play a major role in Aristotle's discussion. In fact the key to the next section of the *Poetics*, from 9.51b33 through chapter 14, is the presence—sometimes more covert than overt—of these two concepts.

Whence did Aristotle draw them, and why just these two? For it cannot be said that pity and fear so occupy the field of view as to exclude the idea of any other tragic emotion. Gorgias speaks of a triad of feelings, "fear-filled shuddering, many-teared pity, and grief-loving longing" (φρίκη περίφοβος καὶ ἔλεος πολύδακρυς καὶ πόθος φιλοπενθής, *Helen* 9, Diels-Kranz 82B11), and although he ascribes them to "poetry" in general there is much to be said for taking this more specifically as a reference to tragedy—and Homeric epic (the *Iliad*). In any case Gorgias can certainly be counted as one of Aristotle's predecessors in this department.

What is certain is that Plato provides the immediate point of departure for Aristotle's thinking. In the *Ion*, 535c, the rhapsode recalls how when he recites something pathetic, ἐλεεινόν τι (from Homer, be it noted), his listeners' eyes fill with tears, and when something fearful, φοβερὸν ἢ δεινόν, their hair stands up on their heads from fright, ὑπὸ φόβου. No other emotion is mentioned. The *Phaidros*, 268c, makes similarly explic-

it mention of pathetic and fearful speeches, ῥήσεις . . . οἰκτρὰς καί . . .
φοβεράς, and this time in specific connection with tragedy. In *Republic*
10.603e–606b, on the other hand, Plato talks at length about our ten-
dency, indeed our craving, to weep and wail and carry on over the
sufferings of the tragic heroes (see especially 606a–b), but says not a
word about fear.

This discourse of Plato's on our weeping over the tragic heroes is
especially interesting in connection with Gorgias's πόθος φιλοπενθής,
"grief-loving longing." Pity is explicitly mentioned only once by Plato, at
606b (ἐλεεῖν), while on the other hand the passage is studded with refer-
ences to grieving: ὀδυρμοί, "lamentations," 604d, 605d; δακρῦσαί τε
καὶ ἀποδύρασθαι, "to weep and lament," 606a; τοῦ θρηνώδους τούτου,
"this lamenting (tendency)," 606a–b; θρηνῳδίαν, "(song of) lamenta-
tion," 604d; πενθεῖ, "he (the tragic hero) grieves," 606b. Moreover the
part of our souls which gives way to the temptation to lament the heroes
is described as the "vexation-prone," the peevish part (τὸ ἀγανακτη-
τικόν, 604e, 605a; cf. ἀγανακτεῖν, 604b); in other words we do not
merely share the heroes' grief, we share their resentment at their suffer-
ings, their sense that they have been wronged.

In Plato's eyes, of course, this vexation at the sufferings in tragedy is
born of ignorance and illusion. At every step in the long exposition (it is
not an argument) we are meant to recall, by contrast, how Sokrates
comported himself in his last hour. In the *Apology*, 35b, he had referred
with disdain to "these pathetic little playlets," τὰ ἐλεινὰ ταῦτα δράματα,
the dramatic performances which other defendants mounted in the
courtroom, weeping and begging for their lives, bringing their children
and relatives and friends to the stand to move the jurors to tears (34c);
and in the *Phaidon*, 117d–e, when his friends burst out weeping at the
approach of the fatal potion, he reminds them gently that that was why
he sent the women away, ἵνα μὴ τοιαῦτα πλημμελοῖεν, "so that they
would not strike this kind of wrong note."

It is clear that much of what Plato reprehends in our reception of
tragedy and Homer (the *Iliad*, as always) falls under the older heading of
lamentation: the kind of mourning which fills the θρῆνοι, the full-dress
laments at the ends of Aischylos's oldest extant plays, *Persians* and *Seven
Against Thebes*—and, significantly, at the end of the *Iliad* itself (the
laments over Hektor, 24.723–776). That pattern of mourning overlaps,
but is not identical with, what Plato describes in *Republic* 10. The chief
difference, aside from the idea of the "peevish part," is that those earlier
lamentations were communal outpourings, mainly from the chorus,

whereas the emotional phenomena described by Plato are exclusively individual feelings, in tragic characters and spectator alike. (It is significant that he speaks of the heroes' weeping and wailing and beating their breasts, 605d, cf. 606b, πενθεῖ, but never explicitly mentions the chorus.)

The same individualism also characterizes Aristotle's presentation of tragic pity, but the hostile bias of Plato's analysis (especially his tracing it to the "vexation-prone," fault-finding element in us) and its total lack of reference to fear suggest that *Republic* 10 was not the immediate source of Aristotle's schema—another indication, perhaps, that that discussion was written after the *Poetics*, as a rejoinder to it, not before. The *Phaidros*, on the other hand, is an unexceptionable source, especially in view of the close connection which it establishes between tragedy and rhetoric.

Aristotle makes it abundantly clear that he considers pity and fear a correlated, indeed a reciprocally conditioned, pair of emotions, and that he thinks they are brought into satisfactory operation only by the tragic action, not just by the display of character and thought. This cardinal point is explicated in chapter 13, in his survey of the possible varieties of the μεταβολή, the tragic shift. Chapter 7, 51a12–15, has already identified happiness and unhappiness (εὐτυχία and δυστυχία) as the poles between which the action can swing. Now, in 13.52b34–53a7, we learn what kinds of men can be involved in what kinds of shift: the proper effect requires an integration of both elements. The shift of a perfectly virtuous man (τους ἐπιεικεῖς ἄνδρας, 52b34–36) from happiness to unhappiness can be ruled out at once: it is neither fearful nor pitiable but μιαρόν, repulsive ("filthy," polluted; see below, p. 146). Shifting the villains (τοὺς μοχθηρούς, "the wicked," b36–37) in the opposite direction is even less acceptable: it is neither φιλάνθρωπον (we shall consider what this means below, p. 157) nor pathetic nor fearful. But the shift of a thorough villain from happiness to unhappiness is also unsatisfactory (53a1–4): it would arouse the φιλάνθρωπον but neither pity nor fear. (We have to note that a shift of the good man to happiness is not even mentioned; it is too obviously untragic.)

Here Aristotle states the criterion which rules out these modes. It is that pity "has to do with the man who *undeserving(ly)* suffers misfortune" (περὶ τὸν ἀνάξιόν ἐστιν δυστυχοῦντα), and fear "with the man *like (us)*" (περὶ τὸν ὅμοιον) who suffers misfortune. But we must move at once to avert a possible misunderstanding. These are not two separate men, they are two aspects of the same person: to earn our pity he must suffer undeserved misfortune; to rate our fear he must be like us (so that we can sympathize with him). The rationale behind this calculus is set forth in chapters 5 (fear) and 8 (pity) of Book 2 of the *Rhetoric*, in the section (chapters 2–11) on πάθη, the feelings. These two chapters establish the correlation which is at the heart of Aristotle's theory: that which we fear in our own case we pity in the case of someone else (2.5.1382b25–26, 2.8.1386a28–29). Both ways, the feeling is self-regarding: the fearful is that danger or evil which we think *may soon* happen to us; the pitiable is that which *might* happen to us (2.8.1385b14–15). But in fact this intimate correlation is a fraud, so far as the tragic fear is concerned. Generations of readers of the *Oidipous* and the *Poetics* have cudgeled their brains in vain to know how we could fear that Oidipous's infinitely picturesque, totally unique fate might be-fall *us*. The real emotion unleashed by the Oidipous story is quite differ-ent. Aristotle lets the cat out of the bag in one word when he says, *Poetics* 14.53b5, that anyone hearing the plot of the *Oidipous* would φρίττειν καὶ ἐλεεῖν, "*shudder* and feel pity." The real tragic emotion, which he elsewhere calls "fear," is not the everyday kind of fear the rhetor deals with in the courts but the *frisson* of horror that comes over us at a tale of parricide and incest.

Thus ἔλεος καὶ φόβος is, if not a misrepresentation, at least a flatten-ing of the real emotional situation in tragedy. Why has Aristotle per-formed this reduction on the facts? Undoubtedly for the sake of symme-try and system. The reciprocal interaction of pity and fear is such a tidy syndrome! In any case he has imported it directly from rhetoric into poetics, and once again, as on a previous occasion, we find him insuffi-ciently sensitive to the differences between real and fictive situations.

"Pity" may seem a simpler, more straightforward concept, but it is not. In a long article over twenty-five years ago, Wolfgang Schadewaldt devoted his formidable learning to demolishing the equation between ἔλεος and the Christian virtue of *Mitleid*, "compassion."[1] More gener-ally, he argued that in speaking of pity and fear Aristotle means a raw, primitive pair of emotions: gut feelings, to employ the American idiom. Unfortunately this is not true either, and exposing the error will bring us very close to the heart of Aristotle's reaction to Plato. It was Plato, not Aristotle, who considered the emotions raw outpourings of the affective,

1. "Furcht und Mitleid," *Hermes* 83 (1955) 129–171 = *Hellas und Hesperien*[2] (Zurich 1970) 1.194–236.

appetitive part of our souls, untinctured by reason. Aristotle's view, clearly visible in his treatment of pity and fear and indeed of all the feelings, in the *Rhetoric*, is that they comport an element of reason. We do not feel fear unless we expect that the evil in question is imminent and likely to befall us (2.5.1382a24–32; cf. b29–34); and we do not pity another unless we think that he does not deserve his misfortune, *and* that we might suffer the same misfortune (2.8.1385b14–1386a3). The proliferation of words for thinking (οἴεσθαι, νομίζειν) in these passages is no accident. The emotions, in Aristotle's view, are not released—not authorized, so to speak—until reason has calculated that they are appropriate to the situation.

This new view of the irrational part of the soul as "partaking of reason in some way" (μετέχουσά πῃ λόγου, *Nikomacheian Ethics* 1.13.1102b13–14, 25–26), or at least potentially obedient to, willing to be commanded by, reason (κατήκοον καὶ πειθαρχικόν, 31), is one of Aristotle's most fruitful innovations not only in rhetoric, poetics, and ethics but in other fields. To it he owes his success against Plato's condemnation of poetry as nurturer of the passions: not so much by refuting it as by turning its flank, so to speak. He does not say outright, in the *Poetics*, that pity and fear are moral emotions; he simply establishes by indirection that their nature, their unimpeded working, excludes tragic outcomes which are morally unacceptable—e.g., the downfall of the righteous, the prospering of wickedness.

We shall have more to say about the role of the spectator or reader of tragedy as a judge. It is more important at our present stage to note what Aristotle has accomplished here. He has demonstrated, at least to his own satisfaction, that the healthy moral sense of the ordinary citizen will reject *ab initio* the outcomes which Plato most reprehended: the defeat of virtue, the victory of vice. Even more ingenious and significant, however, is the way Aristotle has found out of this apparent dilemma. The proper structure for the tragic outcome is (*Poetics* 13.53a7–23) the downfall of a man—one from a prosperous and conspicuous family—who is neither impeccably virtuous nor really wicked, but who comes to grief "because of some ἁμαρτία" (a9–10); to which Aristotle adds, six lines below (a16), "because of a *big* ἁμαρτία," i.e., one pregnant with disaster.

Hamartia is indeed one of the "big" concepts in the *Poetics*, and one of the most controverted (second only to katharsis). I think it can be regarded as established, as a result of the long controversy, that it does not mean a flaw of character. But neither does it refer, in my opinion, to the other term of that facile dichotomy in which the debate on this subject regularly finds expression, "intellectual error."

But we have gotten ahead of our story and must go back to Aristotle's chapters 9 and 10 to pick up the thread. At 10.52a12ff., after a preliminary gesture in 9.51b33, he introduces the concepts of ἁπλοῖ and πεπλεγμένοι μῦθοι. The adjectives are usually translated "simple" and "complex." I prefer "single" and "inwoven," because the idea of the latter is that strands of the plot are woven (πεπλεγμένος from πλέκειν, "weave") *into* each other so that they cannot be cleanly disentangled. The difference between these two types is that in the single plot the change of fortune comes without peripety or recognition; in the inwoven it comes with them. But the mention of these technical devices does not assist our understanding until we begin to see, in chapter 11 (52a38–b1), that their function is to enhance the realization of pity and fear: not to produce them in the first place, but to enhance them.

At the end of chapter 11 (52b9–10) Aristotle finally gets around to saying that the plot has three "parts": peripety, recognition, and the πάθος, the latter being (52b11–13) "a fatal or painful act or happening, such as deaths on the stage (?), paroxysms of pain, woundings, and all that sort of thing." The πάθος ("thing suffered") is actually the hinge of the tragic plot, single *or* inwoven, the source of its pathetic and/or fearful quality. But the single plot, which moves straight along its path without surprise or deviation, realizes only a part of the emotional potential; the voltage, so to speak, remains low. Fearful and pathetic effects are "most," i.e., best, realized, 9.52a4, ὅταν γένηται παρὰ τὴν δόξαν δι' ἄλληλα, "when they come about contrary to expectation (but) because of one another." This combination of logical sequence with unexpectedness raises the emotional power to its maximum effective level. "Inwoven" tragedies are therefore the best ones.

Peripety, in Aristotle's book, is just such a parodoxical yet logical "shift of what is being practiced (τῶν πραττομένων) to its opposite" (11.52a22–23). Considering what was said above about the programmatic connotations of the verb πράττειν ("to be pursuing a certain course or policy"), we have no difficulty applying this to Oidipous. He is out to find the unknown murderer, but events beginning with the arrival of the Korinthian messenger quickly lead—logically but contrary to his expectation—to the opposite of what he intended: the identification of himself as the parricide and incestuous one. "Recognition" is equally germane to Oidipous's case: 11.52a30–31, ἐξ ἀγνοίας εἰς γνῶσιν μεταβολή, ἢ εἰς φιλίαν ἢ εἰς ἔχθραν, "a shift from ignorance to understanding, (leading) to the status either of 'dear one' or of enemy." I have shown elsewhere that φιλίαν here has nothing to do with "friendship" but refers to the ancient ties of blood kinship.[2] Oidipous, when he "recognizes" that the man he slew was his father, enters consciously into those blood ties, whether he likes it or not; but he was involved in them from the beginning, whether he knew it or not.

Aristotle says further, 52a32, that the finest recognition is one that comes together with a peripety, "as in the *Oidipous*"; and he adds, a33–b3, that although there are other kinds of recognitions—for example, of inanimate objects (e.g., Orestes' lock of hair and footprints in Aischylos's *Choëphoroi*), or of chance occurrences, or that one has done or not done something—the best is the recognition-cum-peripety, because it will arouse ("have," possess) pity or fear; ἔτι δὲ καὶ τὸ ἀτυχεῖν καὶ τὸ εὐτυχεῖν ἐπὶ τῶν τοιούτων συμβήσεται, "and furthermore, also unhappiness and happiness will naturally follow upon events of this kind." Why will they naturally or necessarily follow (συμβήσεται, from συμβαίνειν; see above, p. 111)? It is important to state the answer explicitly, since Aristotle does not do so. A sudden revelation like that in the *Oidipous*, of unsuspected offenses against the deep ties of blood, will instantly and automatically destroy all happiness. The moment Oidipous learns the truth, at line 1180, his "happiness"—his wealth, kingly position, marital love, family bliss, and all the rest—is gone forever. Sophokles does indeed deserve Aristotle's admiration (and ours) for so constructing his play that the whole structure of Oidipous's life balances on that pinpoint before toppling into the abyss.

All this reinforces what we said about the importance and necessity of action, to what character and thought cannot do by themselves. And this action is lifted to the final electrifying height by its special "parts," peripety and recognition. At the same time we must recognize that Sophokles was not building this ultra-powerful structure merely for its own sake. There is a further range of thought and feeling in the *Oidipous* which is not dreamt of in Aristotle's philosophy. We shall discuss it hereafter.

Chapter 14, 53b14–22, reinforces and justifies Aristotle's focus on family blood ties. This is a discussion of the possible varieties of the πάθος (at b15, simply τῶν συμπιπτόντων, "the things that happen," a vague phrase; more explicitly αὐτὸ τὸ πάθος, b18, and τὰ πάθη, b19–

---

2. See *Argument* 349–351.

20) from the point of view of their fearful or pathetic character. Here we are told explicitly—at last—that the πάθη work best when they come ἐν ταῖς φιλίαις, "within family bonds" (cf. above on φιλίαν, 11.52a31): when a brother kills or is about to kill a brother, a son his father, and the like. Aristotle cannot resist adding sardonically, ταῦτα ζητητέον, "those (are the things) you must look for."

The second part of chapter 14 surveys the tragic πάθη from a different angle. At 53b15ff. Aristotle had hypothesized that they must be acts of "dear ones" (φίλοι) toward one another, or of enemies, or of "neutrals," and concluded that only the φίλοι would do for tragedy. Here, at 53b27–54a9, he locates the possible πάθη on a different grid, according to whether the tragic deed is performed or not performed and with or without knowledge. In Aristotle's survey of the possible modes it turns out—not exactly to our surprise—that doing is better than not doing and not knowing is better than knowing. Ignorance, leading to the performance of a suitably drastic act (parricide, matricide, incest, or whatever), is the key to the proper tragic effect.

But ignorance of what? In the present passage Aristotle gives only one clue, in the word μιαρόν: shocking, repulsive, literally "filthy," "polluted." The implicit reference is to the whole range of blood pollution and violation of blood taboo which so obsessed archaic Greece. Parricide, incest, and the rest were unimaginably horrible crimes to the archaic sensibility, whether or not they were intended. This ancient set of taboos still colored the fifth century's attitude toward the Oidipous story and is still alive in Aristotle, whether he was conscious of it or not. But he also shows a refinement of the idea, to take account of whether the "polluted" act is performed knowingly or not. This is not Aristotle's personal contribution either; it had already been incorporated into Attic law and legal procedure beginning in the time of Drakon (late seventh century).

We are told here, 53b37–54a2, that to intend the deed (a killing, or whatever, of a family member) knowingly, but not carry it through, is the worst: τό τε γὰρ μιαρὸν ἔχει καὶ οὐ τραγικόν, ἀπαθὲς γάρ, "for it involves (lit. possesses) the μιαρόν *and* is not tragic; for there is no (actual) πάθος." The example given is Haimon's abortive impulse to kill his father, in *Antigone* (related in lines 1231–1234). To do it knowingly (the Medeia pattern) is better; still better to do it in ignorance but then recognize what one has done, 54a2–4: τό τε γὰρ μιαρὸν οὐ πρόσεστιν καὶ ἡ ἀναγνώρισις ἐκπληκτικόν, "for the μιαρὸν does not attach (to it) and the recognition is electrifying." But then Aristotle adds that best of all is to intend the deed in ignorance but subsequently recognize the facts, so that it is not performed. Only one of the three examples cited is from an extant play, Euripides' *Iphigeneia among the Taurians*, but the pattern is clear enough: the recognition intervenes and forestalls the fatal deed.

Why does the recognition forestall the deed? Perhaps the answer is obvious, but it is worth stating because Aristotle does not state it in so many words in the *Poetics*. It is that the tragic hero—the morally serious though not perfect hero—is not the kind of man to carry through a deed of horror when he knows the facts. His pulling back from it at the moment of recognition is in fact an earnest of his goodness of character. For more on this aspect of the total tragic calculus we must go to Book 3 of the *Nikomacheian Ethics*. There, in the course of a discussion of voluntary and involuntary acts (ἑκούσια and ἀκούσια), Aristotle says (1110b18–22) that not every act performed because of ignorance, δι' ἄγνοιαν, is involuntary; only one which brings pain and repentance, μεταμέλεια, can properly be called so. A man "who has done something (bad) out of ignorance (but) shows no disgust or regret (μηδέν τι δυσχεραίνων) over the act" did not act either voluntarily or involuntarily. He may be classified as "nonvoluntary" (οὐχ ἑκών, b23); only the one who repents has a claim to the title "involuntary" (ἄκων, 22).

By this test, and taking into evidence his stabbing out his eyes and what he said on that occasion (*Oidipous Tyrannos* 1268–1274), Oidipous's tragic acts, his twin πάθη, qualify as involuntary. Furthermore (*Nikomacheian Ethics* 3.1.1110b30–1111a2) ignorance of moral principles does not qualify; it has to be ignorance of *details*: "(the circumstances) in which and in connection with which the act exists; for in those (lie) also pity and forgiveness." Here, by implication, as a lawyer might say, Oidipous's case is assimilated to that of a person charged with homicide, φόνος, before an Athenian jury. His behavior after the recognition is admitted into evidence for his character and intent: i.e., that it was not villainous. And that in turn allows "us," the average citizen, to pity *and* fear for him, for he has proved that he is, like us, a moral person, not a villain, and has proved by the same token that he did not quite deserve his fate.

So far Aristotle's theory. It is an ingenious and admirably compact construction, but it has serious defects. We have already spoken of how Aristotle forces the tragic horror into the lesser role of ordinary "fear" for the sake of reciprocity, so that it may work in tandem with pity. Beyond that lies the further range of thought and sensibility (mentioned only fleetingly above) which may have been in Sophokles' mind; it was certainly far from Aristotle's. But Aristotle is not trying to reconstruct tragedy as it was in the Perikleian Age; he is defending it against Plato in the 360s or 350s. In that light we must admire the way he has turned Plato's flank by excluding *ab initio*, on psychological grounds, the outcomes to which Plato most objected: success for the villain, defeat for the virtuous man.

Aristotle brings his flanking movement to a close, 13.53a7–17, by proposing a pattern of outcome which avoids both extremes; it is, he says, μεταξὺ τούτων, "in between these." The tragic shift, to be tragic, must end in unhappiness, not happiness (a9; more explicitly, a13–15), but the new pattern imposes modifications on both the hero and his fate. He must be good rather than bad (a16–17) but not "outstandingly virtuous" (a8)—i.e., not like Sokrates—and his fall must be brought about not by wickedness (a8–9, 15–16) but by some hamartia (a10), in fact a "big" hamartia (a16), i.e., one that leads to dire consequences.

We spoke of hamartia (above, p. 143), but only long enough to say that it pretty certainly does not mean a flaw or failing of character. What *does* it mean, then? A number of surveys have been made of this question, not all of equal value.[3] Earlier usage, especially in poetry, is interesting for the history of the word (it had a broad range of meanings in the fifth century, from mere "error" or "offense" almost to "sin"); but we want to know what Aristotle meant by it. For this purpose we are thrown, for better or worse, on a passage in chapter 8 of Book 5 of the *Nikomacheian Ethics*, 1135b11–25. This comes in Aristotle's discussion of justice—a cardinal fact whose bearing we shall assess later. In the passage in question he distinguishes three grades or levels of involvement in a wrong act (b11, βλαβῶν "damages," torts): ἀτύχημα, "misfortune," accident; ἁμάρτημα, "error," mistake; and ἀδίκημα, "unjust act," crime. Unjust acts are clearly excluded in the *Poetics*; we are concerned here with the distinction between accidents and mistakes. The latter are defined, loc. cit., b12–16, as torts which involve an error as to details: the object (person harmed), the instrument, or whatever is not what the doer thought when he committed the act. On this point *Nikomacheian Ethics* 3.1.1110b32–1111a15 supplies further details, including the case of Merope, which is also mentioned in the *Poetics*, 14.54a5–

3. Cf., e.g., J. M. Bremer, *Hamartia: Tragic Error in the Poetics of Aristotle* (Amsterdam 1969) esp. 4–98.

7: Merope, in Euripides' *Kresphontes*, was about to kill her son under the impression that he was an enemy, but "recognized" him in time.

The crucial distinction for us is the one that Aristotle mentions next, *Nikomacheian Ethics* 5.8.1135b16–19: when the deed is done under the influence of misinformation of the kind already mentioned, and the unfortunate result is contrary to (reasonable) expectation (ὅταν . . . παρα-λόγως ἡ βλάβη γένηται, b16–17), it is an accident; when it is *not* contrary to reasonable expectation it is a ἁμάρτημα. In other words, ignorance of relevant details does not completely exonerate the doer; he is required to exercise reasonable care to foresee them. And one other specification is added, b18–19: when the point of origin of the act—ἡ ἀρχὴ τῆς αἰτίας, "the beginning of the blame (or the charge)"—is within the doer, it is a ἁμάρτημα; when outside, an ἀτύχημα.

This gradation of guilt for harmful acts is, as we said, not Aristotle's invention; it had been incorporated into the Attic legal system long before his time. The most we can ascribe to him is an effort to regularize and rationalize the theoretical basis of the system. Its core remains the concept of legal responsibility; and that is also the core of Aristotle's theory concerning the tragic acts, the πάθη. We have already seen ideas imported into poetic from rhetoric; here we see one imported from the legal system.

In the legal sphere the function of this graduated calculus was to assess the appropriate punishment—also, to some extent, to identify the competent court. In tragedy its function is even more sensitive: to determine the narrow range of judgment and feeling within which the culprit before *this* court can be judged enough "like us" that his fall may inspire fear as if for ourselves, and sufficiently undeserving of his misfortune to inspire pity and forgiveness, i.e., pity and acquittal.

To speak concretely: Oidipous, the offender in this dock, although unmistakably a great man, one of the heroes, has enough common foibles—his testiness, his proneness to suspicion, his readiness to think that he is always right—to qualify him as also one of "us." At the same time he is clearly a good man rather than a bad, and his self-blinding, with his address to his parents and children on that occasion (*Oidipous Tyrannos* 1371–1390), assure us that he would never have killed his father or married his mother had he known what he was doing—in other words, that he does not, or at least not fully, deserve his misfortune. It was a product not of ill-nature but of ignorance.

Or should we say, of hamartia? A peculiar feature of chapters 13 and

14 of the *Poetics* is that the former speaks only of hamartia, the latter only of ignorance. It seems that this fact, if it is not accidental, may be connected somehow with the well-known discrepancy between the two chapters: that 13 (53a9–10, 15–17) recommends an unhappy ending caused by hamartia (we can call it the Oidipous pattern), whereas 14 gives highest marks to a plot in which the dire result is actuated by ignorance but forestalled by a recognition before it happens (the Iphigeneia pattern, from *Iphigeneia among the Taurians*).

There is a further difference between chapters 13 and 14: only the latter mentions recognition (53b31, 35; 54a3, 4, 6–7, 8–9). The relation between recognition and ignorance is indeed direct and obvious, the one being the reversal of the other (11.52a29–31). Hamartia, on the other hand—if our passage in *Nikomacheian Ethics* 5 can be relied on—represents not so much a species of ignorance as a judgment on it, that it could have been avoided by reasonable foresight. In other words, hamartia raises a slight but definite presumption of culpable negligence: slight enough not to obstruct our feeling pity and fear for the hero, definite enough to prevent our feeling that his fall is merely a piece of bad luck, an ἀτύχημα. Aristotle must have performed some such calculus in order to make a place for the tragic hero as neither villain nor mere victim: one who is not wholly guilty but who contributes somehow to his own downfall.

But can we hold Oidipous partly responsible for the fatal occurrence at the crossroads? To do so requires an extension of the hamartia-calculus outside the action of the play to the προπεπραγμένα (18.55b30), the incidents that preceded it. Many an innocent reader of the play has been tempted to ask, "When a man comes straight down the road from Delphoi with Apollo's warning ringing in his ears—'You will kill your father and marry your mother'—might he not be a *little* more careful whom he gets into an altercation with at the first bend in the road?" Such an inquirer will be told sternly by certain scholars that his question is inadmissible: that Sophokles has strictly separated the tragic incidents from the play proper and devoted the latter solely to the discovery of the truth about them. Granted that this is true (and I think it is), was Aristotle aware of the distinction? From the main argument of the *Poetics*— aside from the implications of the word hamartia itself, for surely it is only applicable to the tragic acts, not to the play as such—one would be inclined to say no. But there are some passages in later chapters, especially 15 and 18, which suggest that Aristotle may have had second thoughts about precisely this question. (They also suggest that we may be able to add Homer's greatest hero, Achilleus, as another, different example of hamartia; see below, p. 210.)

To stick to our present argument, hamartia does seem to imply that in Aristotle's opinion Oidipous was to some extent guilty of negligence in not thinking more carefully about whom he might meet on the road. If he had done so, might the outcome have been averted? But this runs squarely counter to an old, indeed a classical pattern in Greek mythology and poetry. Kroisos of Lydia, when he asked the Delphic oracle what would happen if he crossed the river Halys, i.e., entered Persian territory, and was told that he would "destroy a great empire" (Herodotos 1.53), concluded hastily—too hastily—that the oracle meant the Persian empire; in fact, as it turned out, it meant his own. Or, to take a lesser example, Kreon, in *Antigone* 280–289, flies into a rage when the chorus ventures to suggest that the gods might have had a hand in the symbolic burial of Polyneikes. If he had bethought himself in time, might his own disaster have been averted?

The point of these stories—these *exempla*—is that the outcome was *not* averted. The meaning of oracles is normally discovered after the event, not before; and there is something in the nature of things, something the older Greeks called ἄτη, "fatal infatuation" or "doom," which insures that it shall be so. J. M. Bremer and R. D. Dawe have tried to equate Aristotle's hamartia with ἄτη, but in vain.[4] It has at best an analogous relation to the tragic happenings (analogous in the structuralist sense); identity of meaning is excluded by the fact that there is no mysterious "something" in the background—no fate, no destiny, no gods—to control and account for the tragic action. Hamartia is simply an unfortunate error, but one which enables us to feel pity and fear for the hero. We shall consider this point further in the next chapter.

What it comes down to, concretely, is that we have no sure way of adjudicating between chapters 13 and 14, between the Oidipous pattern and the Iphigeneia pattern. That is to say, we have no sure way of telling which represents Aristotle's final judgment in the matter. It is quite true that 13 looks at the tragic action as a whole, 14 only at the tragic act, the πάθος, as such; but that does not help us to a final resolution. Perhaps Aristotle never reached one either.

4. Bremer (above, n. 3) 99–134; R. D. Dawe, "Some Reflections on Ate and Hamartia," *HSCP* 72 (1968) 89–123.

II

The Tragic Side
Peculiar Pleasure (οἰκεία ἡδονή) and Katharsis

WHAT IS the final purpose or end (τέλος) of tragedy? To produce a
certain aesthetic and emotional response in the spectator or reader. This
proposition has been denied on the ground that the purpose of tragedy
ought to be something inherent in the form itself rather than an "exter-
nal" effect upon somebody outside it. But this is absurd. The spectator or
reader—the consumer, to put it in crude modern terms—of a poetic
construct is no more outside it than the person for whom a house is
constructed is "outside" it. A house is something to be lived in, a struc-
ture for people to use. All the arts are teleological, in Aristotle's view (as
in Plato's), and their teleology is grounded firmly in human desires and
needs.

Of course tragedy is not quite as simple a matter as a house. There are
indications in the *Poetics* that the overall purpose or end of tragedy is the
production of a certain kind of pleasure; and then there is katharsis.
These are difficult problems, and Aristotle has compounded the diffi-
culty by being curiously vague and elusive about this side of things.
There are just four or possibly five brief references to an οἰκεία ἡδονή, a
"peculiar" or "appropriate" pleasure, only one of which is really helpful,
and one to katharsis. We must keep these two sets of references separate,
so far as we can, unless and until we gain a clear notion of the relation
between them, if any.

The one helpful reference to the οἰκεία ἡδονή is in chapter 14. Aris-
totle has just been distinguishing between fearful effects attained merely
through ὄψις, the visual appearance(s) of the characters, and those at-
tained through the "structure of the events" as such—e.g., from hearing
the plot of the *Oidipous* (53b1–9). He then speaks of an even lower level
of effect produced by ὄψις: not the fearful but the "monstrous," τὸ
τερατῶδες, b9 (e.g., Grand Guignol shockers; our horror films). He con-
tinues, 53b10–14, οὐ γὰρ πᾶσαν δεῖ ζητεῖν ἡδονὴν ἀπὸ τραγῳδίας
ἀλλὰ τὴν οἰκείαν, ἐπεὶ δὲ τὴν ἀπὸ ἐλέου καὶ φόβου διὰ μιμήσεως δεῖ

ἡδονὴν παρασκευάζειν τὸν ποιητήν, φανερὸν ὡς τοῦτο ἐν τοῖς πράγμασιν ἐμποιητέον, "For one should not seek any and every kind of pleasure from tragedy, but the appropriate (one); and since (it is) the pleasure from pity and fear by means of imitation (that) the poet must endeavor to procure, it is obvious that this must be built into the events." And from that Aristotle goes on to survey the emotional productiveness of the various species of πάθος; see above, p. 146.

This is the only passage in the *Poetics* that approaches a rounded definition of the οἰκεία ἡδονή. It tells us two things about this pleasure (the pleasure appropriate to tragedy, specific to it, *peculiar* to it): that it springs from pity and fear and that it is produced by imitation (διὰ μιμήσεως), i.e., by that process of logical yet startling construction which is the poet's special task. It seems to follow that not every poet or every tragedy will achieve the peculiar pleasure, or achieve it fully, just as not every individual of a species attains the perfect, full development which "belongs to" that species; conversely, and by the same token, the one who does achieve it has reached a pinnacle, a real high point of excellence. Such, presumably, is the case of Sophokles in the *Oidipous*. We must emphasize and hold fast to these propositions, against the facile assumption that anything called "tragedy" automatically attains its goal.

But *is* pleasure the proper aim and goal of tragedy? Plato certainly did not think so. As early as the *Gorgias*, 502a–503a, he established to his own satisfaction that tragedy, like the other poetic arts, is indeed out to please the public, and that in view of this aim it is merely a branch of rhetoric, another piece of low flattery, or toadying (κολακεία, 503a6). As late as the *Laws*, 2.700a–701b, he castigates in sharpest terms the degeneration of music in the musical and dramatic contests, under the spell of pleasure (700d6, e2). (Tragedy is not explicitly mentioned but is certainly to be thought of as tarred by the same brush.) This decline in standards has substituted for the old aristocracy in the theater a "theatrocracy" (701a3), a domination by the mob.

Plato partially, but only partially, redresses these hostile judgments by the careful analysis which he devotes to pleasure in the *Philebos*. In particular, 47e–48a, 50b, he speaks of the mixture of pains and pleasures (cf. 35e–36b) we experience in tragedy and comedy. *Mixture* of pains and pleasures signifies impurity: a concept we shall come back to later. Meanwhile we can ask how it happens that painful feelings (*Philebos* 47e and 50b–c give full lists of them; see above, p. 59) can pass off into pleasure. Aside from philosophical solutions to this problem, we may note that the paradox itself is of long standing in Greek literature.

Homer mentions repeatedly the satisfaction of giving free rein to our craving (ἔϱος) to weep and lament (cf. Plato's remarks in *Republic* 10; and above, p. 140); Achilleus speaks of wrath "swelling in the heart sweeter than dripping honey" (*Iliad* 18.110); and so on. The fact is that the human animal being constituted as it is, giving way to strong emotions can be a powerful source of pleasure to us even though the emotions themselves may seem on analysis to be painful.

Aristotle is clear that pleasure and pain are the master instigators of human behavior and that the emotions are those affections "upon which pain and pleasure follow," *Rhetoric* 2.1.1378a20–21. The order in this listing is not accidental, for pain is an inherent, primitive part of most emotions; e.g., anger, ὀϱγή, is "a craving for revenge, accompanied by pain," 2.1378a30. Yet pleasure can accompany any feeling of anger, from the expectation of getting our revenge, b1–2. Similarly pain is a basic part of the definition of fear, 5.1382a21; shame (αἰσχύνη), 6.1383b12; pity, 8.1385b13; envy (φθόνος), 9.1386b18; indignation (τὸ νεμεσᾶν), 9.1387a9; and jealousy (ζῆλος), 11.1388a32; but pleasure can accompany their reversal or some other change of situation.

This nexus of pain and pleasure, however, is not after all the direct source of Aristotle's specific tragic pleasure. For that, we must return to Plato. *Philebos* 50e–51e describes a class of pleasures which are unmixed, i.e., unmixed with pain: those we experience from beautiful colors, shapes, smells ("most of them," he adds), sounds, and so on. These pure aesthetic pleasures spring from no perceived lack or deficiency. But Plato explicitly distinguishes, 51c, the beautiful shapes he has in mind from those produced by the mimetic arts (ζῷα, i.e., animals, or other painted figures). He means the pure geometrical shapes of straight line, circle, and the surfaces and solids to which they give rise; these entities, he says, 51c6–d1, are inherently (καθ' αὐτά), not relatively, beautiful *"and have certain pleasures native (to them),"* τινας ἡδονὰς οἰκείας. The next sentence, 51d6–9, establishes the same categorization for the pure tones, τὰς ἕν τι καθαϱὸν ἱείσας μέλος, "those that utter a single pure melody." What is meant here is the pure astral music of the heavenly diapason; and the pleasures that these tones give are called, in an equivalent phrase, τούτων συμφύτους ἡδονὰς ἑπομένας, "innate pleasures that accompany these." Finally, in 51e7–52c, Plato extends this line of thought to the pleasures of learning, τὰς πεϱὶ τὰ μαθήματα ἡδονάς, and establishes that they too are "pure" (καθαϱάς, c2), i.e., they do not stem from any lack or deficiency, any pain.

We may recall at this point that at the beginning of *Poetics* 4, 48b4–

22, Aristotle identified two causes which "begat" poetry. The first of these was the innate (σύμφυτον, a5) tendency of human beings to imitate and the concurrent fact that they all take pleasure in imitations, τὸ χαίρειν τοῖς μιμήμασι πάντας, b8–9. We pointed out (p. 89) that Aristotle traces both aspects to the general human desire to learn: *all* men, not only philosophers, get extreme pleasure (ἥδιστον, b13) from learning. I now suggest that these phenomena all cohere. Aristotle is out to convert Plato's "pure" and inherent aesthetic and intellectual pleasures into a justification of tragic poetry, because we learn from it.

But of course tragedy is not only an intellectual, it is also an emotional experience; and Plato had been very explicit that the emotions, the πάθη (παθήματα), contributed a painful quotient to the pleasures that rose out of them. How does Aristotle get around this difficulty? How does he convert the pain-mixed pleasures of tragedy and comedy into something pure?

The first half of the answer has to be that the οἰκεία ἡδονή of tragedy *is* in part intellectual. It is a pleasure based on our observation that the persons of the drama are well drawn: that their speeches and actions do grow plausibly or necessarily out of their characters. And we should note that this pleasure is not exclusively, or even mainly, confined to *new* learning. At least an equally important part is recognition of something we already knew. As Aristotle puts it in 4.48b16–17, συμβαίνει θεωροῦντας μανθάνειν καὶ συλλογίζεσθαι τί ἕκαστον, οἷον ὅτι οὗτος ἐκεῖνο, "It naturally results that in (the course of) viewing we learn and reckon up what each thing is; for example that this (person) is a That." Thus, e.g., during Oidipous's scene with Teiresias (*Oidipous Tyrannos* 316–462) we can say, "Ah yes, this is a Choleric Man."

But identification and classification are not all, even for Aristotle. A further reach of learning is involved in observing how, e.g., anger (since we have just mentioned it) is aroused, and against whom—that whole range of phenomena surveyed in *Rhetoric* 2.5. Literature provides an opportunity to study this phenomenology of the emotions, superior to that offered by any other art, since poetry is more disinterested, more removed from our immediate concerns, than rhetoric or dialectic, and more revelatory of character and thought than are painting or sculpture.

But tragedy not only enables us to understand the passions, it also somehow enables us to feel them, to get at them from the inside. How does it do this? Aristotle is not very clear or explicit on this subject, but we can make out two points, at least in outline. As we have already seen, the specifically tragic emotions, pity and fear, are aroused by the plot/

action, and most effectively when the plot is inwoven with peripety and recognition. Our reaction is conditioned by our perception of the hero as "like us" and not deserving his misfortune; it is actually precipitated by the shock of the change to unhappiness, especially if augmented by peripety and/or recognition; but it must be *based* on a native human kinship, an in-tuneness, which unites us with the sufferer. We vibrate to his string.

This is not only a question of pity and fear but of emotional identification in general. Aristotle says in *Politics* 8.5.1340a12, ἀκροώμενοι τῶν μιμήσεων γίγνονται πάντες συμπαθεῖς, "In listening to imitations all men become fellow sufferers (or simply, feel in sympathy) (with the 'imitated' persons)." Or, as Plato says, *Republic* 10.605d, "You know that when the hero (of tragedy or epic) spreads himself in lamentations, we enjoy it and, surrendering ourselves (i.e., our rational selves), follow along συμπάσχοντες, feeling the emotion with (him)." We may wonder which of the two, Plato or Aristotle, is echoing the other; in any case they are describing the same phenomenon, Plato with deep disapproval, Aristotle with implied approval. Indeed, Aristotle has made it the basis of his theory.

The same idea is alluded to briefly at *Poetics* 17.55a29–30, but this time in specific connection with diction (λέξις): ὅσα δὲ δυνατόν (sc. δεῖ τοὺς μύθους συνιστάναι) καὶ τοῖς σχήμασιν συναπεργαζόμενον, "(one should construct the plots) also working them out (in detail), as far as possible, with the figures." Comparison with a1, τῇ λέξει συναπεργάζεσθαι, makes it clear that Aristotle means figures of speech: not in the usual sense, or not only in that sense, but the figures or forms which speech adopts when under the dominance of strong feelings; we shall document his meaning in a moment, from the *Rhetoric*. He now continues, a30–32, πιθανώτατοι γὰρ ἀπὸ τῆς αὐτῆς φύσεως οἱ ἐν τοῖς πάθεσίν εἰσιν, καὶ χειμαίνει ὁ χειμαζόμενος καὶ χαλεπαίνει ὁ ὀργιζόμενος ἀληθινώτατα, "For those in (the grip of) the passions are most persuasive on the basis of the same natural tendency(ies) (as ours); and (so it is that) the man feeling distress makes (us) feel distress, and the man in anger enrages, most truthfully."

The explication of these ideas is in *Rhetoric* 3.7.1408a10–24. The talk there is about appropriateness in diction, under the two headings of παθητική and ἠθικὴ λέξις. "Emotional" diction is appropriate (and effective) when it employs the turns and modes of expression that are actually used by, e.g., a16–19, the angry man, the one who experiences shock and shame, the one who feels pity. It is obvious that these are examples of people ἐν τοῖς πάθεσιν (*Poetics* 55a31), and that the point at issue is the way people naturally talk when they are in the grip of passion. Aristotle continues in the *Rhetoric* passage, a19–24, πιθανοῖ τὸ πρᾶγμα καὶ ἡ οἰκεία λέξις, "Appropriate diction also makes the business, the effort in hand, plausible"; for the hearer draws a false inference (παραλογίζεται) as a result of it. He knows how people talk when they are angry, etc.; this man before him is talking that way; ergo, this man is really angry, or whatever. Συννομοιοπαθεῖ ὁ ἀκούων ἀεὶ τῷ παθητικῶς λέγοντι, κἂν μηδὲν λέγῃ, "The hearer in each case sympathizes (feels a like feeling together) with the person who talks emotionally, even if (what) he says (is) nothing (i.e., nonsense)."

Of course in the domain of rhetoric all this is a matter of calculation, of deliberate, rehearsed effect, whereas in tragedy we have to assume that the characters—except in out-and-out rhetorical situations—express their real thoughts and feelings. It might seem therefore, once more, that Aristotle has underestimated the difference between the courtroom and the stage, or was not even conscious of it. But in this case that would be an unfair conclusion. Back of the characters stands the poet; *he* writes their speeches; and what Aristotle says (in the very next sentence of the *Poetics*, 17.55a32–34) shows that he *was* aware of the qualities that are required in the poet when he comes to write emotional speeches. In a more general sense, the passage we have been discussing clearly implies an essential basic idea: we human beings share a common emotional constitution which predisposes us to resonate in concert with the tragic characters' sufferings and/or expressed feelings. Not all of us in equal measure, perhaps, or in exactly the same way; that depends on our age, sex, social class and education, and so on. But the tendency to sympathize with other human beings is a part of our generic inheritance. Indeed I would connect it with the inborn human disposition to imitate and to enjoy imitations: 4.48b5–9, τό τε γὰρ μιμεῖσθαι σύμφυτον τοῖς ἀνθρώποις ἐκ παίδων ἐστί, "For imitation is connatural to men from childhood."

This seems the place to redeem a promise we made earlier (p. 141): to discuss the φιλάνθρωπον (*Poetics* 13.52b38–53a3). There are two possible interpretations: (1) the φιλάνθρωπον (the "human-loving") is a general sense of justice, or (2) it is a generalized and primitive kind of human sympathy. It still seems to me, all things considered, that the second meaning fits Aristotle's system better.[1] Thus the fall of the wicked

1. See the detailed discussion, *Argument* 368–371.

man into unhappiness will arouse the φιλάνθρωπον (we feel for him simply as a fellow human being) but neither pity nor fear, because we do not judge him to be "like us" or undeserving of his fate; the change of wicked men to happiness arouses none of the three emotions (there is no place for sympathy). If this line of argument is correct, the φιλάνθρωπον is very close to the general human sympathy we have been talking about, but without the element of judgment which is requisite for pity and fear.

The "peculiar pleasure" of tragedy is mentioned again, or rather implied, toward the end of chapter 14, 53a30–36. Aristotle speaks of the "double plot," with a happy ending for the better characters and the opposite for the worse, and says that although such endings are popular "thanks to the weakness of the audiences," this is "not a pleasure stemming from tragedy but one more appropriate, peculiar (οἰκεία), to comedy."

Two further mentions of the (or a) "peculiar pleasure" come in the chapters on epic, at 23.59a21 and 26.62b14. But although it is tempting to handle them here in order to finish off our discussion of the matter, both passages raise questions which can be properly dealt with only in the framework of Aristotle's whole theory of the epic; see Chapter 12 below. On the other hand we can no longer put off dealing with another problem which is at least equally difficult and much more notorious: the question of katharsis.

The main difficulty regarding katharsis stems from the unfortunate fact that the word appears only once in the *Poetics*, in the last clause of the definition of tragedy (6.49b27–28). According to Aristotle the definition is "gathered up from what has been said previously," but not a word has been said previously about katharsis, or even about pity and fear. Pity and fear later become key concepts in an important section of the *Poetics*, from the end of chapter 9 through chapter 14, and the "peculiar pleasure" puts in its appearance there; but nothing is ever said again about katharsis. Under these circumstances it is not to be wondered at that many, indeed most, interpreters have taken refuge in Book 8 of the *Politics*, 6.1341a21 and 7.1341b32ff., which discusses katharsis at some length and says for good measure that fuller details will be found in the *Poetics*. I protested against this procedure a good many years ago, saying that we must try to interpret the *Poetics* out of itself *if* that is possible.[2] But how is it possible when we have only one isolated phrase to go on, itself of doubtful meaning and bearing? The answer is that we must start

2. *Argument* 441–443.

by working on that phrase, interpreting it as carefully as we can, and then see whether it is indeed totally isolated or can be fitted into the structure of thought in the rest of the *Poetics*.

Here, then, is the phrase we have to interpret: 6.49b24, ἔστιν οὖν τραγῳδία μίμησις πράξεως . . . , δι' ἐλέου καὶ φόβου περαίνουσα τὴν τῶν τοιούτων παθημάτων κάθαρσιν, "Tragedy, then, is an imitation of an action . . . , through pity and fear bringing to completion the katharsis of such παθήματα." I have left several questions unresolved in the translation, so as not to prejudice the interpretation before it starts. I have elsewhere offered a summary of the prevailing understandings of the phrase, i.e., of the elements in it, and a series of new proposals concerning them.[3] There is no need to repeat all that here; it will suffice to indicate the crucial points.

First, as to the usual understandings, most interpreters are agreed that

1. *Δι' ἐλέου καὶ φόβου* means "*by means of* pity and fear."
2. "Pity and fear" are the emotions as we, the auditors or readers, experience them.
3. *Περαίνουσα* means "effectuating, achieving."
4. *Παθημάτων* is (are) again the emotions (of pity and fear) as we experience them.
5. *Κάθαρσιν* denotes an effect produced in or upon those emotions; purgation (the commonest modern interpretation), purification ("lustration"), or clarification.

It will be seen that understandings 2, 4, and 5 share a common presumption, that Aristotle is talking about the emotions of the spectator (or reader); 1 and 3 say that somehow an effect is produced upon them by themselves; and 5 identifies that effect as a purgation or purification.

I have not included the words τῶν τοιούτων, "of such," in this summary because on the usual understanding they involve an insoluble dilemma: either (a) they imply that there are other tragic emotions besides pity and fear—but Aristotle recognizes no other tragic emotions—or (b) they have to be read as equal to "these," which is impossible Greek. Also I have left παθημάτων (genitive plural) untranslated because a translation would prejudice the question at issue.

Against these understandings, I projected a set of proposals:

3. *Argument* 226–231.

1. Δι' ἐλέου καὶ φόβου is equivalent to δι' ἐλεεινῶν καὶ φοβερῶν (πραγμάτων) and means "through, in the course of, pathetic and fearful *incidents*."

2. Περαίνουσα means "bringing to completion," over the course of (διὰ) the pathetic and fearful incidents.

3. Τῶν τοιούτων means precisely what it says: "such," i.e., such as are pathetic and/or fearful.

4. Παθημάτων refers not to the spectator's emotions but to the tragic πάθη, the "fatal or painful" acts which we have identified as the basic stuff of tragedy (above, p. 144). (The longer genitive plural, in place of παθῶν, is perfectly Aristotelian and is in fact used in precisely this sense at 24.59b11.)

These amendments make it harder, not easier, to specify the sense of κάθαρσιν. So long as it denoted something that happened to the spectator's emotions, the choice was relatively simple, between purgation and purification. But if the παθήματα, or πάθη, are the tragic acts themselves impregnated with pity and fear, purgation makes no sense. What might a purification of them be? A clarification of their confused (obscure) significance? A neutralization of their admixture of pain? A purification of their motive? That is the tack I took in my earlier study of this problem.[4] My warrant was the word μιαρόν ("filthy," "polluted," shocking) in 14.53b39, 54a3, which I took to be that which is removed or neutralized by the katharsis. Μιαρόν bears witness to the persistence of the idea of pollution by the murder of blood kin, even in the fourth century and the enlightened mind of Aristotle. This idea had dominated archaic Greece (seventh through fifth centuries), accounting in no small measure for the rise of the Delphic Oracle to international prominence and power (Apollo there acted as the purifier and exorciser of blood pollution). The μιαρόν, it is said here, attaches to the knowing intent to kill a blood relative (e.g., Haimon's lunge at his father in *Antigone* 1232–1234); it does not obtain if the act is performed in ingorance but "recognized" afterward (and followed, we must assume, as in the case of Oidipous, by remorse), and even less if the recognition averts the killing (see above, p. 146).

On the basis of these statements I argued that the "purification" consisted, e.g., in the proof offered by Oidipous that his parricide and incest had been free of the "polluted" character that would have attached to

4. *Argument* 423–447.

them if they had been committed with knowledge of the facts. The proof in question was delivered, I said, by Oidipous's self-blinding and the remorse which he expressed at that moment.

In short, my solution of the katharsis problem consisted in bringing together in one consecutive pattern the ἄγνοια and ἁμαρτία, the ignorance and error which led to the tragic acts; the peripety and recognition which reversed the ignorance; and the movement of revulsion which followed that revelation. It was only natural that this solution should be accused of myopia, i.e., of being limited essentially to one play, the *Oidipous Tyrannos*. But the accusation ignores the substantial evidence in the *Poetics* that the *Oidipous* was Aristotle's ideal play, by which he set more store than any number of others; and it ignores the evidence of 13.53a18–22. Aristotle there lists six heroes, Alkmeon, Oidipous, Orestes, Meleagros, Thyestes, and Telephos, as exemplars of "the few houses around which the finest tragedies are constructed." A striking feature of this list is that we know of at least sixty-six tragedies devoted to the stories of these heroes (not counting further plays dealing with their *Nachkommen*), but of these sixty-six-plus only eight are extant: *Choëphoroi, Eumenides, Oidipous Tyrannos, Oidipous at Kolonos*, the *Elektras* of Sophokles and Euripides, *Orestes*, and *Iphigeneia among the Taurians*. Not all those are directly concerned with the main tragic acts (Oidipous's parricide and incest, Orestes' matricide), and only three of them (the *Elektras, Iphigeneia*) display anything like the inwoven structure of the *Oidipous Tyrannos*.

Thus an objection to my suggestion concerning katharsis on the ground that it applies to only one tragedy is itself myopic. Aristotle apparently knew dozens of plays which embodied his favorite pattern or patterns, and he explicitly rates them as "the finest." The discrepancy with our extant stock of tragedies is due, presumably, to the fact that the person or persons who made our selection (probably in the second century A.D.) did not employ Aristotle's criteria. There are still plenty of blood-and-guts, melodramatic plots in the extant repertory, but Aristotle's favorite "inwoven" structures, complete with ignorance, peripety, and recognition, are very sparsely represented. Presumably they did not appeal to the taste of the second century A.D.—and anyhow the selection appears to have been made for use in the schools, for much younger readers.

One other point needs clarification. My interpretation of katharsis was objective, in the sense that it applied the concept to the tragic πάθη—an *exculpation* of them, demonstrating that they were free of any "polluted" intent—rather than to the spectator's emotions. But this in no way contradicts what was said at the beginning of this chapter, that the final purpose of tragedy is to produce a certain aesthetic *and* emotional response in the spectator. He is still the final judge, the one who permits himself to feel the "peculiar pleasure" because he has become convinced that the tragic acts were "pure."

Yet I confess that my explanation may have been tailored too closely to the specific pattern of the *Oidipous*. I would now be inclined to accept some broader and looser definition, perhaps the "cleansing" suggested by H. D. F. Kitto.[5] But I would still resist the solution offered by Leon Golden,[6] that katharsis is simply an intellectual clarification of the *meaning* of the tragic happening; as I would resist any attempt to find a metaphysical dimension in Aristotle's theory.

Above all, I would emphasize again the isolation of the katharsis phrase. It has the air of something tacked on to the definition rather than an organic part of it: perhaps tacked on as an added response to Plato? However that may be, Aristotle has given us no clue to the vital question of how—if at all—katharsis is related to the οἰκεία ἡδονή. The latter appears only rarely in the *Poetics*, but often enough that we can form some idea of it; katharsis is never mentioned again after that one place in chapter 6. Nevertheless, it is reasonably clear that Aristotle thought the function (the "work," ἔργον) of tragedy was a special kind of pleasure and that this pleasure was produced by the poet's "structuring of the incidents," the σύστασις τῶν πραγμάτων, but with a specific emotional component stemming from pity and fear.

5. "Catharsis," in Luitpold Wallach, ed., *The Classical Tradition: Literary and Historical Studies in Honor of Harry Caplan* (Ithaca, N.Y. 1966) 133–147.

6. "Catharsis," *TAPA* 93 (1962) 51–60. Golden's view was repeated and expanded in O. B. Hardison's commentary to Golden's translation of the *Poetics*, *Aristotle's Poetics: A Translation and Commentary for Students of Literature* (Englewood Cliffs, N.J. 1968) 114–120, and by Golden himself in a number of subsequent articles.

12

Homer and Epic

THE *Poetics* contains no definition of epic to match that of tragedy. This is not an accident. Tragedy is the master genre, the model of serious mimetic art. Hence the discussion of it is put first, is very much longer (seventeen chapters, compared to three), and subsumes a large part of what Aristotle has to say about epic, leaving only the special properties of the latter to be treated separately. In other words the main body of the *Poetics*, through chapter 22, deals with serious poetry as a whole and with tragedy as its paramount specimen; chapters 23–25 are a kind of appendix.

Instead of a definition of epic there are several *comparisons* of epic with tragedy in which the latter serves as standard for the former—a standard to which epic as such never quite measures up. On the other hand Homer is Aristotle's model poet—a standard to which no other serious poet ever quite measures up.

Between the two terms of this paradox, the epic genre as such does not receive its due: not that it is weighed in a fair scale and found wanting, but that it is never really measured at all by criteria appropriate to it. The skewed verdict grows naturally out of Aristotle's youthful, one-sided thinking about mimetic poetry and his enthusiasm for drama.

We have already spoken of Plato's and Aristotle's conflicting views on Homer. The conflict goes very deep, to the roots of their respective intuitions of poetry; we shall therefore come back to it in Chapter 14. Let it suffice here to remind the reader that for Plato Homer is the master seducer, speaking to the soul of the listener with an uncannily compelling voice; to Aristotle he is a supremely gifted master builder. Aristotle never admits, except once by indirection, that Homer has done anything less than perfect; Homer is the only poet he ever calls "divine" (θεσπέσιος, 23.59a30). But let us begin our survey of this paradoxical subject at the other end, with the concept of epic.

Epic is one branch of the "nameless art," the one that uses a single kind of verses, without music (1.47a28-b9); it is serious, thanks to the σπουδαῖοι who are its chosen object (2.48a1–18); and it is a narrative genre (3.48a22–23). Here the difficulties and ambiguities begin, but we shall hold them off for a bit while we pursue the narrative idea. The first comparison of epic and tragedy is in 5.49b9–12. According to that passage, epic "followed" tragedy (see above, p. 102) up to the point of being a (1) sizable (2) imitation of (3) serious matters (4) in verse. In all these respects it is like tragedy; it is unlike it in having its verse "single," i.e., unmixed with song, and in being narrative; also in having no norm of length, whereas tragedy holds to a single circuit of the sun. As we saw, these stipulations mark epic as the inferior genre.

Parallel specifications are offered in chapters 23 and 24, those devoted specifically to epic, but with significant differences. Aristotle begins, 23.59a17, περὶ δὲ τῆς διηγηματικῆς καὶ ἐν μέτρῳ μιμητικῆς, "Concerning the mimetic art (which is) narrative and in verse (i.e., in verse only)," but goes on at once to requirements which, as he himself points out, are drawn from tragedy: a18–21, ὅτι δεῖ τοὺς μύθους καθάπερ ἐν ταῖς τραγῳδίαις συνιστάναι δραματικοὺς καὶ περὶ μίαν πρᾶξιν ὅλην καὶ τελείαν ἔχουσαν ἀρχὴν καὶ μέσα καὶ τέλος, ἵν' ὥσπερ ζῷον ἐν ὅλον ποιῇ τὴν οἰκείαν ἡδονήν, δῆλον, "That one should make (put together) the plots dramatic as in the tragedies, namely about a single whole and complete action having a beginning, middles"—note the plural—"and end, so that like a single whole animal it may produce its *peculiar pleasure*, is obvious."

Our first comment on this must be, it is by no means obvious that epics should be constructed like tragedies. That is not a description of epic, it is a prescription springing from Aristotle's love affair with tragedy and facilitated by the inverted order he has given to his treatment of the two genres. Epic, as the senior form, and especially with the great Homer leading its train, ought to have been treated first; but no, tragedy must come first and epic must follow in *its* train. As for Homer, he will turn out to be not really an epic poet but essentially a dramatist.

On the other hand, in our present passage the adjuration to make the epic structures "dramatic" does not mean that they are to consist of direct speech and action only, since Aristotle has just said, and emphasizes again in the next chapter (see below, p. 170), that epic is a narrative genre. Rather, as the context makes clear, the reference is to tightness of structure, strict logical sequence; and this is reinforced by a contrast between poetry and history: 23.59a21–24, "and that the structures (poems) not be like histories, in which it is necessary to give a report not of a single action but of a single time, all the things that happened during it to one person or many: events each of which has a chance relationship to the others." The particular bearing of these statements, and of the reference to the battles of Salamis and Himera, which immediately follows, does not concern us here; the important thing is the remark about Homer, 59a30–34. He showed his "divine" superiority to the other poets in not choosing to "make," compose, the Trojan War as a whole, although it had a beginning and an end. If he had, the plot would have been too "big" and not easy to survey in a single glance, or if it had kept to moderate length it would have been "complicated, obstructed, choked, by its multifariousness." That is, it would have lacked concentration and clarity.

We now come to what Aristotle puts forward as Homer's greatest achievement: 59a35–37, νῦν δ᾽ ἓν μέρος ἀπολαβὼν ἐπεισοδίοις κέχρηται αὐτῶν πολλοῖς, οἷον νεῶν καταλόγῳ καὶ ἄλλοις ἐπεισοδίοις οἷς διαλαμβάνει τὴν ποίησιν, "Instead, he has separated out one 'part' (the Wrath of Achilleus) and used many (others) of them as episodes, for example, the Catalogue of Ships and other episodes with which he intersperses his composition." Διαλαμβάνει does not mean "varies," "diversifies"; its sense is that the "episodes" are inserted between the successive stages of the central action and hold them apart, thus converting its relatively modest bulk into a long poem. Why Homer did this, and why—and to what extent—it is a good thing, will concern us hereafter.

In this special commendation of Homer Aristotle has invented a new use for an old word. Ἐπεισόδιον, from ἐπείσοδος, a "following entrance" (the entrance of a new character when others are already onstage), natively means simply an act or scene in drama between choral odes. This sense seems to attach to the derived verb ἐπεισοδιοῦν, 17.55b13: "to episodize," i.e., turn parts of the plot into actual scenes (the reference is to the writing of a play like the *Iphigeneia among the Taurians*). But Aristotle has extended ἐπεισόδιον to cover sections of any poem, epic or dramatic, which are dispensable, not an organic part of the central action. It is used in this derived sense in 17.55b13, 16, 23 in connection with the *Iphigeneia* and the *Odyssey*. The reference to the latter is clear enough: Aristotle considers only the return of Odysseus to Ithake and his final vengeance as belonging to the central plot; "the rest"—including, then, all of the Wanderings!—"are (just) episodes." The case of the *Iphigeneia* is less clear; Aristotle appears to waver between the two senses of ἐπεισόδιον. In any case the larger aspects of his innovation are not in doubt. The distinction between central action and

episodes in epic enables him to bring Homer's epics—but only Homer's
—into direct comparison with tragedy, almost as if they were specimens
of the same genre. In chapter 4, 48b34–49a6, the relationship is that
of model and imitation. In the *Iliad* and the *Margites* Homer "sketched"
(ὑπέδειξεν, b37) the essential forms, τὰ σχήματα, of tragedy and
comedy, and once their outlines had "just appeared" (παραφανείσης τῆς
τραγῳδίας καὶ κωμῳδίας, a2–3), the epic and iambic poets rushed to
develop them, "because these (new) forms were greater and more to be
prized than those (old ones)," a5–6. What Aristotle is doing here de-
serves attention. He is rating artistic ideas higher than primitive rituals
or tribal taboos in the development of poetry, offering not only a histori-
cal thesis about the development of tragedy but a general idea of artistic
forms as stimulating and controlling the growth of literature.

Homer appears here in his greatest role. Not content with producing
two major works of art, he inspired future generations to realize a new
ideal. Aristotle's Homer is in fact a model of self-transcendence. He is no
mere epic poet but the harbinger of something better than epic: the
drama. And not only on the serious side: Homer is also the animating
spirit in comedy (see Chapter 13 below). No other poet plays such a
seminal or commanding role. And he is able to do it because the struc-
tures he creates are already quasi-dramatic, in two senses. First, the per-
sons he presents in his mixture of direct speech and narrative are to
all intents and purposes dramatic characters. Aristotle makes this explic-
it in 23.60a5–11. Homer "alone of the poets"—presumably, the epic
poets—understands that the poet himself should talk as little as possible.
The others ἀγωνίζονται, are "in competition," onstage themselves,
the whole time; ὁ δὲ ὀλίγα φροιμιασάμενος εὐθὺς εἰσάγει ἄνδρα ἢ
γυναῖκα ἢ ἄλλο τι ἦθος, καὶ οὐδέν' ἀήθη ἀλλ' ἔχοντα ἦθος, "while he,
after a few words of preface, immediately brings on a man, a woman, or
some other character, and none characterless but (all) having character."
This introduces Aristotle's new term ἦθος for the dramatic persons and
uses it for a neat oxymoron: if Homer's characters have character, it is
clear many characters in other poems do not. We are reminded of their
"characterless tragedies" of 6.50a25: evidently many of their characters
had no character.

But dramatic directness and force are not the whole of Homer's legacy.
The other part is dramatic economy, tightness of form: what Aristotle
designates by "dramatic" in 4.48b35–36 and 23.59a19. This refers to
his special invention which is attributed to the *Iliad* in 23.59a35–37: the
structural pattern of central action plus episodes. As we have already

seen, 17.55b16–23, Aristotle also finds this structure in the *Odyssey*. There the central story is called the λόγος, the "argument," or the ἴδιον, the "special" part; "the rest is episodes." A similar commendation of the *Odyssey* was issued in 8.51a22–29. The authors of *Herkleïds*, *Theseïds*, etc., thought that unity of the hero would assure unity in the poem; but Homer, "either through art or through nature," saw that it was not so and therefore did not "compose," include in his poem, everything that befell Odysseus such as his being wounded on Parnassos when young or his feigning madness in order to dodge military service when the troops assembled to sail for Troy.

Alongside these errors peculiar to the biographical epic we can set others specific to the chronicle epic. Aristotle characterizes these at 23.59a21–30 as histories-in-verse. The poets of the Epic Cycle (presumably the main ones Aristotle has in mind) considered it their duty to report "everything that happened to one person or more during a single time span" (a23–24). Homer's procedure is praised in contrast to theirs (a31–32): he did not "compose the (Trojan) War as a whole either," i.e., any more than he "composed" Odysseus' life as a whole.[1]

But here doubts and cavils begin to arise. The Cyclic poets did not misconceive their mission. They were in fact historians; their job was to preserve the early history of the Greek nation (that they did it in verse is a function of their times, not of the content), and virtue in that kind of pursuit consists in preserving everything, so far as possible. Aristotle shows no awareness of these governing principles, although he must have been aware that the Greek myths, or at least the heroic legends, were historical at bottom.

There is, however, another possibility. In view of the prescriptive note with which chapter 23 begins ("One should make the plots 'dramatic,'" etc.) it is possible that Aristotle is not thinking of the Cyclic poets after all or not only of them, but of somebody closer to home. Antimachos of Kolophon, an older contemporary of Plato, wrote, along with poems in other genres, a *Thebaïd* in twenty-four books. An epic poem of that length (as long as the *Iliad* or *Odyssey*), if it was not constructed on the Homeric plan, and it pretty clearly was not, must have included every scrap of material Antimachos could find in the archives concerning the Tale of Thebes. In other words, his poem would appear to have been a Cyclic epic long after its time, and without the historical justification which the Cyclic poets could claim for their work. But the most signifi-

---

1. Else's interpretation of this phrase is set out in detail at *Argument* 581–582.

cant thing about Antimachos, for our purpose here, is that Plato admired the *Thebaïd* excessively: he even sent Herakleides Pontikos to Kolophon after the poet's death to secure a reliable copy of it.[2] Thus, although the work must have been written well before Aristotle's time, around the turn of the fourth century, it was perhaps seen in the Akademy as an embodiment of Plato's ideal of poetry: inclusive, not mimetic in his sense, respectful toward the gods (?), conscientious about the "facts" of the tradition. All this, if even approximately correct, might account for Aristotle's decisive but discreetly veiled rejection of chronicle epics. (Were persons unknown starting to write them again?)

Another question pertains to Homer himself and his superior method of "picking out" one part and using it as an armature on which to drape episodes. It has been noticed, independently of Aristotle, that the chronology of the Trojan War is seriously distorted in the *Iliad*. Most of its events (from the arrival of the Achaians at Troy) are crowded into a few weeks in the tenth year, leaving very little visible content for the other nine. The distortion is most evident in the large number of incidents which would necessarily or naturally have come at the beginning of the war: the Catalogue of Ships (actually a record of the muster of Achaian contingents of men and ships at Aulis, with a much shorter and obviously secondary muster of the Trojans and their allies at Troy); the abortive duel of Paris and Menelaos, which was to decide the conflict in place of the war; the scene that became known as the τειχοσκοπία, the Viewing from the Wall, in which Helen for the first time identifies the chief Achaian leaders for the benefit of Priam (this after more than nine years of conflict!); the first review of the troops by Agamemnon, with the treacherous bow-shot of Pandaros and the symbolic wounding of Menelaos; the first actual meeting in battle and killing of Simoeisios (4.473–489), the first young sacrifice to the cruelty of war; the parting of Hektor and Andromache; and Hektor's first duel, with Aias.

Among them, these episodes fill most of the first third of the poem. "Episode" was not their natural status; Homer made them into episodes to follow his new ἀρχή. Ἀρχή, "beginning," was defined in 7.50b27–28 as "that which itself does not necessarily follow something else, but after it some different thing naturally is or happens." Aristotle's theory of "beginning," "middles" (plural in 23.59a20), and "end" seems to me one of the most brilliant and original of his insights in the *Poetics*; but back of it stands the creative genius of Homer. As his new ἀρχή Homer had selected, or perhaps invented, the Quarrel, which has nothing to do with the beginning of the war. And since it "does not necessarily follow something else," he was free to locate it anywhere he chose within the agreed-on time frame of the war—preferably as close to its end as possible, so as to partake of the atmosphere of doom that hangs over the whole. But with this last remark we have passed the boundary of what can properly be called Aristotelian. Aristotle does not recognize "doom."

We saw that Aristotle found in the *Odyssey* the same structure, central action plus episodes, as in the *Iliad*. But the *Odyssey* works differently. A master time frame is established at the beginning of the poem, with the assembly of the gods. We then go successively (although the events of the two sequences are to be understood as virtually contemporaneous) with Athene to Telemachos in Ithake and with Hermes to Odysseus on Kalypso's isle; Books 1–4 bring Telemachos to Sparta; 5–8 and 13 move Odysseus via Scheria (but with a long central interlude, 9–12, in which with Odysseus as narrator we go back to the beginning of his Return) to Ithake, where Telemachos will at last join him; and so toward the final denouement. The play with time here is several degrees more sophisticated than the simple inversions and compressions of the *Iliad*. But was Aristotle aware of the problems of time in either poem?

An answer may be implied in what Aristotle says about the length of poems in 24.59b18–28. The passage begins by recalling the ὅρος τοῦ μήκους (μεγέθους), the norm of length which was set up in 7.51a9–15 (see above, p. 107): that length in which a shift from adversity to prosperity or the reverse can be accomplished plausibly or necessarily. That was offered as a norm for tragedy, and we were already told in 5.49b14 that epic has no such norm. Now Aristotle seems to accept the norm for epic, too: "For beginning and end must be capable of being seen in one view." And he suggests that this would happen "if the (epic) structures were shorter than the ancient ones and approximated to the bulk (or quantity) of the tragedies offered at a single sitting." Whether Aristotle is referring to connected trilogies or simply to the established practice that each poet offered three plays in the competitions, it is an interesting fact that the Wrath of Achilleus does approximate fairly closely to this length (about 4,200 lines). But of course the *Iliad* (15,693 lines) and *Odyssey* (12,105) as wholes enormously exceed the norm. So Aristotle adds at once, ἔχει δὲ πρὸς τὸ ἐπεκτείνεσθαι πολύ τι ἡ ἐποποιία ἴδιον . . . διὰ τὸ διήγησιν εἶναι ἔστι πολλὰ μέρη ἅμα ποιεῖν πραττόμενα, "But epic has a very large special capacity for extra extension of its size . . . , because it is narrative, it is possible to insert many parts at the same time they are done," whereas (the omitted part says) tragedy can only represent the action that is enacted onstage at any one time.

Aristotle is referring here to what we may call the "magic carpet" aspect of the narrative mode: since the time of narration is equally removed from *all* the events narrated, the narrator can move among them, backward or forward or sideward, with sovereign freedom, whereas in the theater the action going forward onstage at any one moment establishes a master time frame which makes other actions relatively past or future and so less easily accessible to the poet. The dramatist, in spite of his freedom in other directions, is in bondage to one of those "perceptions that necessarily attend upon the poetic (i.e., the dramatic) art," 15.54b15–16 (see above, p. 137). This thesis is subtle, but with an analytical subtlety which I think we can safely attribute to Aristotle (in contradistinction to *aesthetic* subtlety, which was not his long suit).

We must not pass over one brief remark, the only place in the *Poetics* where Aristotle ever admits or even implies that Homer was less than perfect. It is the statement quoted just above from 24.59b20–21, that epics would observe the norm of length if they were "shorter than the ancient ones," with the immediately following assertion that epic has a special license to expand its bulk additionally by episodes. This is special pleading; for the awkward fact is that the *Iliad* and *Odyssey*, Aristotle's favorite "ancient poems," were also much the longest, at least twice as long as any of the Cyclic epics. We noted some time ago, in connection with 5.49b12–14, that Aristotle seems to waver between two different conceptions of the respective lengths of tragedy and epic: (1) that one is shorter, the other longer, (2) that the one is of relatively unvarying, the other of widely varying length—i.e., it has no effective norm of length. And now Aristotle compounds the apparent confusion by saying that the norm of length is valid and would apply if epics were shorter than the "ancient ones."

Actually, these two views are not necessarily incompatible; they simply look at different aspects of the total situation. Epics as a class did indeed vary enormously in length, and the Homeric epics were indeed enormously longer than any tragedy (or any other epic, at least before Antimachos's *Thebaïd*). But Aristotle is not about to admit this embarrassing state of affairs in explicit terms, or to mention Homer's name outright. The result is his thesis of the *extra* extension of epic bulk (by episodes). But that gets him into a new and even more serious contradiction.

The reason alleged for the optional expansion is that epic is a narrative genre. But Homer is not a typical epic poet; he is more a dramatist than a narrator. This point was implied in 3.48a21–22, if my emendation there was justified (see above, p. 83), and is made with all possible explicitness in a passage just below, 24.60a5–9: Ὅμηρος δὲ ἄλλα τε πολλὰ ἄξιος ἐπαινεῖσθαι καὶ δὴ καὶ ὅτι μόνος τῶν ποιητῶν οὐκ ἀγνοεῖ ὃ δεῖ ποιεῖν. αὐτὸν γὰρ δεῖ τὸν ποιητὴν ἐλάχιστα λέγειν, οὐ γάρ ἐστι κατὰ ταῦτα μιμητής. οἱ μὲν οὖν ἄλλοι αὐτοὶ μὲν δι' ὅλου ἀγωνίζονται, μιμοῦνται δὲ ὀλίγα καὶ ὀλιγάκις, "Homer deserves praise in many other respects, but particularly because he alone of the (epic) poets is not unaware of what it is necessary to compose. Namely the poet himself should say as little as possible; for in those parts he is not an imitator. Now the others are (on view) competing all the way through, and imitate few things and seldom." The interpreters, by and large, have not known what to make of this passage; some have declared it eccentric or even suspect.[3] On the contrary, it states with exemplary clarity what made Homer the supreme poet in Aristotle's eyes: that he was essentially a dramatist.

Although the tension between Homer the dramatist and epic as narrative pervades Aristotle's chapters on epic, it has been insufficiently noticed. Whenever he formulates a prescription for epic, it derives from Homer: that the plots should be "dramatic," not like histories, 23.59a18–24; that a central plot plus episodes is the proper structure for an epic, 59a30–37; that epic should have the same species as poetry, 24.59b7–16; that the poet should not talk himself but "bring on" characters, 60a9–11; that the marvelous, τὸ θαυμαστόν, is required in both genres but has special opportunities in epic, 24.60a11–18; that epic needs to "tell lies *comme il faut*," 60a18–26; that λέξις should take a back seat to character and thought, 60b2–5.

These prescriptions share two recurrent features. First, most of them are introduced by the word δεῖ, "it must," "it is necessary," "one should": 23.59a18; 24.59b8, 11, 60a11, 19, 23, 26, 34, 60b3. But δεῖ never denotes an external or mechanical necessity imposed simply by the fact that one is writing something called "epic"; in every case it means an inward, an ideal necessity derived from the example of Homer and projected as a preachment: "one should," "one must." In every case

3. E.g., D. W. Lucas, in his commentary on the *Poetics* (Oxford 1968) 226: "This has nothing to do with likenesses or differences between epic and tragedy; the passage stands in isolation."

Homer is named or implied as the model, and Aristotle remarks several times (23.59a29, 37; 24.60a8), disparagingly, that "the others" do not follow his example. This tension, as I have called it, betrays a very curious state of affairs: that most of Aristotle's theory of epic is deliberately not based on a study of the genre per se, or of its normal practitioners (we cannot even be sure how many of them he had read), but on the solitary genius of Homer.

There are some places where the definition of epic is drawn from its normal status as a narrative art. One of these we have already discussed: 24.59b18–27, on the difference between epic and tragedy with respect to length. But we did not discuss the sequel, 59b27–31: ὑφ' ὧν οἰκείων ὄντων αὔξεται ὁ τοῦ ποιήματος ὄγκος. ὥστε τοῦτ' ἔχει τὸ ἀγαθὸν καὶ τὸ μεταβάλλειν καὶ ἐπεισοδιοῦν ἀνομοίοις ἐπεισοδίοις. τὸ γὰρ ὅμοιον ταχὺ πληροῦν ἐκπίπτειν ποιεῖ τὰς τραγῳδίας, "by which (the episodes), if they are germane, the weight (or dignity) of the (epic) poem is increased. So it has this advantage, and (that of) varying, and 'episodizing' it with dissimilar episodes; for the similar, quickly satiating (the spectator), is what makes tragedies fail (fall out, i.e., from the competitions)."

So says Aristotle in chapter 24. In the final judicial comparison of epic and tragedy he sings a different tune: 26.62a18–b3, "Furthermore (tragedy is superior) in that the end of the imitation is (comes) in less length; for the more concentrated is more enjoyable than that which is diluted with much time: I mean, for example, if one should put the *Oidipous* in as many verses as the *Iliad*." Here the question is strictly and solely between the two genres (Homer is not a direct issue), and epic's extra length is accounted a handicap rather than an advantage. And the next, closely related, argument tells even more heavily against epic (62b3–11, given in summary here, because the text is in some disarray): still less enjoyable (than an overextended *Oidipous*) is the kind of unity we find in epic. Several tragedies can be made from any epic, of whatever quality; thus the *Iliad* is as unified as an epic can be and yet has episodes which bulk large in themselves. The result, even if someone produces an epic with a single plot like the *Iliad*, is that if kept short it appears truncated, and if of suitable length, diluted. (The admission that the *Iliad* lacks unity after all is made even more explicit at 18.56a12, where Aristotle says forthrightly, ἐποποιικὸν δὲ λέγω τὸ πολύμυθον, "By 'epic' "— i.e., having epic character—"I mean that which has many μῦθοι," and the *Iliad* is cited as an example.)

Epic has suffered a peripety here, since chapter 24. It appears that

Homer's brilliant experiment was a failure after all. What has happened? To attempt an answer (by no means an assured one), we must see what Aristotle has to say in the rest of chapters 24 and 26, and to some extent in chapter 25 as well.

One of the quiet sectors of the field is the domain of meter. Aristotle broaches this subject in 24.59b31–60a5. The hexameter (the "heroic verse") became wedded to epic ἀπὸ τῆς πείρας, "as a result of trial (and error)," 59b32. The reason is that the heroic verse was inherently suited to narration—"the nature (of the genre) itself" conducted the trial, 60a4–5; cf. 4.49a24—by virtue of being στασιμώτατον καὶ ὀγκωδέστατον τῶν μέτρων, "the most stationary and majestic (weightiest) of the verses," b34–35. These two epithets must not be taken as mere synonyms. "Stationary" refers to the relative slowness of dactylic verse, from its "even," 2 + 2 rhythm (one long syllable paired with another, or with two shorts). The other adjective speaks of the dignity, majesty, which inheres in the steady pace of the "even" rhythm, in contrast to the κινητικά, the rhythms of movement, the iambic and trochaic (1 + 2), 59b37–60a1.

Obviously Aristotle is projecting epic here as the leisurely genre, the one with all the time in the world at its disposal. But how does Homer, with his "dramatic" plots and his tightening of the knot, fit into this picture? Not very well. Except for his long, leisurely similes—perhaps the most conspicuous feature of his style to one approaching it from outside—Aristotle's Homer sorts ill with the idea of "stationary" majesty, especially as his dramatic qualities are asserted so sharply in the very next section, 60a5–11 (see above, p. 166). If his dramatic vein was so pronounced, why did he not take up iambic trimeter as his appropriate medium, like tragedy (4.49a23–28; see above, p. 93)? Alas, Aristotle was ultimately the prisoner of reality. The hexameter was once and for all the chosen medium of epic as the trimeter was of tragedy (and comedy)—nothing to be done about it.

The concept of epic as narrative winds in and out of the rest of chapter 24 but cannot quite be called a controlling theme. (Actually this part of the chapter has an episodic air, as of miscellaneous short paragraphs thrown together more or less at random; but this impression may be deceptive. Thus 60a5–11, on "Homer the dramatist," stands between two sections which emphasize the narrative character of epic—perhaps to emphasize Homer's dramatic prowess by way of contrast.)

The section 60a11–18 introduces the concept of τὸ θαυμαστόν, the marvelous. This, says Aristotle, is an effect legitimately sought by both epic and tragedy, but the ἄλογον, the irrational or illogocal, "through which the marvelous is most (best) achieved," is more available in epic because one doesn't actually see it, 60a14, διὰ τὸ μὴ ὁρᾶν εἰς τὸν πράττοντα, "on account of not seeing (in to, all the way to) the doer." For example, the pursuit of Hektor by Achilleus, *Iliad* 22.131ff., with the Achaians standing back, not attacking him because Achilleus waves them off (205), would appear ridiculous on the stage, but in epic λανθάνει, "it escapes notice."

The topic of Homeric "lies," ψευδῆ, 60a18–26, has a certain affinity with what precedes and follows, but gains piquancy from the attacks Plato had made in *Republic* 2 and 3 on Homer's "lies" about the gods and heroes (see above, p. 19). There, as we have seen, Plato singles out as "ugly lies," lies badly told, stories about gods and heroes which in no way resemble their originals, like painted portraits which give no likeness (2.377d–e). A poetic example of failure to achieve likeness (ἀνομοίως μιμήσασθαι) is the lamentation of Zeus over Hektor, *Iliad* 22.168, "Ay me, I see with my (own) eyes a dear man being pursued around the city, and my heart laments (for him)." This portrait, says Plato, has no resemblance to the original: high gods do not disturb their peace by lamenting over mortals.

To this kind of attack on Homeric ψευδῆ Aristotle makes no direct rejoinder either here or anywhere else in the *Poetics*. He says nothing at all about Homer's portraits of the gods. The example he chooses for commendation (24.60a18–19, "Homer has taught the others also how to lie *comme il faut*," ψευδῆ λέγειν ὡς δεῖ) is of an altogether different character.

In *Odyssey* 19, the book which the Greeks called Νίπτρα, the (Foot) Washing, the disguised Odysseus tells Penelope a false tale about having seen Odysseus on his way to Troy and buttresses it with some true details of how the hero was garbed at that time. From these true details Penelope draws a παραλογισμός (a20), a false inference: not that he *is* Odysseus but that he *saw* Odysseus (and therefore is not Odysseus). This whole scene plays on earth, between human beings; gods are not involved. Leaving aside its importance to Odysseus (to maintain his disguise), we can see that it touches on a theme especially interesting to Aristotle precisely in his Akademy period: the difference between true and false inference. (See the *Topics*, passim, and especially its concluding book on paralogisms, the so-called *Sophistic Refutations*.) But there is more.

Odysseus tells six false tales in all, to as many different people, beginning with the goddess Athene, at various points on his homeward journey and on Ithake. They all have one master trait in common: though literally false to Odysseus' own case (he usually claims to be a Cretan; he has been a pirate, a merchant; etc.), they are all set in the real, perilous world of commerce and seafaring in the eastern Mediterranean in the eighth to seventh centuries. In other words, although the events Odysseus narrates do not happen to have happened to him, they did happen to many real people and *could* have happened to him. They are οἷα ἂν γένοιτο and, in an important sense, more real that the fictive adventures which Odysseus retails at such length in the Wanderings. Indeed the relationship between "reality" and "lies," fictions, myths, dreams, is far more subtle and complex in the *Odyssey* as a whole than in most literary works. That is one reason for its perennial fascination.

Now, out of this complex Aristotle has chosen to draw one feature which obviously interested him. Did he perceive the depth and subtlety of the whole? It is a risky question, but I for one should like to give him the benefit of the doubt and think that this is his tribute to Homer the magician; and I am encouraged in this by the last section of chapter 24, to which we now come. It begins with a paradox (60a26–29) by which Aristotle obviously set some store, since he will quote it again in chapter 25 (61b11–12): προαιρεῖσθαί τε δεῖ ἀδύνατα εἰκότα μᾶλλον ἢ δυνατὰ ἀπίθανα, τούς τε λόγους μὴ συνίστασθαι ἐκ μερῶν ἀλόγων, "One should choose probable impossibles rather than unpersuasive possibles, and the plots (arguments) should not be constructed out of irrational 'parts.'" Here Aristotle begins with "possibles" and "impossibles" and then substitutes ἄλογα, "irrationals," but the meaning is the same. The basic point was made in chapter 9, 51b15–32 (see p. 113 above). "Possibility" has two senses, one according to the standard of ordinary reality, the other according to "probability or necessity," and we saw how energetically Aristotle worked to establish the paradox that only some of the things that have actually happened are probable and therefore possible in this second, higher sense. The final test, always, is not what can actually happen but what the poet can make us believe (ἀπίθανα, "unpersuasive," makes the contrast clear).

Aristotle next proceeds, 60a27ff., to set up a scale of alternatives. Best of all (μάλιστα, "preferably," a28) is that the λόγοι, the plots or arguments, have nothing irrational about them. Next best: if they do have, the irrational should be placed ἔξω τοῦ μυθεύματος (a29), "outside the plot structure," as with the *Oidipous* (the implausibility in question is Oidipous's not knowing the manner of Laios's death). This is contrasted with two cases where it is ἐν τῷ δράματι, one to the charge of Sophokles, the other of Aischylos. Another alternative is, a34–35, ἂν δὲ θῇ, καὶ φαίνηται εὐλογωτέρως, ἐνδέχεσθαι καὶ ἄτοπον, "But if he does put it (in), and it comes through more plausibly (than not), even an absurdity is admissible." Θῇ is a strong word, almost equivalent to ὑποθῇ, "posits"; φαίνηται (φαίνεσθαι) is used elsewhere by Aristotle to signify something "coming across" to the listener or reader; and ἄτοπον is (deliberately) stronger than ἄλογον but not essentially different— something like "wildly improbable." The example (a35–b1) makes Aristotle's meaning clear: "The irrationalities in the *Odyssey*, surrounding the setting ashore (of Odysseus on Ithake), would obviously be intolerable if an inferior poet composed them." As D. W. Lucas suggests,[4] Aristotle probably has in mind the whole sequence 13.70–196: the stowing of Odysseus and his gear in the Phaiakians' ship; his magical deep sleep ("most like unto death," 80); the preternatural speed and sureness of the ship's passage; the off-loading, with Odysseus still asleep; the return journey and metamorphosis of the ship into a rock by the vengeful Poseidon; to the moment of the hero's awakening in the homeland which he (magically) does not recognize.

The sequence is indeed magical, especially the lines (86–88) that evoke the rapid running of the ship, "swifter than any hawk." It is a bravura specimen of Homeric art. And Aristotle puts his finger—for once—squarely on the secret. It is in the language: 60b1–2, "The poet conceals the gross improbability by sweetening (ἡδύνων) it with his other excellences." Ἡδύνων recalls the ἡδυσμένος λόγος in the definition of tragedy, and the next sentence confirms the identificaton: "One should put forth one's best effort with λέξις in the parts that are neither full of character nor of thought"—an excellent description of the Voyage and Setting Ashore. But Aristotle's point is not really a negative one. He does not mean to say, "Just make sure that a passage has no character or thought in it, and you may spread on the poetic language at will." This third alternative is available only to supreme poets—in fact, only to Homer.

This completes our survey of what is said about epic in the main body of the *Poetics*. It remains to consider two chapters, 25 and 26, which stand a little apart from the main body. We shall begin with 26. This σύγκρισις or comparative evaluation of tragedy and epic might seem to be a natural conclusion to a study of the two genres; but chapter 26 does

4. Commentary (above, n. 3) 229.

not quite provide a full summary of the argument of the *Poetics*. Another beginning tack will be more fruitful.

We discovered in chapter 4, 49a7–9, a remark which pointed in the direction of chapter 26; see above, p. 95. Aristotle had said, just before that, that epic poets turned to tragedy (and iambic poets to comedy) because these forms outlined by Homer were superior to the old ones. He then said, in the passage that interests us here, that "a review of the question whether even tragedy is adequate to the forms, . . . , is another story." We pointed out that the phrase ἄλλος λόγος, "another story," is normally a signal that the topic in question will be discussed later, in another place. We also pointed out that the question did not so much concern epic as tragedy: whether it "already," even it (i.e., in comparison with epic), was adequate to the master forms adumbrated by Homer. These forms were (1) "dramatic" imitation of (2) serious persons, or rather their actions.

We now find that chapter 26 fills these specifications. It institutes a final comparison between epic and tragedy, but in the interest of tragedy. And we can discern the reason, or at least the occasion, for the comparison. It is that certain unspecified people (τις, "somebody," 61b27; φασιν, "they say," 62a3, subject unstated) have rated epic above tragedy as "less vulgar"; and we can guess with considerable confidence that these unnamed critics are—Plato. Our warrant for this identification is in the *Laws*.

The *Laws* does not return to Plato's open attacks on Homer and tragedy, in the vein of *Ion*, *Gorgias*, and *Republic* 2 and 3. On the other hand the work still envisions a strict control of all literature in the state and proposes a formal apparatus of censorship, δοκιμασία, 6.763ff. More relevant to our immediate concern is a passage in Book 2, 658a–659c. Plato imagines an open competition for all comers, in "music," sports, or racing, but devoted to pleasure only (ἡδονῆς πέρι, 658a9), so that "whoever pleases the spectators most" (b1) shall win. He then distinguishes the various kinds and levels of offering according to who would be pleased by them: little children would vote for the jugglers and prestidigitators; bigger children for comedy; teenagers, educated women, and "more or less the whole common crowd," for tragedy; "but we old men would no doubt award the pleasure-prize to the rhapsode who presents artistically (καλῶς) the *Iliad* or *Odyssey*, or something from Hesiod" (658d). And the Athenian suggests to his elderly colleagues that their age-mates would be judging correctly, ὀρθῶς (658e).

This passage supplies the clue we need for understanding chapter 26. Aristotle is responding either to the *Laws* or to oral statements of like tenor in the Akademy, and this accounts for the particular physiognomy of the chapter. Its first section, 61b26–62a4, is devoted to the charge made by those who favor epic; but the burden of the charge, as reported here, is not the merits of epic but the deficiencies of tragedy, and these deficiencies boil down to just one: tragedy is vulgar, φορτική. The word is repeated four times in this short passage, thrice near the beginning (61b27, 29, 33) and then again, lest we miss it, at the end (62a4). Although Aristotle, as usual when he is criticizing or correcting Plato, mentions no name, the section is strewn with coded references to Plato. Thus the "spectators" of epic are twice called "better" by its partisans (61b28, βελτίους; 62a2, ἐπιεικεῖς, "morally superior" = βελτίους); Plato had characterized his old judges as βελτίστους καὶ ἱκανῶς πεπαιδευμένους, "best and adequately educated," *Laws* 658e9.

Again, tragedy is called ἡ ἅπαντα μιμουμένη, "the (art) that imitates anything and everything," 61b28–29—a clear allusion to *Republic* 3.397a–398b, with its insistent leitmotiv, the contrast between the imitator of the morally superior man (τοῦ ἐπιεικοῦς, 397d4) and the one who is willing and able to imitate absolutely everything (πάντα διηγήσεται, 397a2; πάντα ἐπιχειρήσει μιμεῖσθαι, a3—the "everything" then specified in rich detail: thunder, the soughing of winds, noises of wheels, pipes, trumpets, animal cries, etc., etc., etc.—and again at the end of the passage, μιμεῖσθαι πάντα χρήματα, 398a2).

It is insinuated, though not actually said, in this astonishing passage in *Republic* 3 that the tragic poet is this figure of contempt, the person who is able and willing to sink so low as to imitate everything. The lower he is on the moral scale, ὅσῳ φαυλότερος ᾖ, 397a1–2, the more willing he will be to do so. Nor is the theme of pleasure missing. The interlocutor Adeimantos, when asked which character to admit into the new state, votes for the "unmixed imitator of the good man," 397d4–5, but Sokrates points out that the opposite type will be "much the most pleasing to children, their accompanying slaves, and most of the *canaille*." We see that Plato has not essentially changed his mind about tragedy in the interval between *Republic* 3 and *Laws* 2, he has only moderated the violence of his attack and moved part of its audience up a notch, from children and slaves to young teenagers and educated women—but the mob (ὁ ὄχλος, τὸ πλῆθος) is still there.

The clinching piece of evidence, however, is in the statement, 62a3, that the superior "spectators" of epic οὐδὲν δέονται τῶν σχημάτων, "have no need of the figures." It is not said explicitly what figures these are. They must include dance figures, but need not be limited to them: gestures and movements of the body in acting are surely to be thought of also. Now, Plato in *Laws* 2 makes much (653d–e, 657d, 664e, 672c) of the tendency of the young—of all species—to skip and hop and jump and run, whereas the elderly have lost their spryness (τὸ ἐλαφϱόν, 657d4) and are content to watch the young at their play. The connection is not made explicit in the *Poetics* but must be implied in the remark about the figures; no other reason is as probable.

Aristotle fills out his account of the charge against tragedy with some details about flute-players and actors which are not very luminous to us, except that two of the three actors mentioned (Mynniskos and Kallippides) were famous in the fifth century and thus may, as I once suggested,[5] spring from oral reminiscences by Plato about the theater of his youth.

The indictment is stated briefly (61b27–62a4, thirteen lines), Aristotle's counterargument even more succinctly (62a5–b15, twenty-nine lines, but broaching seven different points). Here we find the peripety already alluded to (above, p. 172). Up to now we have heard repeatedly about Homer's genius and how it held up a beacon not only for epic but for tragedy. Now he is not mentioned, except in the penultimate argument, 62b7–11, and there it turns out that even his work was not sufficiently unified. Epic now stands naked before the bar of judgment: she can no longer hide behind Homer.

This argument in rebuttal puts forward seven points in briefest possible compass (except the sixth):

1. 62a5–8: The accusation lodges against the art of acting, not poetry, and can be brought equally against epic and lyric delivery.
2. a8–11: Not all movement is to be "censored out" (ἀποδοϰιμαστέα, a reference to the *Laws*), but only that of low characters.
3. a11–14: Tragedy does not have to have "movement" (performance) to reveal its characters.
4. a14–17: Tragedy has all the "parts" that epic has, and music (source of the "most vivid pleasures") besides.
5. a17–18: Tragedy has vividness, τὸ ἐναϱγές, in reading as well as on the stage.

5. *Argument* 637–638.

6. a18-b11: Epic is less unified (more "diluted") and therefore less pleasurable—even a work like the *Iliad*.

7. b12–15: What appears to be meant as a clinching argument: εἰ οὖν τούτοις τε διαφέρει πᾶσιν καὶ ἔτι τῷ τῆς τέχνης ἔργῳ (δεῖ γὰρ οὐ τὴν τυχοῦσαν ἡδονὴν ποιεῖν αὐτὰς ἀλλὰ τὴν εἰρημένην), φανερὸν ὅτι κρείττων ἂν εἴη, μᾶλλον τοῦ τέλους τυγχάνους τῆς ἐποποιίας. "If, then, it (tragedy) is superior in all these respects and also with respect to the function of the art—for they should produce not any chance pleasure but the one (already) specified—it is evident that it must be superior, since it achieves the end more than epic (does)."

This final drawing of the balance in favor of tragedy tells us that it does a better job at producing the "peculiar pleasure" than epic, but implies *eo ipso* that epic too is obligated to produce it so far as it is able. This is the place in the *Poetics* where epic is most explicitly associated with the emotional work of tragedy (but see below, p. 183 on 25.60b24–26). We may also recall 24.59b14, where the *Iliad* is called ἁπλοῦν καὶ παθητικόν, "single," i.e., not having a structure full of peripeties and recognitions, and based on a *pathos* (not merely "emotional"); and we may recall further the passage at the end of chapter 15, 54b14–15, with its mention of Achilleus as "good and 'like' (ὅμοιον)." (The latter word is a supplement proposed by me.)[6] If it is correct, Achilleus is identified there as both a hero (ἀγαθόν = σπουδαῖον) and "like us," i.e., a candidate for our pity and fear. This would be a significant extension of Aristotle's tragic canon, to include the greatest of Homer's heroes—an eminently suitable extension, but can we ascribe it to Aristotle? I think we can. Earlier in chapter 15, 54a26–28, Aristotle has proposed the category of consistency or uniformity, τὸ ὁμαλόν, for tragic characters, and says that even if the person being imitated is inconsistent, ἀνώμαλος, he must be presented as *consistently* inconsistent. Aristotle perhaps saw Homer's Achilleus as an example of the "melancholic" temperament, which is consistent in and indeed accounts for the extreme variations of mood we find in him.[7]

The idea of the *Iliad* as not only a protodrama but a prototragedy is further recommended by 24.59b15, where the *Odyssey* is described by way of contrast as "inwoven" and ἠθική, "ethical." What does this latter

6. *Argument* 475–480; cf. below, p. 210.
7. For this point, see the discussion at *Argument* 462–463.

word mean? Surely not simply that the *Odyssey* has more, or more successful, portrayals of character than the *Iliad*. Rather, both here and in 18.56a1 "ethical" seems to mean "moral" in the sense of the "double structure" mentioned at 13.53a31–36: a structure in which, "as in the *Odyssey*," the better and worse characters experience the opposite fates that are morally appropriate to them—good for the good, bad for the bad. And since Aristotle goes on to say that the poets (of tragedies) cater to the weakness of the audiences when they produce such endings, but that this pleasure is more appropriate ("peculiar," οἰκεία) to comedy, it follows that the *Odyssey* is an analogue of comedy rather than tragedy.

This idea may seem paradoxical; on the other hand, of the nine places in the *Poetics* where the *Odyssey* is mentioned (4.49a1; 8.51a24, 29; 13.53a32, our current concern; 17.55b17; 23.59b3; 24.59b15, 60a35; 26.62b9), only the first explicitly identifies it as a prototype of tragedy, and precisely that case is suspect. Symmetry of reference calls there for *one* poem, Ἰλιάς, for tragedy, to match ὁ Μαργίτης for comedy, whereas καὶ ἡ Ὀδύσσεια, "also the *Odyssey*," has the air of intrusion after the fact. A like suspicion attaches to the same words at 26.62b9. In all the other passages, except the one in chapter 13, the point at issue has nothing to do with tragedy or comedy as such but simply with poetic structure (unity, etc.) or style.

It must be admitted that one swallow does not make a summer and one reference to the *Odyssey* as an analogue to comedy does not establish the point beyond doubt. Indeed it could hardly be more than a passing analogy, at best. To incorporate it into the basic fabric of Aristotle's theory would have necessitated revisions so drastic as to defy imagining.

Finally, we should look briefly at chapter 25. This is even less an organic part of the *Poetics* than 26; the organization of the chapter is especially confusing; and the points of contact between it and the rest of the work are few and uncertain. Its origin was in the popular critical activity or parlor game called Ζητήματα or Ἀπορήματα or Προβλήματα Ὁμηρικά, "Homeric Questions" or "Problems." These Questions or Problems were mostly directed at Homer in a hostile, nitpicking spirit which hardly deserves to be dignified with the name "criticism." The most prominent practitioner of the art was Zoïlos, "the Homer-Scourge" (Ὁμηρομάστιξ). So far as we can divine from the scattered evidence, he and his ilk went at Homer with any weapon that came to hand, looking for material inconsistencies, moral failings, real or alleged, deficiencies of characterization, etc. By and large, it was a petty-minded, spiteful exercise, out to destroy or impair the credit of the Prince of Poets. The lurking motive was almost certainly the jealousy which small minds feel at the reputation and influence of great ones. The genre was naturally calculated to spur Aristotle to rebuttal in defense of his idol, but there was nothing in it to spur him to a *philosophical* rebuttal. As he himself says, *Sophistic Refutations* 175a31, "Sophistries are fitly answered by sophistries." Aristotle here plays a game that is not really to his taste, but he does so with bravura.

Under these circumstances we need not be surprised to find very little of Aristotle's larger theory of literature on display in chapter 25. However, two principles of more than routine interest are invoked, one having to do with the content of poetry ("what they imitate"), the other with the concept of "correctness," ὀρθότης.

The principle on content is outlined at 60b8–11: Ἐπεὶ γάρ ἐστι μιμητὴς ὁ ποιητὴς ὥσπερανεὶ ζωγράφος ἤ τις ἄλλος εἰκονοποιός, ἀνάγκη μιμεῖσθαι τριῶν ὄντων τὸν ἀριθμὸν ἕν τι ἀεί, ἢ γὰρ οἷα ἦν ἢ ἔστιν, ἢ οἷά φασιν καὶ δοκεῖ, ἢ οἷα εἶναι δεῖ. "For since the poet is an imitator, like a painter or any other image-maker, it is necessary (for him) to imitate things in one of three ways in any particular case (ἀεί): either the way they were or are, or the way they are reported or thought to be (the way they say and it seems [to them]), or the way they ought to be." This opens up a considerably wider focus on the objects of imitation than we found at the beginning of Aristotle's theory, in chapter 2 (see above, p. 81), and puts the center of gravity in a different place. There Aristotle promulgated a division of persons as being better or worse in relation to a moral average. Here the way those persons really are is but one term in a scheme that encompasses reputation at one end and an ideal standard at the other. The remark quoted from Sophokles below, 60b33–34, αὐτὸς μὲν οἵους δεῖ ποιεῖν, Εὐριπίδην δὲ οἷοι εἰσίν, "(He said) that he portrayed (his characters) the way one should, but Euripides the way they are," is generally though not precisely congruent with the principle as here stated. Aristotle offers it as a gambit for defense if the portraiture in a poem is criticized as οὐκ ἀληθῆ, "not true (to life)": in other words, as a defense of older authors like Sophokles.

The other pronouncement, on "correctness," involves a response to Plato as well as to the vulgar crew of Homer-haters. In *Laws* 2 Plato repeatedly invokes the concept of ὀρθότης in artistic representation. It embodies much the same moral-political critique as he brought to bear in *Republic* 2 and 3: that the poets do not represent the gods and heroes "correctly," according to the best (i.e., Plato's) intuition of their nature. "Correctness" is there distinguished from beauty or artistic finish, τὸ καλόν (καλῶς): a poem may have the latter without the former, but Plato wants both. To this Aristotle responds, 60b15–21, with a distinction between two kinds of correctness, that of poetry itself and that of another art such as medicine (b20) or politics (b14). This reply delivers the deathblow to Plato's holistic criticism, as well as to much of the niggling criticism of the "Homer-scourges." Art is now an autonomous realm with its own standards and criteria. (The whole *Poetics* carries the same implication, but it is not stated so explicitly elsewhere.) But what *are* its own criteria? Chapter 25 does not give a fully satisfactory answer to this question. Thus the pursuit of Hektor in *Iliad* 22 is cited again, this time as an error, ἁμάρτημα. The solution, 60b23–29, is to admit the error (ἀδύνατα πεποίηται, ἡμάρτηται, "impossibilities have been composed (put into the poem): an error has been committed") but plead that that is all right (ὀρθῶς ἔχει, "the procedure is correct") if the emotional effect which is the goal of the art is achieved better or at least as well thereby. On the other hand, if the goal could be achieved just as well καὶ κατὰ τὴν περὶ τούτων τέχνην, "also in accordance with the art that is concerned with these things," it is not all right; "for if possible one should not commit any errors at all."

Surely there is some lack of clarity here. The "art that is concerned with these things" must be the art of war, but it is not clear how the fantastic scene in *Iliad* 22 is or should be related to the art of war; it is too idiosyncratic. How would it have run if Achilleus had *not* waved the Achaians back? On the other hand we have here, at last, a more or less unambiguous affirmation that epic—at least the *Iliad*—has the same emotional purpose as tragedy (cf. the reference to "peculiar pleasure," ἡδονήν τὴν εἰρημένη, at 26.62b12–15). And the passage confers another advantage: the double mention of the Pursuit of Hektor (here and in 24) establishes it as a chief exhibit in the indictment of Homer for his ἀδύνατα and ἄλογα and thereby opens up for us a precious glimpse into the pettifogging minds of Zoïlos and his ilk. Obviously they had no organ for the grandiose architecture and other beauties of this, the supreme climax of the *Iliad*; all they could see was the absurdity of the mass of Achaians being stopped dead by a gesture from one man. This is fifth-century rationalism with a vengeance: a worthy companion piece to Protagoras's reproof of the opening phrase of the *Iliad* as a ἁμάρτημα (19.56b15–18): the poet has issued the Muse a command ("sing, goddess") which he mistakes for a prayer. In that instance Aristotle does not quite conceal his irony and his indignation: "Who could suppose that this is an error?" Answer: Protagoras, or Zoïlos.

The theme of impossibility, τὸ ἀδύνατον, is resumed later in chapter 25, at 61b9–15. Aristotle's general advice is to solve the problem by reference to the poetic composition, τὴν ποίησιν, or to "the better," or to "opinion." With respect to the first category he repeats the paradox he had put forward in 24.60a26–27, that a plausible impossibility is preferable to an implausible possibility. In other words, the final test is the poet's sovereign art: what he can make us believe. "The better" has already been elucidated, 60b33–35, by Sophokles' *bon mot* about his characters, and "opinion" by a suggested retort to Xenophanes' attacks on the Homeric gods, 36–61a1: "Anyway, that's the way they say (they are)."

These Homeric Problems give us an unpleasant aftertaste of the Sophists' involvement with Homer: rationalistic, captious, unwilling and unable to grant the poet any credence above the lowest level of real life. The contrast is valuable because it puts in relief Aristotle's nobler rationalism, which for all its limitations was still genuinely devoted to the old Homeric ideal. He still believed in heroism, and he inspired Alexander to pursue it. That is the practical side of Aristotle's theory.

13

Comedy

THE *Poetics* originally had two books, and comedy was treated in the second. These facts have been denied or disputed, but for no sufficient reason.[1] Since the second book is lost, we must do what we can with the scattered references to comedy in the extant first book, chiefly in 3.48a28–b2, 4.48b22–49a13, and 5.49a32–b9. There is also an anonymous Byzantine treatise dealing with comedy, the so-called *Tractatus Coislinianus*, which clearly has some relationship to the *Poetics*: just what, is not certain. We shall survey this evidence, but first a general point calls for mention. Aristotle's treatment of each of the major genres is dominated and to some extent distorted by a prejudice, an *idée fixe*. Tragedy is seen through the prism of the *Oidipous Tyrannos*. For epic, the corresponding idea is the preternatural genius of Homer. For comedy, the controlling factor is Aristotle's aversion to fifth-century Attic comedy, with its political orientation, its vituperativeness, and its foul language. Aristotle did not enjoy, he saw no reason to enjoy, political satire or unbridled attacks on individuals. His disapproval of this "iambic" kind of poetry (5.49b8, ἡ ἰαμβικὴ ἰδέα) led him to a tendentious slanting of the definition of comedy (in chapter 5) and a gross distortion of its history (in chapter 4), including total suppression of the two most important persons in the story (according to our lights), Archilochos and Aristophanes.

Aristotle did not invent this attitude. The iambic or comic poet's readiness to attack anybody, his lack of respect for constituted authority, dignity, and status, were deeply repugnant to the "best people," that is, the Greek aristocracy. Thus Pindar (*Pythian* 2.54–56) does not hide his

1. E.g., by A. P. McMahon, "On the Second Book of Aristotle's *Poetics* and the Source of Aristotle's Definition of Tragedy," *HSCP* 28 (1917) 1–46; Daniel de Montmollin, *La Poétique d'Aristote: texte primitif et additions ultérieures* (Neuchâtel 1951) 188–193.

contempt for "the carping Archilochos, so often in desperation"—i.e., because he could not *do* anything to satiate his spite—"fattening himself on hatefully spoken insults"; and Perikles or Alkibiades may have felt no different, in their hearts. Plato, the blue-blooded aristocrat, shows an interesting variation. We might have expected him to dislike Aristophanes and not to forgive the caricature of his master in the *Clouds*; the *Symposion* is on view to show that he did forgive. Of course Plato's own genius was comic rather than tragic. There is no tragic dialogue, except the *Gorgias*, to match the long line of comic masterpieces: *Protagoras, Ion, Euthyphron, Euthydemos, Menexenos, Symposion*; and the whole point of the *Phaidon* is that it is *not* a tragedy. Tragedy is impossible in the presence of Sokrates; comedy is not only possible with him, it is, so to speak, built in. But not obscenity, not personal attack, except on out-and-out sophistic types like the fatuous pedant Euthyphron, the puffed-up rhapsode Ion, or the eristic pair of brothers in the *Euthydemos*; and even there, except in the latter case, the satire is tempered by an almost affectionate smile, and Protagoras is treated with notable respect.

The *Philebos*, 48a–50a, establishes the root motive of comedy—Attic comedy—as φθόνος: jealousy, malice, *Schadenfreude*. It is noteworthy that Plato nevertheless accepts the comic motive as one that obtains between equals: we laugh at our *friends* (49e–50a). That is not the way Pindar took the comic (iambic) impulse, and not the way Aristotle took it. He makes it amply plain in the *Politics*, 7.17.1336b3–35, especially 20–21, that he wants iambic poetry and comedy—their foul language, their schooling in slander and character assassination, their low view of human nature—kept far away from the young until they are ready to take part in the men's symposia, i.e., until long after puberty. Plato in the 370s was worried about the nefarious influence of Homer and tragedy on the young; Aristotle twenty years later is even more exercised over comedy.

These concerns go far toward explaining the twist which Aristotle gives to his definition of the comic (τὸ γελοῖον, the laughable) in chapter 5. He had begun in chapter 2 with a flat distinction between σπουδαῖοι, the serious people, and φαῦλοι, those of no account. He now wants to refine the distinction in such a way as to remove all pain and hurt from the workings of comedy. But Plato in the *Philebos* had put his finger on the comic nerve and defined it as φθόνος, jealousy, spite—an inherently painful emotion. How can Aristotle undo this and say that the laughable is "a fault, an ugliness which is painless and not destructive" (49a34–35, ἁμάρτημά τι καὶ αἶσχος ἀνώδυνον καὶ οὐ φθαρτικόν)? Very simply; by turning his back on Attic, "iambic" comedy and taking as his norm the Dorian variety: not personal attacks on individuals but harmless spoofing of comic types, far from any political motive.

That this gambit of Aristotle's has not been much noticed by the commentators does not detract in any way from its originality or its significance. He has wiped the Attic Old Comedy out of his theory and his "history." Neither Aristophanes nor his recognized predecessor, Archilochos, has any place in the story. Instead we begin, immediately after the original improvisational stage (4.48b25–26), with the *Margites*, a minor work among the epic παίγνια ("playthings," playful works) which made fun of—what else?—a comic type, the learned but ineffectual fool. Aristotle seized on this spiritual forebear of Dorian comedy with some insistence, as a product of Homer himself. The man who saw that the Cyclic epics were not by Homer should perhaps have had wit enough to see that the *Margites* was not genuine either. But no matter; it represented the right kind of comic form, dramatic representation of the ludicrous (4.48b37–38, οὐ ψόγον ἀλλὰ τὸ γελοῖον δραματοποιήσας), and it came at the right time—or so Aristotle must have thought—to block Archilochos from the competition. At any rate there is no mention of Archilochos anywhere, and no room for him in the narrative. He cannot be put back with the primitive improvisations, and his proper place in the history is preempted by Homer with his invention of a different kind of iambic poem devoted to "painless" humor.

After the *Margites*, the next significant stage in the comic line of development—that is, in Aristotle's version of it—is the Dorian comedy of Epicharmos at Syrakuse in the early fifth century. The links between these two stages are not only obscure, they are nonexistent. Who *were* the iambic poets who according to 4.49a4–6 abandoned iambic and went over to the comic forms which Homer had adumbrated, because they were "greater and more estimable"? Aristotle has to confess that he does not know: 5.49a37–b5, the advances in tragedy were recorded, those in comedy were not, because comedy was originally not taken seriously (διὰ τὸ μὴ σπουδάζεσθαι: almost a pun, since comedy is nonserious by definition). Comedy turns up—in Sicily, be it noted; we have not reached Athens yet—"already possessing certain forms when the first to be called poets of it (i.e., the first to be called comic poets) are recorded" (5.49b2–3). The forms in question are then specified, b4–5, as "masks, prologues, actor's companies, and the like."

What this means concretely is that Epicharmos (for he is next in Aristotle's line of succession) inherited a complete form of comic drama, with actors, masks, etc., when he began to work. But there is another discrepancy here, besides the lack of any visible connection between the *Margites* and Epicharmos, and that is the term "comic poet," κωμῳδοποιός, itself. The Dorians did not call their comic poets κωμῳδοποιοί, for the simple reason that they had no "comedies," κωμῳδίαι. Κωμῳδία is an exclusively Attic product and Attic word until at least the time of Aristotle. We do not know for sure what the Dorians called their comic playlets (they were much shorter than the Athenian variety, averaging around three hundred or four hundred lines each); certainly not κωμῳδίαι, more likely simply δράματα, "acts, plays." (They had no need of a word to distinguish comedy from tragedy, for they had no tragedies.)

This unfortunate terminological discrepancy stimulated someone— whether Aristotle himself, is not clear—to some etymological and historical reflections which are on view in the second part of chapter 3, 48a25–b2. The transition to this section is provided by a27–28, which say that Sophokles and Aristophanes (more on him below) both imitate men acting, πράττοντας καὶ δρῶντας ἄμφω, and this leads in turn to the statement, a28–29, ὅθεν καὶ δράματα καλεῖσθαί τινες αὐτά φασιν, "whence also certain people say that they are called 'dramas,' because they imitate men doing, δρῶντας." Who are these "certain people"? Certainly not Athenians; it would not occur to an Athenian to call serious *or* comic plays δράματα. There is a certain amount of skewing here which could lend a handle to a particular claim. The Dorians had some plays, which they probably called δράματα; but only comedies (i.e., what we call comedies). Athens on the other hand had plays of three kinds, tragic, satyric, and comic, but did not apply the term δρᾶμα to any of them except satyr drama—and that precisely was a Dorian genre, introduced by Pratinas from Phlious in Peloponnese toward the end of the sixth century. But the point of the etymological play with δρᾶν, δρῶντας in a28–29 is to lead up to the Dorians' claims to the origination of tragedy *and* comedy in the lines that follow, a29–b2. In other words, either the "certain people" are those Dorians or they are in close collusion with them.

The claims themselves come down to two: a general one to drama as such, based on δρᾶν, which is claimed to be a Doric word, and a special one to comedy, κωμῳδία, which is claimed to derive from κώμη, "village," which is alleged to be a specifically Doric word as against the Attic

δῆμος, "deme." We shall survey these claims, but only briefly.[2] The
Dorian claim purports to be divided into two, historically and geographi-
cally, one for comedy from Megara (both Megaras, the one in old Greece
and the one in Sicily) and one for tragedy from "some of those in
Peloponnese" (this, we happen to know, meaning primarily Sikyon). To-
gether these formed one argument, put forward by persons who were
"Dorians" in a special scholarly sense.

The Megarian claim, especially the one from old Megara, had a solid
basis. Megarian farce (called τὸ δρᾶμα τὸ Μεγαρικόν in a fragment of
Attic comedy) did exist there from an early date and was still flourishing
in the fifth century (the connection with Epicharmos will occupy us
shortly). The Sikyonian claim to tragedy is a different kettle of fish en-
tirely. It was not based on an existing tragic drama—no Dorian city had
such a thing—but solely on dubious inferences from a passage in Hero-
dotos about "tragic choruses" at Sikyon in the seventh century. And the
etymologies put forward in support of these two very unequal claims are
both fallacious. Κωμῳδία is not from κώμη, "village," but from κῶμος,
"revel(-band)," and δρᾶν was not an exclusively Doric word, although
there may have been an impression at Athens that it was.

Nevertheless there is a good deal of learning in the passage, and learn-
ing with a noticeable bent toward social and cultural history. Thus we
hear about the early democracy at old Megara, 48a31–32; the relative
chronology of Epicharmos and the earliest Athenian comic poets, Chio-
nides and Magnes, 33–34; that κωμῳδοί were so called because they
wandered through the villages (κῶμαι), "being driven from the city in
disgrace," 37–38; and lastly there is a philological note on δρᾶν (alleg-
edly Doric) and πράττειν (Attic), 48b1–2. Moreover the reference to the
villages probably implies a story which turns up at several places in later
antiquity, about some rustics who went to town to air their grievances
against the townsfolk: an early case of social protest.

This cluster of cultural and social allusions does not particularly re-
semble Aristotle—the Aristotle of the *Poetics*—but it *is* reminiscent of his
pupils and later colleagues Dikaiarchos of Messene and Aristoxenos of
Taras (Tarentum). They were both deeply interested in such matters,
and both were spirited, even belligerent, partisans of Dorian culture.
This attribution would have important consequences for our passage. It
would necessitate a dating no earlier than the period of the Lykeion, for
Dikaiarchos and Aristoxenos were certainly not associated with Aristotle

2. Details in *Argument* 101–123.

in the Akademy. In any case, whatever the authorship of the passage (and there is nothing that necessarily excludes Aristotle), one thing about it seems clear and deserves emphasis: it is not, as the commentators tend to say, a purely neutral comment, merely calling attention to the Dorian claims. Its purpose is partisan, to back those claims.

There are several indications of this. As we said, the only visible purpose of the remarks on δρᾶν, δράματα at 48a25–29 is to lead up to the Dorian claims; and δρῶντας is in clear thematic harmony with the key word δρώντων in the definition of tragedy (649b26), not merely in the general sense in which all mimetic poetry imitates men in action, but in the specific sense of drama. Again, in the statement, 48b1–2, that the Dorians say δρᾶν for "do" but the Athenians say πράττειν, the *Poetics* text presents the latter in the nominative case, 'Aθηναῖοι, which means that the writer of the sentence makes the statement on his own authority: in other words, he accepts the Dorian claim. Generations of editors and commentators have emended the remark into something merely quoted: this solely in order to rescue Aristotle from approving a false or imperfect statement (δρᾶν is *not* exclusively Doric).

But the most significant piece of evidence has to do with Epicharmos. (As Alfred Gudeman suggests, he was undoubtedly the trump card in the Dorians' deck all along.)[3] The statement, 3.48a33–34, ἐκεῖθεν γὰρ ἦν 'Eπίχαρμος ὁ ποιητής, πολλῷ πρότερος ὢν Xιωνίδου καὶ Mάγνητος, "For Epicharmos the poet was from there (Sicily), being much earlier than Chionides and Magnes," is of doubtful validity. It is not certain that Epicharmos was earlier, not to say "much earlier," than these first attested Athenian comic poets; but it is clear that the writer of the passage set great store by his being earlier, because that was the way to establish not only an honorable place for Epicharmos but the chronological priority of Dorian comedy over Athenian. Again the purpose is not purely documentary but engaged, partisan.

Epicharmos appears again in the text at 5.49b6, but in a peculiar way. The names 'Eπίχαρμος καὶ Φόρμος stand in a sentence with which they have a connection in meaning but none in grammar. Whoever put these names into the text did so in an informed spirit. Epicharmos (we know very little about Phormos except his name) was undoubtedly the originator or at any rate the most conspicuous practitioner of regular plot-making (τὸ μύθους ποιεῖν, 49b5–6) in Dorian comedy. This, according

3. See Gudeman's edition of the *Poetics* (Berlin 1934) 114–115.

to Aristotle, was his inheritance from Homer. From Epicharmos the torch was passed to Athens, but only well after the official beginnings of comedy there (Chionides and Magnes): 49b7–9, τῶν δὲ ᾿Αθήνησιν Κράτης πρῶτος ἦρξεν ἀφέμενος τῆς ἰαμβικῆς ἰδέας καθόλου ποιεῖν λόγους καὶ μύθους, "But of those at Athens Krates first began, giving up the iambic manner, to compose general arguments, i.e., plots." Krates (who flourished ca. 440, some forty-five years after the official beginnings of comedy at Athens, and perhaps fifteen years after Kratinos) had a fondness for harmless subjects like animal masquerade and mythological burlesque; he was not as typical of Old Comedy as Kratinos, nor as influential, but he fitted Aristotle's definition of comedy better. (This is the place where Aristophanes should have been mentioned but is not.)

Into this sequence an alien note has been interpolated: 5.49b1–2, "For in fact (only) late (i.e., ca. 484) the archon gave a chorus of comedians, but (before that) they were volunteers." The reference is certainly to Athens: Syrakuse did not have an archon who "gave a chorus," indeed its comedy did not have a chorus at all. Then what is the point of the "late" (ὀψέ) giving of the chorus? I suggest that it means late in relation to Epicharmos: in other words that the sentence is a pendant to 48a33–34, which said that Epicharmos was "much earlier than Chionides and Magnes." The two sentences then claim, between them, that Epicharmos was in business at Syrakuse, with a completely formed art of comedy, long before the official competition in comedy (under the presidency of the archon) was established at Athens.

The note is of the same learned variety as 3.48a25–b2, on the Dorian claims to tragedy and comedy, and seems to reflect the same kind of anthropological-sociological interest in cultural institutions. This allies it further with 4.49a10–13, which can likewise be identified (see Appendix 2, no. 12) as an intrusion into the text of the *Poetics*. Τὰ φαλλικά ("the phallic performances") originally stood there; even if it did not, we can find parallels in a long passage of Athenaios going back at least to one Semos of Delos in the second century B.C., on phallic performances in several Greek cities including Sikyon and Thebes.[4] (It is perhaps only a coincidence that according to Athenaios the phallic performers at Thebes were called ἐθελονταί, "volunteers.")

---

4. Athenaios 14.621f–222d; cf. Aristophanes, *Acharnians* 241–249 and A. W. Pickard-Cambridge, *Dithyramb, Tragedy and Comedy*², rev. T. B. L. Webster (Oxford 1962) 134–147.

Finally, the passages we have been studying seem to have a family resemblance to the mixed matter at 4.49a18–21 (interpolated: see Appendix 2, no. 13). Mention is made there of the troupe of tragic actors, scene-painting, and the derivation of tragedy from σατυρικόν, satyr drama—the only mention of this genre in the *Poetics*. Here again we see an interest in details of cultural and institutional history: an interest which contrasts sharply with Aristotle's more abstract and philosophical approach. Moreover the derivation of tragedy from satyr play has affiliations with a theory which derived all three forms of drama—tragedy, comedy, and satyr play—from an undifferentiated primitive performance allegedly called τρυγῳδία (must- or new-wine-song: a nonce word modeled on τραγῳδία).

The notion that tragedy, comedy, and satyr play were all derived from a single primitive jollification was certainly not Aristotle's theory, but one can conjecture with a good deal of probability that it came out of the Peripatetic school. Chamaileon, a learned Peripatetic of the second generation who wrote voluminously on literary, especially dramatic, history (*On Homer*; *On Hesiod*; *On Thespis*; *On Satyr Play*; *On Aischylos*), is said to have stated that tragedy developed out of the σατυρικά; a *Suda* article implies that at least one other source put forward the same idea; and we find analogues to it in three epigrams of the Hellenistic poet Dioskorides (see below).[5]

Here is a tantalizing mass of testimony. Confused and inconclusive though it is, it seems to point to a theory developed in the Peripatos in the first or second generation after Aristotle which derived all drama from a single root, a primitive celebration of the fruits of the vine. From one point of view this is a far cry from Aristotle's own theory, which strictly separated the lower improvisatons from the higher (4.48b24–27). But from another point of view the distance is not so great. If you are looking for a source of drama in popular practices and institutions— and Aristotle seems to authorize this—you may well be led to the lower rather than the upper end of the scale: its manifestations are that much more numerous and conspicuous, especially in fourth- and third-century Greece. And this theory utilizes a genuine Aristotelian idea, that of evolution, development. If tragedy could develop out of primitive performances, why not out of humorous performances—especially if the humor was harmless, unsatirical, like that of the φαλλικά and σατυρικά?

---

5. And see discussion and documentation in *Argument* 172–179.

It is possible, then, to assume a single motive behind the interpolations in chapters 3, 4, and 5. Persons in Aristotle's school in the 320s, or not long after, may have been moved to justify his prejudice against the Attic Old Comedy by assigning chronological and ideological priority to Dorian comedy (Epicharmos). And in doing this they may well have thought that they were not drastically altering their master's theory but simply improving or clarifying it.

If these speculations (for they cannot be anything more than that) are correct, or even on the track of truth, still another inference may be possible. For at least a century now a spectral body called the "satyric dithyramb" has haunted all efforts to reconstruct a plausible early history of tragedy out of the *Poetics*. The idea was of course based on a combination of "those who led off the dithyramb" (4.49a11) with "its having developed out of a σατυρικόν" (49a20). It has been quite adequately shown, over and over again, that no such thing ever existed; and Aristotle's own theory is not likely to have embraced it, with its corollary of a late and radical shift from gay (σατυρικόν) to grave (tragedy). But the supplement which we have been postulating may have embraced such an idea.

There is a startling collection, or conglomeration, of these ideas in a triad of epigrams by Dioskorides, an Alexandrian poet of the late fourth century. Thespis appears here (*Anthologia Palatina* 7.41, no. xxi Page) as the inventor of country games and revels (κώμους) which were then "raised" and perfected by Aischylos; the latter also made some innovations on the stage. Another epigram (7.410, no. xxii Page) speaks of the new "graces" which Thespis invented for his fellow villagers when Bakchos led the dance. Finally, a satyr is presented (7.37, no. xxii Page) as guarding the tomb of Sophokles because the latter had brought him, an "oaken" creature, from Phlious still eating nettles, changed his aspect to gold, and clothed him in purple, i.e., in the tragic actor's garb.

These epigrams do not present a consistent, coherent picture of the early stages of tragedy, but they do suggest an idea of its having developed out of something entirely different, something much humbler and gayer, something as close to home as village revels, and of its doing this very late in its history, as late as Sophokles. Such a dating runs so counter to our ideas of the development as to seem grotesque, but it has a certain rationale of its own, and in fact it gives lines 49a18–21 for the first time a consistent grammar and message, *if* we read them throughout as focused on Sophokles: τρεῖς δὲ καὶ σκηνογραφίαν Σοφοκλῆς, ἔτι δὲ τὸ μέγεθος, ἐκ μικρῶν μύθων καὶ λέξεως γελοίας, διὰ τὸ ἐκ σατυρικοῦ μεταβαλεῖν, ὀψὲ ἀπεσεμνύνθη, "But three (actors) and stage-paintings Sophokles (introduced); and moreover (he introduced) the (tragic) grandeur: out of little (insignificant?) plots and comic language, on account of having developed out of a (the?) σατυρικόν, it turned serious late." Everything is in order except that the grandeur (μέγεθος, ὄγκος, ὕψος) which we are accustomed to attribute to Aischylos is assigned to Sophokles. As for the "little plots" and comic language, Wilamowitz was prepared to find them in the *Suppliants, Persians,* and *Prometheus.*[6] That his "discoveries" were mistaken does not prove that ancient scholars could not have made them also.

Finally we may notice that Dikaiarchos, like *Poetics* 4.49a18–19, and against what seems to have been the canonical view, attributed the introduction of the third actor to Sophokles.[7]

We end not with anything like certainty, but with a possibility that Dikaiarchos was the source of the interpolated passages we have been discussing. They have in common Dorian patriotism, a sociological interest in comedy, and a desire to trace the origin of tragedy to something gay and popular. Although none of these attitudes is Aristotelian per se, none is entirely incompatible with Aristotle's ideas.

Of course if any part of the *Poetics'* text comes from Dikaiarchos or another member of Aristotle's school, that has implications for the text itself. It must have remained "open," that is, accessible to additions by other hands, for a while after it left Aristotle's. But this is no longer properly a question of comedy. We devote some further consideration to it in Appendix 1.

Our final problem concerning Aristotle's theory of comedy as such has to do with the brief and anonymous *Tractatus Coislinianus.* It is one of a number of late-antique and Byzantine treatises on comedy but is distinguished from the rest by the fact that it is obviously derived more or less directly from the *Poetics.* The question is, from which part? If from the lost second book, the *Tractatus* would be a precious, indeed a unique treasure. Lane Cooper wrote a whole book based on that premise;[8] unfortunately it seems not to be true. What the treatise offers is either

6. Ulrich von Wilamowitz-Moellendorff, "Die Spurhunde des Sophokles," *NJbb* 29 (1912) 468–469 = *Kleine Schriften* I (Berlin 1935) 373–377.

7. *Vita Aeschyli* 15 = frag. 76 in Fritz Wehrli's edition of Dikaiarchos, *Die Schule des Aristoteles,* Heft I (Basel 1944) 30.

8. *An Aristotelian Theory of Comedy* (New York 1922).

crude pastiches based on tragedy, from the extant first book, or rhetorical commonplaces or rags and tags of philological knowledge: e.g., about the three divisions of comedy, Old, Middle, and New (section 10). There is nothing in it that has any genuine Aristotelian savor; in particular, nothing to reflect Aristotle's crucial distinction between the right and wrong kind of comedy. The *Tractatus* offers us nothing really useful or usable.

14

Résumé
Aristotle's Theory of the Poem and the Poet

WE ARE NOW in a position to sum up and appraise the theses which together constitute Aristotle's theory of literature. We shall do so by contrasting the fundamentally different views held by Plato. The cardinal point in Aristotle's theory is the concept of the poem as a construct and the poet as a constructor. This runs squarely counter to Plato's deepest intuition, which was that poetry is a communication from one soul to another. Whether this latter perception goes back to Plato's early poetic experiments or simply reflects his experience in writing his own "trage-dies" and "comedies"—the major dialogues—it never left him. So far as we can trace his attitude to poetry, it remained faithful to that intuition. Indeed the inner reason for his lifelong resistance to Homer was that he perceived Homer as a great and powerful but misguided soul, propagating a false view of human life.

We already noticed in discussing the *Republic* the special meaning which Plato attached to μίμησις in connection with Homer: that in pre-senting his characters Homer slyly pretends to *be* them, making as if they were doing the talking instead of himself. Another part of the charge has to do with the content rather than the form or method of Homer's μίμησις in the *Iliad*. That content is, to put it in a nutshell, the tragic view of life.

The task which Sokrates undertakes beginning in *Republic* 2 is to show that justice is not merely beneficial to its practitioner in external ways but is truly, inwardly good for him. This demonstration is not complete when the subject of μίμησις comes up in *Republic* 3, at 392c. At 392a–b Sokrates has rehearsed the popular view (which he had previ-ously said, 2.364cff., was propagated by the poets): that justice is a nuisance to oneself, a benefit only to others, and that many unjust men are "happy," many just men are wretched. Then, at 392c, he says that we cannot maintain the opposite view until we have proved our major the-sis, that justice is naturally good in itself. Once that is done we can consider that the question of the poet's stories, λόγοι—i.e., their content—will have been settled; meanwhile we turn to their λέξις, the way the stories are presented, and that means μίμησις.

With the unfinished business concerning men's happiness and unhappiness we may contrast Plato's certainty about the gods, that they are good and the cause of good only (2.379bff.). This is actually a part of the same complex of ideas, for a large part of the sufferings that afflict the just were traditionally—especially by the poets—ascribed to the gods. The paradigm is Priam.

Actually the discussion of men's unhappiness is only technically unfinished; Plato's opinion on the matter is in no real doubt. He had learned once for all from Sokrates—both from his teaching and from the example of his death—that the good man, i.e., one who is like Sokrates, cannot be made unhappy by any external cause; a poet who represents such a thing as happening is either ignorant or guilty of willful deception. Either way, the Homer of the *Iliad* is a prime offender. (The passage which draws Plato's heaviest fire is of course the parable of the two jars on Zeus's doorstep, *Iliad* 24.527–533. It is damnable in his eyes precisely because it puts the tragic view in such memorable terms.)

Thus Homer's mimesis, his dramatic gifts, are not the substance of his offense; they are only an adjunct to it. His worst sin is to present human happiness as tragically incommensurate with goodness.

There is no trace of any of this in Aristotle; above all, no hint that he ever felt himself as a rival of the poets. His theory approaches the problem from the opposite end, the poem. Poems are structures made by the poet; indeed his leading task is that of construction. Conveying ideas or intuitions is no part of his job. Poets, in Aristotle's view, do not think; they build. Presumably they need to think about what they are building, but general thought about life or fate or the human condition is not a part of their duty or their art. The exclusion of this factor from Aristotle's theory is in fact so complete that many interpreters have not missed it; they have taken for granted it must be there somewhere, perhaps under another name.

Aristotle's theory, then, quite unlike Plato's, is a theory of poetic structures, and of the poet as a maker of such structures. The "metaphysical" element, if we wish to call it that, inheres not in the structures as wholes but in the universals, the plausible or necessary human acts or utterances which go to make up the structures.

Aristotle lays down a series of general requirements for the poetic action, the μῦθος or σύστασις τῶν πραγμάτων: that it must be unified, be logically coherent, and have a certain size. These are three distinct but inseparable aspects of a single desideratum, which can best be designated by the word "unity." We must guard, however, against the facile and partly misguided Renaissance schema of the Three Unities. One of these, unity of action (of the πρᾶξις or the μῦθος), is fundamental; unity of time, referring to an alleged limitation of the clock or calendar time which may be presumed to elapse during the poetic action, has only a limited standing in the practice of the Greek dramatists and none in Aristotle's thought; unity of place, though not infrequently observed in the plays, has at best a marginal place in his theory, as we shall see.

Aristotle introduces unity in chapter 7, 50b26–31 (cf. 23.59a20–21) as an attribute which appertains to any beautiful thing, whether a natural creature (ζῷον) or a construct made of parts. The allusion to ζῷον is an echo of Plato's famous demand in the *Phaidros*, 264c, that "every λόγος"—every utterance: speech or poem—have the unity of a ζῷον. In spite of the "organic" suggestions of the word, Aristotle develops the concept of unity and wholeness purely in abstract rhetorico-logical terms, in the sequence ἀρχή, beginning; μέσον, middle(s) (μέσα, 23.59a20); and τέλος, end. Only after the pattern has been laid down does he establish, at the beginning of chapter 9, 51a36–38, that the poet's job is not to tell the things that have happened but those that *might* happen, that are possible according to probability or necessity, because only they can be combined into a unified whole. These elements are subsequently, 51b8–10, defined as "universals": "the kinds of things that a certain kind of person will naturally do or say under given circumstances." Poetry tends to "say" or report these things, while history rather reports what has actually been said or done; and Aristotle adds that poetry is therefore more philosophical and to be taken more seriously than history. The aphorism is famous; its importance is in the energetic way it counters Plato's allegation that poetry has no philosophical grasp or dimension. Aristotle does not claim that it *is* philosophy, but he gives it an honorable, quasi-philosophical status.

We pointed out that Aristotle's poetic "universals" have an affinity with the premises of the syllogism. In both cases a complex of general elements is combined in a synthesis which is an individual whole. The poetic synthesis is logical but also creative; it is precisely in connection with the making of the σύστασις τῶν πραγμάτων, the structur(ing) of the poetic events, that Aristotle speaks most insistently of the poet (ὁ ποιητής) as a maker. It is not a creation *ex nihilo*, but a creation nonetheless, the highest reach of the poet's art and the one that brings him most honor. (Aristotle's prime example would presumably be Sophokles' *Oidipous Tyrannos*.)

Of the three general requirements for the poetic structure, the one most often ignored and/or misinterpreted is that of a limit or norm (ὅρος) of length. What is said about it, in 5.49b12–16, was long misassigned to the alleged unity of time. But Aristotle's prescription (for it is a prescription, not merely an observation of poetic practice) has nothing to do with the alleged "dramatic" time of poetic works; it refers to their real duration, which can be experienced either primarily, in performance, or secondarily, through reading. Which measure we use does not matter greatly so long as we are clear that Aristotle is talking about real length of the structure and/or the work, not its supposed internal time. Of the two possible measures, the original and basic one is surely length of performance, and, closely connected with that, the concentrated intensity of experience which comes from viewing a masterpiece like the *Oidipous*. It must be confessed that Aristotle does not often talk in this vein. In 7.51a6–15 he rejects any limit which is defined by "the competitions and sense-perception" as "not belonging to the poetic art." But this seems to refer to an external, purely arbitrary limit. He proposes instead a definition "according to the very nature of the subject," in two parts: (1) the larger the structure the more beautiful, so long as it remains "clear as a whole" (σύνδηλος; cf. εὐσύνοπτον, a4, εὐμνημόνευτον, a5–6); (2) a general definition (ὡς δὲ ἁπλῶς διορίσαντας) would be "that length in which, with things happening in sequence according to probability or necessity, a shift naturally follows (συμβαίνει) to good from ill or from good to ill fortune." At 24.59b18–22, speaking of epic, he refers with approval to the first of these formulations as "adequate" (ἱκανός) and says that the condition would be met "if the (epic) structures should be shorter than the ancient ones and approximate the quantity (πλῆθος) of tragedies which are presented for a single hearing."

This last phrase pretty clearly refers to the established practice whereby each poet in the competitions offered three plays. It is not so clear whether Aristotle is thinking of unified trilogies like the *Oresteia*, though his point would be strengthened if he were. In any case the experiential basis of the remark, its reference to actual performance, seems pretty close and direct. Aristotle must mean that sovereign concentration of feeling and affect which we experience from a dramatic masterpiece like the *Oidipous*—and experience best from actual performance. (If Aristotle tries to tell us that he gets the same concentrated effect from reading the play, or from hearing the bare plot, we shall lend a respectful but skeptical ear.) As for the substance of the passage, Aristotle is struggling here with a difficulty which he has brought upon himself. Epics in general, old or new, were not overwhelmingly long. The longest by far were precisely the Homeric poems. But Aristotle had decided, for better or worse, to base his theory of epic not on a statistical average or on a broad survey of the field, but on Homer, whose works, as he himself repeatedly emphasizes (e.g., 60a5–11), are entirely different from—and superior to—the rest. His solution of the immediate problem is to declare, 24.59b22–28, that epic has a special capacity for extra expansion of its bulk. But just as the problem of extra length was occasioned by Homer, the solution speaks to Homer and Homer alone. It is predicated on a special view of Homer's greatest achievement: the construction of a central action (the Wrath of Achilleus; the Return of Odysseus) comparable in size and unity to the πρᾶξις of a tragedy, around which the rest of the poem is draped as a series of ἐπεισόδια, episodes (in a special sense of the word). This compound structure is identified for the *Iliad* at 23.59a35–37, for the *Odyssey* at 17.55b16–23 (cf. 8.51a24–29). What it signifies is that Aristotle sees Homer as achieving the nearly impossible: within the ample bosom of "epic breadth" he has secured something like the unity and concentration of tragedy. Upon inspection it even turns out that these central actions have approximately the same length as that indicated for tragedy at 24.59b21–22, about 4,500 lines.

Thus Aristotle's procedure with epic is to equate it as far as possible with tragedy; but as he himself indicates, that can be done only for Homer. Homer appears here as the master builder, the precursor and model (4.48b34–49a–b) of tragedy. This is Aristotle's solution of a larger problem also: how and in what sense tragedy developed out of epic. This solution is an outgrowth of his almost limitless admiration for Homer. In any case, Aristotle is a convinced evolutionist in his view of the development of poetry. Not that either of the two species, high and low (or serious and trivial), grows out of the other. They remain distinct throughout their history, entering at most into a kind of personal union in Homer, who produced both serious epic(s) and the farcical *Margites*. But within those fixed limits each kind developed and evolved toward its own natural culmination (its "nature," 4.48b27). For tragedy, Aristotle's evolutionary stages include early serious poems, 48b33 (examples not given); Homer's *Iliad* (and *Odyssey*?); early tragedy, 4.49a5; "numerous changes," 49a14; and finally, with Aischylos, the victory of speech over song and dance and the concurrent victory of iambic trimeter over trochaic tetrameter, 49a14–18, 21–24. A similar concurrence of metrical developments with those in method or style is seen at the very beginning of the story: the first serious narrative poems (as distinct from improvisations) were in hexameters (ἡρωικῶν, 48b33); more detail at 24.59b31–60a5.

The development on the comic side is parallel to the other but more difficult to trace, partly because, as Aristotle says (5.49a38–b1), it was less known, but also because of his rejection of the "Attic" or iambic species of comedy. What is left is a jejune and disjointed sequence: the primitive flytings, ψόγοι, 4.48b27; the *Margites*, 48b30, 38; Dorian comedy, especially that of Epicharmos at Syrakuse, 5.49b5–7; at Athens, Krates and other writers of unsatirical comedy; and then—nothing. Aristotle in 360 could not foresee Menander, and without him there was nobody to serve as τέλος of the development, to match Aischylos and Sophokles in tragedy. In other words, the history of comedy, so far as it was visible to Aristotle, offered nothing definitive to back up his intuition as to the right kind of comedy. The chief eccentricity on view in his schema is the importance it assigns to the Dorian variety. (Although it seemed to us that the passage on the Dorian claim to the invention of comedy, 3.48a29–38, might stem from Dikaiarchos or Aristoxenos, it is perfectly consonant with Aristotle's strong preference for unsatirical comedy.)

In spite of these deviations and insufficiencies, the general bent and rationale of Aristotle's evolutionism are clear enough. His theory is entelechic (although the word ἐντελέχεια does not appear in the *Poetics*): he believes that the process was purposive and somehow impelled *a fronte*, by some influence which steered it toward the final result.

One consequence of this entelechic bent is the peculiar position of epic in the story, vis-à-vis tragedy. At 5.49b9–10 Aristotle tells us that epic "followed (ἠκολούθησεν) tragedy up to the point of being a large-scale imitation of serious matters by means of verse." The verb ἠκολούθησεν cannot be, as is sometimes claimed, a gnomic aorist meaning "agrees with." It has to mean that epic "accompanied" tragedy along the same path of development, but only far enough to become a (1) sizable (2) imitation of (3) serious matters (4) in verse.[1] Aristotle adds at once, b11–

---

1. The text discussed here is defended in *Argument* 204–205. Else, adopting Lasson's emendation, reads μέτρῳ μεγάλη μίμησις ("a sizable imitation in verse"); Kassel in his Oxford text prints his own μετὰ μέτρου λόγῳ ("by speech with metre"). In Aristotle, μέτρον (almost always in the plural, μέτρα) refers to concrete verse(s), not to abstract meter or verse form. When he calls μέτρα

12, "But in its (the epic's) having its verse plain (ἁπλοῦν, simplex, i.e., unmixed with music) and being narrative, there they differ," and he subsequently adds—as at 24.59b17ff.—the difference in length.

Within the narrow bounds of his definition, Aristotle is very conscientious about registering the relationship between poetic mode or method and verse form. In principle, the genre (the poetic mode) leads the way and "teaches (the poets) to choose the (verse) that suits it" (24.60a4–5).[2]

The three general requirements for the tragic structure (and, by later extension, the epic structure) are presented with clarity and emphasis, 7.50b21–9.51b32. Unity, logical coherence, and limit of size are deduced by a fairly direct process of inference from the concept of an action: in other words, from the definition of tragedy in 6.49b24–31. Moreover, as Aristotle says, these specifications in the definition are drawn directly out of the preceding chapters.

The derivation of the special requirements for tragedy is neither so clear nor so direct. Pity and fear are mentioned in the definition, and katharsis besides, but the clause that contains them is *not* drawn from what precedes and, as we saw, its meaning is anything but obvious. The reference at 6.50a30 to what "was (defined as) the work (function) of tragedy" does not clarify the situation appreciably; indeed the emotional side of tragedy does not receive any explicit discussion until the end of chapter 9, 52a1ff., and Aristotle never makes quite clear whether it extends to epic, although the end of the *Poetics*, 26.62b12–14, points in that direction. So far as tragedy is concerned, the most illuminating passage is 14.53b11–13, from which we learn that the οἰκεία ἡδονή, the specific or "peculiar" pleasure of tragedy, stems from pity and fear and must be consciously produced (παρασκευάζειν) by the poet. Combining this with the survey of tragic μεταβολαί, "shifts," at 13.52b34–53a17, we see further that this achievement is tied up with the σύστασις τῶν πραγμάτων, i.e., is a part of the poet's constructive function, with the important corollary that the poetic construction serves emotional as well as aesthetic purposes.

It is by such means that the threat represented by poetry in Plato

---

"portions of the rhythms" (4.48b21–22), he implies that they are segments of speech in a particular rhythm.

2. Cf. 4.48b30–34, 49a23–24. In these passages, dealing with iambic as the verse of both comedy and tragedy, there is some ambiguity; the common factor seems to be the need of a verse that will carry conversation, verbal interchange, and that need may be felt to override the difference in ἦθος.

is subdued in Aristotle's theory of literature. Aristotle's soul was not haunted by poetry. He looked it in the eye and saw, not a Gorgon face, but a rationally observed, rationally delineated human countenance. In the *Poetics* there is one reference, a minor and oblique one, to the poetic madness (chapter 17). We do not even know for sure how to read the passage: whether as saying that the manic psyche is, or is not, to be preferred to the plastic, imaginative one. But it does not matter. However the poet comes to his rendering of reality, it *is* a rendering of reality as we see it and know it around us. Imitation, in a new and wholly objective sense, has won the day; inspiration has retired to the dubious heaven whence it came. Poetry—such is Aristotle's message—is a benign possession for good and all; it belongs to this world and to us.

Appendix 1
Aristotle's Revisions of the *Poetics*

I HAVE ARGUED that the *Poetics*, at least in the main, belongs to Aristotle's Akademy period, and more particularly to the years around 360–355. It was intended (along with certain satellite works, the lost dialogue *On Poets* and the *Homeric Problems*) to present a new theory of literature in response to Plato, and to a lesser extent to the hostile critics of Homer answered in chapter 25. Although the high intellectual vigor of the *Poetics* is evident on every page (nobody, to my knowledge, has ever disputed Aristotle's authorship), its ultra-concise, tortuous, elliptical manner really leaves us no choice but to perceive it as a lecture script, meant to be supplemented by the "satellite" works.

Lecture scripts are not usually produced for a single occasion only. Their normal function is to serve as a guide to *repeated* presentations of a given body of material; and in this normal functioning they normally pick up a certain accumulation of additional memoranda, notes from the lecturer to himself, possible objections, *bons mots*, anecdotes, interesting questions raised by the hearers, and so on. We would assume, in default of evidence to the contrary, that the *Poetics* lectures (the work is clearly too long for a single hearing) were repeated more than once, in the Akademy if not later in the Lykeion; and we have indeed discovered in our study of the text a number of insertions of varying length and character. Some, we thought, were from Aristotle himself, others not. The question immediately before us is whether the insertions that seem to stem from Aristotle's own hand—including some that we have not yet studied—add up to a substantial revision of his theory or remain at the level of minor supplements, notes, queries, and the like.

We can distinguish three possible kinds of addition to the *Poetics* text:

1. Supplements by Aristotle himself.
2. Supplements or revisions by other persons close to him, either in the Akademy or the Lykeion.
3. Interpolations from other sources throughout the transmission of the text in antiquity (through the Byzantine period).

And we can further divide the first category into two:

    1a. Supplements by Aristotle which appear to involve a major revision (this is the variety chiefly referred to in the title of this appendix).
    1b. Those which appear not to involve such a revision.

The words "seem" and "appear" are of the essence here. This kind of discrimination is a ticklish business; our work will have to be conducted with all possible circumspection and will not be able to claim, at best, more than a certain degree of probability.

An inventory of all passages in the *Poetics* which seem to have been added to the text, by Aristotle or others, can be found in Appendix 2. Each item carries an inventory number and, in the margin, a tentative assignment to one of the categories mentioned above: 1a, 1b, 2, or 3. Items under 1a and 1b are discussed here in Appendix 1; of the three assigned to category 2, no. 8, which is chiefly on comedy, was taken up in Chapter 13.

Category 1b (to begin with the easiest) embraces just four items, nos. 3, 9, 10, and 28, and one of those (no. 28: chapter 16) is assigned to the group merely on technical grounds. It pretty clearly is from Aristotle's pen, and there is no necessary reason to designate it as "late" in any sense; it is simply an odd block which has been thrust into the text at a somewhat arbitrary place. I say "somewhat arbitrary" because Aristotle's review of the techniques of recognition does have some affinity with his other prescriptions for the "writing stage" of tragedy; yet it does not fit where it is and would not fit better anywhere else. The proof that it does not fit where it is, is that it stands squarely in the middle of a passage dealing with "the perceptions which necessarily attend upon the poetic art" (15.54b16). This subject is broached at the end of our present chapter 15 and directly continued at the beginning of 17—another indication that our inherited chapter divisions of the *Poetics* are often crude and misleading.

No. 3 (1.47b13–22) is an equally clear case, although the damage it has done (through not being recognized for what it is) is more extensive. The passage is a long footnote which Aristotle urgently wished to append to his *diairesis* of the "nameless art," to urge that mimesis, not verse, is what makes poetry; but since the ancients did not have the convenient device of putting footnotes at the bottom of the page to distinguish secondary from primary matter, he had to put it directly in the text. The length and complexity of the footnote (three clauses, dealing with mimes, etc., possible mimesis in spoken verses such as trimeters, elegiacs, etc., and possible ones in "all the verses") led to secondary—actually tertiary—corruptions of the text at 47b22–23; see above, p. 78.

In spite of all this, the case remains in principle a simple one. Nothing requires us to suppose that the addition was made "late" or as part of any major revision in theory; on the contrary, it speaks to the heart of Aristotle's original thinking. It would of course be possible to assign it to a redactor, an editor who inherited

Aristotle's manuscript and was faced with the task of putting it in order. That is Montmollin's hypothesis;[1] but it is not required in this case.

Equally simple, in principle, is the added matter near the beginning of chapter 4 (no. 9: 48b6–8, 9–20). The additions have caused some confusion as to the sequence of argument in the text, but they spring directly from one primal intuition of Aristotle's, that the source of the mimetic impulse in man is his innate desire to learn. There is no ground at all for designating this intuition as late, or for attributing the added matter to an editor.

Similarly the three lines on pre-Homeric "comic" poetry (no. 10: 4.48b28–30, "Of those before Homer . . . and poems of that kind") seem to represent an afterthought by Aristotle himself which has gotten into a wrong place in the text; no need to invoke a redactor.

We now turn to bigger game: the four passages in the *Poetics* (leaving chapter 25 aside as a special problem) which we have assigned to 1a as seeming to imply a major revision of Aristotle's theory. The discussion begins with no. 32 and goes on to nos. 26, 37, and 6, in that order. But some brief prolegomena may be helpful here. Three of these four sections cluster near the middle and toward the end of the *Poetics*, and that placement seems not to be accidental. After chapter 14, and especially after 15, the treatise loses some of its theoretical vigor and tapers off into a medley of prescriptions for what I have elsewhere called the "writing stage" of poetic composition: in other words, after the all-important matter of plot/action has been handled in detail and with care, other problems of more practical nature come up for briefer discussion. Also, Aristotle's treatment of epic now looms before us. This, then, would seem to be a good place for second thoughts on tragedy and its relation to epic, and Aristotle seems to have had such thoughts just here.

Two new ideas appear in these passages: (1) the concept of ὅλος (ὁ) μῦθος, the "whole story" or rather "the story (as a) whole," with a new pair of subdivisions, δέσις and λύσις; and (2) a shift in definition of the object of serious poetry, away from the superior (heroic) person in the direction of the average man, one "like us."

It is evident that the concept of a "whole story" brings μῦθος back toward its original meaning. Up to now, in the *Poetics* it had denoted strictly and solely the poet's work: his σύστασις τῶν πραγμάτων, structur(ing) of the events. Now it means something more like "myth" in its usual acceptation: the preexisting body of material out of which the poet makes his structure. Let us illustrate the difference by two examples, one from tragedy, the other from epic.

In *Oidipous Tyrannos* Sophokles has managed a sort of miracle: he has put the πάθη, the tragic events, *outside* his structure and devoted the play entirely to the discovery of the truth about them. The chemical purity, so to speak, of this solution—separating the tragic base as far as possible from the dramatic struc-

---

1. Cf. above, chap. 13, n. 1.

ture, but in such a way as to saturate the latter with the emotional power of the former—is a stunning achievement. Aristotle admired it enormously, perhaps even excessively, but it is not quite clear whether he perceived its full dimensions. The phrase ἔξω τοῦ δράματος, "outside the drama," appears twice, at 14.53b32 and 15.54b3, and congeners of it three times more (ἔξω τῆς τραγῳδίας, 54b7; ἔξω τοῦ μύθου, 17.55b8; ἔξω τοῦ μυθεύματος, 24.60a29), but only in the first of these is there an explicit reference to emotional factors (τὸ δεινόν, 14.53b30); the rest are concerned with irrationalities, ἄλογα, or "particulars," τὰ καθ' ἕκαστα. But ἔξωθεν is used in our passage in the requisite sense (18.55b25), and we will return to it below.

The other example may be more helpful. Homer's "divine" superiority over the other poets is shown, 23.59a31, τῷ μηδὲ τὸν πόλεμον . . . ἐπιχειρῆσαι ποιεῖν ὅλον, "by the fact that he did not undertake to compose the (Trojan) War (as a) whole either"; and in the central passage (no. 32) among those we are currently studying, at 18.56a10–13, the tragic poet is advised "not to compose an epic mass (as a) tragedy," οἷον εἴ τις τὸν τῆς Ἰλιάδος ὅλον ποιοῖ μῦθον, "as, for example, if someone should compose the story of the *Iliad* (as a) whole." Μῦθος here is clearly neither Homer's central action nor his central action plus episodes, but the whole story as a Cyclic poet might have told it, from end to end. This is the mass from which Homer "picked out one part" (23.59a35), using the rest as episodes. But as Aristotle points out (18.56a13–15; cf. 17.55b15–16, 26.62b8–10) epic—Homeric epic—is long enough to give its episodes breathing room, whereas in tragedy they have to be brief. The tragedian who puts a whole epic mass, ἐποποιικὸν σύστημα, into his play is going to fare badly in the competitions. He has in fact produced an episodic drama, and episodic tragedies are the worst (9.51b33–34; *Metaphysics* 11.10.1076a1, 14.3.1090b19).

It is evident upon reflection—or even without much reflection—that these necessities bear much more heavily on the tragic than on the epic poet. Suppose the tragedian wants to dramatize (as we know Aischylos did) the terrible moment of Achilleus's hamartia, when he sends Patroklos to his death. The actions precedent to this one must be shown somehow; but how? In the *Iliad*, no problem: the Quarrel and the Embassy have already been narrated in Books 1 and 9. But the tragic poet must summon all his cunning to achieve the same end by other means. The one thing he knows or should know is that he cannot achieve it the same way his brother poet has, by massive blocks of narration.

The physiognomy of Arisototle's new idea appears most clearly at the beginning of our key passage, no. 32, 18.55b24–29: Ἔστι δὲ πάσης τραγῳδίας τὸ μὲν δέσις τὸ δὲ λύσις, τὰ μὲν ἔξωθεν καὶ ἔνια τῶν ἔσωθεν πολλάκις ἡ δέσις, τὸ δὲ λοιπὸν ἡ λύσις, λέγω δὲ δέσιν μὲν εἶναι τὴν ἀπ' ἀρχῆς μέχρι τούτου τοῦ μέρους ὃ ἔσχατόν ἐστιν ἐξ οὗ μεταβαίνει εἰς εὐτυχίαν ἢ εἰς ἀτυχίαν, λύσιν δὲ τὴν ἀπὸ τῆς ἀρχῆς τῆς μεταβάσεως μέχρι τέλους, "Of every tragedy one part is tying and the other untying: the things outside (the play), and in many cases some of those inside, are the tying, and the rest is the untying; I mean that 'tying' is the section from the beginning as far as the last part before the shift toward good or bad fortune takes place, and 'untying' that from the beginning of the shift to the end."

We have not previously had anything like this combination of breadth of view with precision in detail. The new whole of which δέσις and λύσις are the parts is larger than the play, and yet its articulations are traced with great exactitude. The most obvious gain is that the events "outside"—τὰ προπεπραγμένα, "the things done beforehand," b30—now become a definite, measurable part of the whole: they are in a sense no longer "outside." But the events "inside" also gain in definition. The "last part (last episode) before the tragic shift takes place" is, in the case of the *Oidipous*, the arrival of the Korinthian messenger, who purports to bring good news but actually sets the last tragic development in motion; and although we do not have the *Lynkeus* we can tell that its δέσις similarly ended with the capture of the child Abas and the "guilty" pair Lynkeus and Hypermestra. That which seemed to point to disaster for them was the darkness just before the dawn (a specially Sophokleian conjuncture).

The concept of λύσις turns up later in our passage and also in no. 26 (15.54a37–b15), the only other place in the *Poetics* where it appears. That the "untyings" of the μῦθοι should result naturally from the character (of the chief hero) is presented there as an additional (καί, a37) corollary of the principle that probability or necessity should operate in character portrayal just as much as in plot construction. Here, however, we must take note of a split in the text tradition. The Arabic version implies ἐξ αὐτοῦ . . . τοῦ ἤθους, "from the character itself"; the rest of the tradition gives ἐξ αὐτοῦ . . . τοῦ μύθου, "from the plot itself." I have elsewhere given reasons for preferring ἤθους, and they still seem to me valid.[2] In particular, Aristotle's objection to the employment of gods to solve problems of λύσις (54b1–6) seems to fit better with an invocation of character: the "untyings" should come from people rather than from gods. And we shall find this preference for the reading ἤθους supported from another quarter.

The section of no. 26 comparing character portrayal with the procedures of the portrait-painters (54b8–14) starts out from the basic premise we had in chapter 2 (48a4, 18), that tragedy imitates persons "better than we (are)," but quickly modulates it in a new direction. The procedure of the εἰκονογράφοι is not to begin with superior persons and then tone them down to make them more lifelike, but the opposite: καὶ γὰρ ἐκεῖνοι, ἀποδιδόντες τὴν ἰδίαν μορφὴν ὁμοίους ποιοῦντες, καλλίους γράφουσιν, οὕτω καὶ τὸν ποιητήν, μιμούμενον καὶ ὀργίλους καὶ ῥαθύμους καὶ τἄλλα τὰ τοιαῦτα ἔχοντας ἐπὶ τῶν ἠθῶν, τοιούτους ὄντας ἐπιεικεῖς ποιεῖν, "For in fact they, while making them 'like' by rendering their individual looks (τὴν ἰδίαν μορφήν), paint them better-looking; so also the poet, in imitating persons wrathy or easy-tempered or having other characteristics of that kind as to their characters, should, while they are such

2. See *Argument* 473–474.

(while leaving them such), make them good." It is a new approach: begin realistically; then you may add some idealistic touches.

The emendation I proposed at 54b14 would fit very well into this line of thought. Kassel's text reads †παράδειγμα σκληρότητος οἷον τὸν Ἀχιλλέα ἀγαθὸν καὶ Ὅμηρος†. The first step toward healing the passage is to remove the gloss παράδειγμα σκληρότητος. It was meant to characterize, perhaps to stigmatize, Achilleus's stubbornness ("example of hardness"), but σκληρότης cannot have been applied to Achilleus by Aristotle: for him it is a hard-shelled, boorish trait, fit for a peasant. What he wrote, I suggest, is οἷον τὸν Ἀχιλλέα ἀγαθὸν καὶ ⟨ὅμοιον⟩ Ὅμηρος, "as, for example, Homer (portrayed) Achilleus as good and like (us)." That is, in line with the recommendation to imitate the good portrait-painters, Homer made his Achilleus good and also (but also) like the average man, namely in his propensity to anger.

This reading not only is consonant with the preceding sentence, it also provides a connection, and a significant one, with the first statement in our passage (54a37–b1), that the "untyings" of the μῦθοι should result naturally from "the character itself" (of the hero). Achilleus's irascibility, while it establishes a link with "us," the average man, and thus may earn him our sympathy, will still not permit him, at the beginning of *Iliad* 16, to accept Agamemnon's gifts and be reconciled with his fellow Achaians, and this leads directly to his hamartia in sending Patroklos out to his death, against his (Achilleus's) own premonitions of disaster (which are clearly expressed in the passage). In other words his fatal step is not taken παραλόγως, contrary to reasonable expectation (see above, p. 149); it is a true hamartia in Aristotle's terms.

But this line of thought leads still further. Achilleus's mistake is not a hamartia in the sense of a mistake about the identity of persons; it is a miscalculation as to what is likely to happen, and is followed by a recognition (18.22–27, 107–111), with the marks of repentance which we recognized in Oidipous (above, p. 147). Do these considerations suggest that Aristotle is beginning to find a way out of his narrow preoccupation with the Oidipous pattern (and the Iphigeneia pattern), toward a broader understanding of the maze of human ignorance and error? It is an idea worth considering, and surely if any human work is fitted to stimulate such thoughts it is the *Iliad*.

The second section of our passage no. 32, 55b32–56a10, may or may not be a separate entry; that it belongs to the same stratum is pretty well proved by the presence of δέσις (here called πλοκή, "weaving," 56a9) and λύσις. The chief novelty here is a theory of four species of tragedy, which looks as though it may have some affiliation with no. 37 (24.59b7–16), as the latter says that epic should have the same species as tragedy; but the two sets of four do not quite match. There is no agreed-on way to make them do so; but perhaps the problem is not entirely desperate.

The discrepancy lodges in one corner of the board. Three of the species are the same, point to point: πεπλεγμένη ("inwoven," usually translated "complex"), παθητική, and ἠθική. In no. 37 (chapter 24) the fourth species is the ἁπλῆ, "single"; in no. 32 it is obscured by a textual corruption: τὸ δὲ τέταρτον †οης. Since the neuter phrase is inconsistent with the style of the other three (e.g., ἡ δὲ παθητική, sc. τραγῳδία, etc.), I once conjectured ἡ δὲ ἐπεισοδιώδης, "and the episodic"; †οης would then be a distorted remnant of -δης.[3] This guess was prompted in part by Aristotle's reference to the *Prometheus*. Which *Prometheus*? Probably the one we have, and it certainly is episodic. A less venturesome surmise would be ἁπλῆ, to match 24.59b9. Actually, the episodic is one variety—the worst—of the ἁπλῆ, 9.51b33; but a difficulty in the way of any interpretation is that in chapter 18 each play is assigned to one category only, whereas in 24 the *Iliad* and *Odyssey* belong to two each: the *Iliad* is single and παθητικόν (based on a tragic πάθος, Achilleus's sacrifice of Patroklos), and the *Odyssey* inwoven and "ethical." Does this difference perhaps stem from the greater length of epics, especially the Homeric epics, which gives them a chance to embody more than one class? The next section of chapter 24, 59b17–31, is precisely the one that most dwells on the theme of "extra length" and emphasizes that this gives epic greater variety (59b29–30, μεταβάλλειν καὶ ἐπεισοδιοῦν ἀνομοίοις ἐπεισοδίοις; see above, p. 172).

A final obstacle to interpretation of the key passage in chapter 18 is the assertion that the four classes are based on four "parts": 55b32–33, τοσαῦτα γὰρ καὶ τὰ μέρη ἐλέχθη, "For so many have also the parts been said (to be)." It was natural to take this as a reference to the six "parts" of tragedy in chapter 6 (cf. also 5.49b16–17), but no forward movement is possible along that line. Let us take our clue rather from the three "parts of the plot": 11.52b9–10, δύο μὲν οὖν τοῦ μύθου μέρη ταῦτ' ἐστί, περιπέτεια καὶ ἀναγνώρισις· τρίτον δὲ πάθος, "So then, these are two parts of the plot: peripety and recognition; a third is (the) πάθος." The "inwoven" species is then the one "of which the whole is peripety and recognition." (Cf. 24.59b15, where the *Odyssey* is described as πεπλεγμένον ἀναγνώρισις γὰρ διόλου, "inwoven (for it is recognition throughout"). The παθητικόν (examples: *Aias, Ixion, Iliad*) is that which has only a πάθος, or only πάθη (in the *Iliad*, perhaps embracing not only Achilleus's fatal act but Hektor's death and the multitudes of other deaths). We have already conjectured (above, p. 181) that "ethical," in connection with the *Odyssey*, may refer to its comedy-like character (13.53a36): its ending is "moral," presenting the endings which we think *ought* to come to the two groups of characters, good to the good and bad to the bad. Finally (and, frankly, least satisfactory under this solution), the "single" plot is that which has no other marked characteristic—at least in the case of tragedies.

It remains to point out that if we adopt this interpretation we must mark ἔξω

3. *Argument* 524–528.

μελοποιίας καὶ ὄψεως, 24.59b10, as an interpolation stemming, presumably, from an honest reader who thought that the "parts" referred to here were those of chapter 6.

It must be admitted that this solution of the "four species" problem involves a certain amount of roughness. If someone believes that Aristotle, or his text, was not that consistent, I shall not gainsay him.

We are left with no. 6 in our inventory of possible 1a interpolations. The three short phrases in chapter 2 that mention τοιούτους or ὁμοίους, persons "like (us)," as objects of poetic imitation do seem to have some affinity with no. 26, where Aristotle recommends following the model of the good portrait-painters: starting with average men but then touching up the portraits to make them better-looking (καλλίους, 15.54b11). But it is by no means clear that the phrases really belong here (see above, p. 81).

Appendix 2

Inventory of Interpolations in the *Poetics*

Items are classified 1a, 1b, 2, or 3 according to criteria outlined in Appendix 1.

2? 3?   1. 1.47a26–28, on the dance as representing imitation through rhythm alone, seems to have no relevance to Aristotle's theory or to any art form in his time. It may be connected with a theory of Aristotle's pupil Aristoxenos, or with the pantomime of the Imperial Roman period. See p. 77.

3   2. 1.47a28, ἐποποιία is a simple gloss which interrupts Aristotle's sentence but betrays a correct intuition of his meaning, since τοῖς μέτροις (sc. ψιλοῖς), a30, does indeed refer to epic.

1b   3. 1.47b13–22 is a long footnote by Aristotle to enforce his point that the criterion of poetry is μίμησις, not the use of verse.

3   4. 1.47b22 and 22–23, μικτὴν ῥαψῳδίαν and καὶ ποιητὴν προσαγορευτέον, "mixed recitation" and "also to be called a poet" (referring to Chairemon), are, respectively, a gloss like no. 2, and an attempt to make sense of Aristotle's footnote (no. 3).

3   5. 2.48a3–4, κακίᾳ γὰρ καὶ ἀρετῇ διαφέρουσι πάντες, "for with respect to vice and virtue all men differ": an honest but stupid attempt to paraphrase the preceding clause.

1a? 2?   6. 2.48a5, ἢ καὶ τοιούτους, 6, Διονύσιος δὲ ὁμοίους, and 12, Κλεοφῶν δὲ ὁμοίους, "or also such (as we are)," "and Dionysios 'like' (people)," "and Kleophon 'like,' " jointly establish a third class of *imitandi* "like" (us): ordinary citizens. We found no room for such persons in Aristotle's original theory, but room may have been made for them later; see p. 81.

3   7. 3.48a21–22, ἢ ἕτερόν τι γιγνόμενον, "or becoming something different," is a Platonic intrusion into Aristotle's quite different theory. See p. 83.

2?   8. 3.48a25–b2, on δρᾶν, δράματα, and Dorian claims to tragedy and comedy, see p. 188.

1b   9. 4.48b6–8, καὶ τούτῳ διαφέρουσι . . . τὰς πρώτας, and 12–19,
            αἴτιον δὲ καὶ τούτου . . . τινὰ ἄλλην αἰτίαν, are two explicative
            passages added, undoubtedly by Aristotle, to identify the mimetic
            impulse with man's special, innate desire to learn and his enjoy-
            ment of knowledge.

1b?   10. 4.48b28–30, τῶν μὲν οὖν πρὸ Ὁμήρου . . . καὶ τὰ τοιαῦτα,
            "Now then, of those before Homer . . . and poems of that kind":
            the lines are out of place; they belong three lines below and may
            be a supplementary note added by Aristotle which has gotten into
            the text at a wrong place.

3?   11. 4.49a1, καὶ ἡ Ὀδύσσεια, "and (or, also) the *Odyssey*": in view
            of 13.53a31–36 (see p. 181) it is doubtful whether Aristotle
            would have cited the *Odyssey* as a prototype of tragedy specifi-
            cally. Cf. no. 43.

2?   12. 4.49a10–13, καὶ αὐτὴ καὶ ἡ κωμῳδία . . . νομιζόμενα, and 14–
            15, ἡ τραγῳδία, "both it and comedy . . . practiced in many of
            our cities, . . . tragedy," are a pair of notes perhaps stemming
            from the same source as no. 8.

2? 3? 13. 4.49a18–21, τρεῖς δὲ καὶ σκηνογραφίαν Σοφοκλῆς . . . ὀψὲ
            ἀπεσεμνύνθη, "three (actors) and scene-painting Sophokles; . . .
            it (tragedy) acquired seriousness late": this obscure series of
            phrases (it is not clear that they are sentences) dislocates Aris-
            totle's argument seriously by introducing the conception of a late
            and drastic shift from σατυρικόν (here almost certainly meaning
            satyr drama) to tragedy. For a possible clue to this puzzling devel-
            opment see *Argument* 175–179.

3?   14. 5.49b1–2, καὶ γὰρ χορὸν κωμῳδῶν . . . ἀλλ' ἐθεθονταὶ ἦσαν,
            "And in fact a chorus of comedians (the archon 'gave' late) . . . ;
            (before), they were volunteers": the interpolated sentence has to
            do with Athens, whereas Aristotle's genuine narrative does not
            bring in Athens until b7 (τῶν δὲ Ἀθήνησιν). See p. 191.

3?   15. 5.49b6, Ἐπίχαρμος καὶ Φόρμος: the two names are apposite to
            Aristotle's story but out of place in the text just here. That the
            names are merely a gloss is demonstrated by a note in the Arabic
            translation; see *Argument* 197–199.

3?   16. 6.49b29, καὶ μέλος, "and song": an intrusive gloss; see *Argu-
            ment* 233 n. 6.

3   17. 6.50a1–2, πέφυκεν αἴτια δύο τῶν πράξεων εἶναι, διάνοια καὶ
            ἦθος, "There are naturally two causes of acts: thought and char-

acter," is a crude and inaccurate paraphrase of the clause that precedes it. See *Argument* 240–241.

3   18. 6.50a12–13, οὐκ ὀλίγοι αὐτῶν, ὡς εἰπεῖν, "not a few of them, more or less": Aristotle's deduction operates from the characters of the drama; this phrase refers, misguidedly, to the poets. See *Argument* 249–250.

3   19. 6.50a17–19, καὶ εὐδαιμονία καὶ κακοδαιμονία ἐν πράξει ἐστίν, καὶ τὸ τέλος πρᾶξίς τίς ἐστιν, οὐ ποιότης, "Both happiness and unhappiness are (lie) in action, and the goal is a certain action, not a quality": Aristotle's argument is concerned with the dramatic characters; this is a statement about human life in general. See p. 114.

3?   20. 6.50b9–10, ἐν οἷς . . . ἢ φεύγει, "in which . . . or avoids": a pointless duplication of the genuine text, perhaps springing from scribal error.

3   21. 12. 52b15–27, from κατὰ δὲ τὸ ποσόν to end: this witless farrago of faulty and/or irrelevant information (irrelevant, that is, to Aristotle's argument) is the product of some grammarian, more likely from Byzantion than from antiquity. See *Argument* 359–363.

3   22. 13.53a5–6, ἔλεος μὲν περὶ τὸν ἀνάξιον, φόβος δὲ περὶ τὸν ὅμοιον, "pity to do with the undeserving (sufferer), and fear with the one 'like' (us)," is an unnecessary gloss which gets in the way of Aristotle's sentence.

3   23. 13.53a25–26, αἱ πολλαὶ αὐτοῦ εἰς δυστυχίαν τελευτῶσιν, "Most of his (Euripides') (tragedies) end in misfortune," is a note like the last one, from a reader who thought that the only point here was Euripides' unhappy endings.

3   24. 13.53a36–39, ἐκεῖ γάρ . . . ἀποθνῄσκει οὐδεὶς ὑπ' οὐδενός, "For there . . . nobody gets killed by anybody," is a note like the preceding two, but stupider. If there ever was a comedy in which Orestes and Aigisthos (!?) walked off arm-in-arm at the end, it would prove nothing for Aristotle's point about "double endings."

3   25. 15.54a23–24, οὕτως ἀνδρείαν ἢ δεινὴν εἶναι, "(inappropriate for a woman) to be brave or eloquent in that way": the inappropriate eloquence was that of Euripides' Melanippe (cf. 54a31); we do not know what woman was unsuitably brave.

ia 26. 15.54a33–b15, χρὴ δὲ καὶ ἐν τοῖς ἤθεσιν . . . . Ἀχιλλέα
ἀγαθὸν καὶ ⟨ὅμοιον⟩ Ὅμηρος, "One should also in the charac-
ters . . . . Homer (makes) Achilleus good *and* ⟨like⟩ Homer,"
seems to belong to a major revision. Chief signs: (1) the circum-
stantial care with which the concept of necessity or probability is
applied to characters, as it had previously been (chapter 9) to
plots/actions; (2) the appearance, a37, of a new word in plot
analysis, λύσις ("untying," denouement); (3) the suggestion of a
new approach to character-drawing, starting from the ordinary
man—ὅμοιος, "like" (us)—instead of the superior one. Cf. no. 32
and see p. 210.

3 27. 15.54b14, παράδειγμα σκληρότητος, "specimen of hardness," is
intended to characterize Achilleus's refusal of Agamemnon's of-
fers, but it cannot be from Aristotle. See p. 210.

1b 28. 16 (entire), 54b19–55a21: there is no reason to assign this chap-
ter to a later period; it is simply an odd block, a technical analysis
of "recognitions" which does not fit in smoothly anywhere. It
presumably represents a note by Aristotle that has been inserted
arbitrarily here. See *Argument* 484–485.

3 29. 17.55a27, τὸν θεατὴν, "(escaped) the spectator('s notice)": a
simpleminded and erroneous identification (the person intended
is the poet); meant to be helpful, like nos. 5, 11, 22, and 27.

3 30. 17.55b7–8, διὰ τίνα (sic scribendum) αἰτίαν, ἔξω τοῦ καθόλου,
"for what reason, (is) outside the 'universal,' " is a paraphrase of
the next line, καὶ ἐφ' ὅτι δέ, ἔξω τοῦ μύθου.

3 31. 15.55b14, ἐν τῷ Ὀρέστῃ, "in the *Orestes*": the preposition must
be deleted; the reference is to the person Orestes in the
Iphigeneia.

ia 32. 18.55b24–56a10, Ἔστι δὲ πάσης τραγῳδίας τὸ μὲν δέσις τὸ δὲ
λύσις . . . δεῖ δὲ ἀμφότερα ἀρτικροτεῖσθαι, "Of every tragedy
one part is 'tying,' the other 'untying' . . . but both must be fitted
smoothly together," is a key passage embodying a significant re-
adjustment of Aristotle's concept of tragic structure: (1) δέσις
and λύσις between them include portions of the story which are
outside the play proper; and (2) one element ("part") is classified
over the others. No. 26 seems to belong to this new stratum also.
See p. 210.

3 33. 18.56a21, τραγικὸν γὰρ τοῦτο καὶ φιλάνθρωπον, "for this is
tragic and 'philanthropic' ": the clause is isolated, its reference
weak and implausible.

3   34.   19.56b1–2, καὶ ἔτι μέγεθος καὶ μικρότητας, "and also importance and unimportance (bigness and smallnesses)": this *topos*, which has to do with blowing up your own facts, arguments, etc., and talking down your adversary's, is already included in "proof and refutation" (56a37–38). Cf. no. 29.

3   35.   21.58a8–17, αὐτῶν δὲ τῶν ὀνομάτων . . . εἰς ταῦτα καὶ Ν καὶ Σ, "of nouns themselves . . . (ending) in these (letters) and *n* and *s*," is a minor grammatical appendix, breathing the same kind of pedantry as no. 21.

3   36.   23.59b5–7, [πλέον] ὀκτώ . . . [καὶ Σίνων καὶ Τρῳάδες], (from *Little Iliad* are made) "eight (tragedies) [more] . . . [also *Sinon* and *Trojan Women*]": in *Argument* 588–593, I showed that most of the first eight titles, given supposedly as those of tragedies derived from the *Little Iliad*, are not titles of plays but simply designations of sections of the epic material, drawn from Proklos's *Chrestomathy*; and that the word "more" and the titles *Sinon* and *Troades* are a supplement from another grammarian, trumping his colleague's act. Thus the passage contains an interpolation within an interpolation.

1a   37.   24.59b7–16, Ἔτι δὲ τὰ εἴδη, . . . πάντας ὑπερβέβληκεν, "Furthermore the species . . . he has surpassed all (his rivals)": the paragraph again invokes the concept of species of tragedy and epic (whether they are the same ones is a question) and proposes a new classification of the *Iliad* and *Odyssey*. It belongs with nos. 26 and 32 and is discussed together with them (p. 210).

3   38.   59b10, ἔξω μελοποιίας καὶ ὄψεως, is a note by an earnest but misguided explicator who thought that the "parts" mentioned here were the six "parts" of tragedy in chapter 6. Cf. no. 29 and p. 212.

3   39.   24.59b29–30, εἰς μεγαλοπρέπειαν and τὸν ἀκούοντα, "for (lit. into) magnificence" and "the hearer": the first interpolation invokes a virtue which Aristotle ascribes only to persons and explicitly rejects as a description of style; the second distorts the meaning of the verb μεταβάλλειν (from "changes" to "diverts") in an un-Aristotelian way.

3   40.   24.60a30, Οἰδίπους, is a relatively harmless explanatory gloss but cannot be a part of Aristotle's sentence.

1a?   41.   25 (entire), 60b6–61b25: the chapter involves us in a number of problems, which we briefly discussed in Chapter 12. On the basis of a very thorough analysis Daniel de Montmollin finds in it evi-

218 Appendix II

dence of a second edition; see *La Poétique d'Aristote: texte primitif et additions ultérieures* (Neuchâtel 1951) 99–117.

3   42.   26.62a16, καὶ τὰς ὄψεις, "and visual appearances": the following clause, δι' ἧς (singular) κτλ., makes it clear that only music is included in the genuine text.

3   43.   26.62b9–10, καὶ ἡ 'Οδύσσεια and καίτοι ταῦτα τὰ ποιήματα, "also the *Odyssey*" and "and yet these poems": the first phrase has the air of something tacked on to Aristotle's sentence, like the same words in no. 11 (4.49a1); the second is textually dubious. The genuine text seems to be καὶ τοιαῦτ' ἄττα ποιήματα, "and some (other) such poems," i.e., poems like the *Iliad*, having parts which are sizable in themselves: thus there is no clear reference to the *Odyssey*. It seems advisable to consider the first phrase an interpolation from the same source as no. 11.

Index